Praise for *From Sund*

In my evangelistic work around the world, thousands have accepted God's end-time truth of the Bible Sabbath. They clearly understand our Lord's invitation to keep the Sabbath holy, but they often ask, "How do I keep the Sabbath?" May-Ellen Colón's book will help many of these new Sabbath keepers to see the beauty of the Bible Sabbath. This Christ-centered, practical presentation can make a difference.

You may not be a new Sabbath keeper. You may have understood the biblical command to keep the Sabbath from the time when you were a child. There is something in this book for you as well. You will see the Sabbath through new eyes and have a deeper appreciation for this gift from God. It is my prayer that you will be richly blessed as you read these pages.

Mark Finley, general vice president
General Conference of Seventh-day Adventists

A great book is one you believe and which you consider valuable because it offers a life-changing experience. This is what I found in Dr. Colón's book *From Sundown to Sundown: How to Keep the Sabbath . . . and Enjoy It!* I personally have been blessed by reading the manuscript, and I believe that many will have the same experience. I recommend that all Sabbath keepers take this opportunity to make Sabbath keeping as enjoyable as the Lord wants it to be. This is a book that by the power of the Holy Spirit can change your life as it has changed mine.

Jonathan Kuntaraf, director
Sabbath School/Personal Ministries Department
General Conference of Seventh-day Adventists

As a youth I'm relieved to know others around the world struggle with the same question I have: What is appropriate

Sabbath activity? I appreciate that *From Sundown to Sundown* recognizes biblically based patterns that apply to our world today—the *whole* world. Finally, there's a Sabbath guide that takes different cultures, different times, and different age groups into consideration. It's like touring the world, growing up, and time traveling all at the same time, *on Sabbath!* Who ever heard of Sabbath as a vacation with God *and* the family? Dr. Colón has taken the complicated subject of appropriate Sabbath behavior and balanced it for our busy lives today, whether you're an Asian pastor, Hispanic mother of three, or a young American kid.

Rudy Estanque, young adult

FROM
SUNDOWN
TO
SUNDOWN

How to Keep the Sabbath...
and Enjoy It!

MAY-ELLEN COLÓN

Pacific Press® Publishing Association
Nampa, Idaho
Oshawa, Ontario, Canada
www.pacificpress.com

Cover design by Lars Justinen
Cover design resources from Lars Justinen
Inside design by Aaron Troia

KING JAMES VERSION (KJV)

Additional copies of this book are available by
calling toll-free 1-800-765-6955 or by visiting http://www.adventistbookcenter.com.

Library of Congress Cataloging-in-Publication Data
Colon, May-Ellen Netten, 1949-
From sundown to sundown : how to keep the Sabbath...and enjoy it! / May-Ellen Netten Colon.
p. cm.
Includes bibliographical references.
ISBN 13: 978-0-8163-2261-9 (pbk.)
ISBN 10: 0-8163-2261-9 (pbk.)
1. Sabbath 2. Seventh-day Adventists—Doctrines. I. Title.
BV125.C65 2008
263'.2—dc22
2007050222

08 09 10 11 12 • 5 4 3 2 1

Dedication

I dedicate this book to my best friend,
my supportive and patient husband, Gaspar,
and to my grown children, Ivan and Sara-May,
with whom I have enjoyed many delightful Sabbaths.

Table of Contents

Foreword

As you open the cover of this book, you will probably find it unlike any that you have read before. You have read doctrinal books about the Sabbath. You have read historical evidence about the change of the Sabbath. You have been clear on the *what*. This book, *From Sundown to Sundown,* is the clearest presentation of the *why* and particularly of the *how* that we have ever read. It skillfully combines the statistical (the data is massive), theological, historical, relational, experiential, rational, and spiritual. Drawing from surveys completed in fifty-one countries across the globe, tapping into the motives and practices of more than thirty-five hundred Seventh-day Adventists, the author finds that 96 percent of the respondents believe that the seventh-day Sabbath is the true day of worship. But as they enter this temple carved in time every week, how many know how to gain the blessing inherent in the celebration of this birthday of the world? How many know it's all about Him and their faith relationship with Him?

Dr. May-Ellen Colón is disarmingly open and honest as she shares her family's experiences of wrestling with Sabbath dilemmas. But if you're looking for a cookbook approach to the dos and don'ts of Sabbath keeping, you will be disappointed. Dr. Colón goes beyond the precepts to the principles, and beyond the principles to the Person.

Let us give you a hint of good things to come. Do you *Sabbath*? Is Sabbath exclusively a noun, or can it be a verb? Do you *keep* Sabbath or can you also *make* Sabbath? Have you noticed that there is another word hidden within *Sabbath*? Have you found *Abba* in your Sabbaths? Dr.

Colón notes that the Bible doesn't say, "Remember the Sabbath day to keep it gloomy." Abraham Heschel, the great Jewish writer, says that it is a sin to be sad on the Sabbath.

We have been told that at a given point in history we would go forth and proclaim "the Sabbath more fully." *From Sundown to Sundown* is epochal. We believe it marks a fuller view of the Sabbath for such a time as this. As you read these pages, may you feel, as we have, that you are experiencing the Sabbath "more fully" and that as world troubles deepen, you can find and share a fresh beauty, meaning, and strength that gushes forth from your weekly family vacation with Jesus.

John Youngberg, EdD,
Millie Youngberg, EdD
Professors Emeriti of Andrews University

Preface

It was a warm, sunny afternoon in the early 1990s. Hundreds of Adventists were packed into a church on a hill in Kigali, Rwanda. My husband, Gaspar, and I were in the middle of presenting a seminar on family spirituality. Though the seminar wasn't focused on Sabbath keeping, one mother in the audience raised the subject. She was frustrated; she wanted to make the Sabbath a happier, more holy experience for her family, but she didn't know how. Others in the audience jumped in, sharing their questions and comments about Sabbath keeping, which launched us into a full-blown discussion that took us down a different path than I had planned for our seminar.

That day in Rwanda I realized that I needed to understand the Sabbath experience better myself. I wanted to be able to give better, more practical answers the next time someone asked me about Sabbath practice. So, I began a quest that ultimately led me to write a doctoral dissertation on the practice of the Sabbath across several cultures.[1]

For that dissertation, my teammates and I circulated surveys in five different languages to fifty-one countries in five geographical areas of the world. This allowed 3,221 Seventh-day Adventist families to speak to me about their Sabbath observance. Throughout this book I'll be suggesting ways to learn from the data.

I've written this book from within the confines of Adventism. However, it is meant not only for Seventh-day Adventists but also for members of other communities of faith—for anyone who is concerned about the issue of Sabbath keeping. As needed, I will supply background for

readers who are not Seventh-day Adventists. Keep your Bible handy as you read this book, for I will list Bible references that will deepen your understanding of the subject.

Acknowledgments

Though they may not realize it, the wise and helpful people who helped me with my doctoral dissertation indirectly helped me with this book as well. Many of them appear in the endnotes. I am especially indebted to my dissertation committee: John B. Youngberg, chair; Dorothy Bass, external examiner; Jo Ann Davidson, Roger Dudley, Jimmy Kijai, and Jane Thayer. John and Millie Youngberg, my longtime mentors, are religious educators par excellence. After I defended my dissertation, they gently nudged me to continue writing about the Sabbath and provided inspiration that helped me stick with this project.

Tim Lale gets much of the credit for motivating me to start this book project. Shortly after I defended my dissertation in 2003, he challenged me to write a practical book on keeping the Sabbath using my dissertation as the springboard. It was no small challenge to shift gears from writing dissertation-type language to writing the simpler and more vibrant vernacular of a popular book. Tim bore with me for a long time and has been a helpful source of encouragement during the whole journey.

My family has seen me through yet another monasticlike season of my life. Thank you, Gaspar, Ivan, and Sara-May for your infinite patience, support, and encouragement during this writing project. We had all breathed a sigh of relief when I finished my dissertation, anticipating a return to normalcy, and then, unexpectedly, this book project rose up.

I am blessed with many friends who carried their friendship to a new level by giving me wise counsel along the way. A special thank you goes to the members of my writing group, the "Inking Angels": Lyndelle

Chiomenti, Jean Kellner, Ella M. Rydzewski, Bonita Shields, and Rebecca Timon. Other loyal friends also came to my aid with helpful input: Kathy Beagles, Karen and Ron Flowers, Ben Maxson, Tim Lale, Ekkehardt Mueller, Jon Paulien, Gerhard Pfandl, Tim Poirier, and my husband, Gaspar—my very best friend.

The Sabbath School and Personal Ministries Department at the General Conference has been very supportive throughout this project. Thank you to Jonathan Kuntaraf, Gary Swanson, and Jim Zackrison for allowing me to take Fridays to focus on this project. That enabled me to finish it.

Kaye Bass, Kathy Beagles, Kathleen Kuntaraf, Tim Lale, Ella Rydzewski, and Jim Zackrison graciously shared personal stories that found their way into this book. And I am grateful to several helpers who contributed to chapter 11 by replying to my e-mail survey about Sabbath fog, bumps, and confusions: Marjorie Baldwin, Richard Bauer, Stephen Bauer, Nick Brightman, Lyndelle Chiomenti, Faith Crumbly, Richard Davidson, Afia Donkor, Debbie Eisele, Claire Eva, Linda Farley, Ron Flowers, Falvo Fowler, Carl Friday, Patricia Habada, Madeline Johnston, Kay Kuzma, Diane Levy, Carol McHenry, Milton McHenry, Eliezer and Gloria Melendez, Lourdes Morales-Gudmundsson, Ekkehardt Mueller, Judith Peters, Sara Porter, George Rice, Benjamin Schoun, Dick Stenbakken, Jane Thayer, Rebecca Timon, Michael Tomlinson, Cindy Tutsch, John Youngberg, and Tim Zollbrecht.

A big thank you goes to Rudy Estanque, Cliff Goldstein, Tyson Shaw, and John and Millie Youngberg, who read the complete manuscript draft and provided valuable input.

Most of all, I am eternally grateful to the Lord of the Sabbath, Jesus Himself, for His help and for giving me the gift of the Sabbath to enjoy in this life and in the life to come.

Introduction
Conundrums, Confusion—
What's a Sabbath Keeper to Do?

One Friday afternoon while Kathy, a friend of mine, was busy moving some African artifacts from one wall to another and trying to arrange them tastefully, her adult son came into the room talking with someone on her cell phone, which had rung in another part of the house. When Kathy heard him say "But they will just be looking, and you won't be transacting any business yourself," she realized that her son was talking with her aunt, who had her North Carolina property up for sale while she was living sometimes there, sometimes in Tennessee, and sometimes in Florida.

Soon Kathy quit her chore and took the phone to speak with her aunt, who repeated the conundrum about which she had called for input. A couple was very interested in her property, had seen it a couple of times, and had even taken a video of it. They wanted to come by again but had specified Saturday as the day that worked into their schedule. The realtor claimed to have forgotten that Kathy's aunt had specified no Sabbath showings.

Taken from a "precept"—or rule—perspective, this situation posed a question. As Kathy's son had said, her aunt wouldn't be doing business. She would, in fact, be in another state at the time. If the realtor hadn't mentioned the showing to her, she would have been none the wiser. And what if she were to lose this sale? There had been little interest in the property, which was somewhat off the beaten track.

Kathy didn't know what to say. Sticking to the letter of the law seemed to be safe. But she was tired of Sabbath keeping being a matter of guessing whether or not a certain action was on some hidden master list of rules for the Sabbath.

Kathy hedged a bit, saying that the problem was indeed an interesting one. Her aunt replied that others had told her the same thing. Then Kathy started sharing the train of thought she was learning to use in dealing with issues such as this one. That train of thought is the main theme of this book.

Sabbath—a problem?

Through the years, my personal pursuit of Sabbath keeping has sometimes been fraught with conundrums, especially when I have factored in the cross-cultural dimension. My family and I have traveled all over the world, and we have lived in Africa and Russia. Our experience has been enriching, but it has also resulted in confusion when I tried to come to grips with the issue of keeping the Sabbath. I've observed that while nearly all Adventists agree on the time frame of the Sabbath, there is considerable divergence of opinions about the practices of and motivations for Sabbath keeping.

Twenty years ago, Rob Gorle, an English teacher from New South Wales, Australia, highlighted samples of diverse Sabbath activities from various cultures. In Sydney, Australia, some Adventists might engage in car talk or comparing the latest fashions, and Adventists in Papua New Guinea might discuss the best place for the Saturday-night fishing expedition, while discussions in college cafeterias might range from politics to the fruits of the Spirit. Gorle noted that Sabbath keeping in various parts of the world may also mean scuba diving, Bible study, soccer games, distributing religious literature, or visiting people in a retirement center. He viewed the diverse activities he recorded in a positive light, stating that they "are signs that the Adventist church has started coming of age. A variety of cultures are finding room for expression within the church."[1]

Should Adventists view the existence of varied and sometimes contradictory practices in a positive light? Or should we consider this reality as evidence of problems in our Sabbath keeping?

Then there is the conundrum of Sabbath as a stressor for Adventist Church leaders. Sabbath is often their busiest "work" day, and many say it leaves them very fatigued. One weekend, my husband, Gaspar, and I were in charge of Sabbath School, and Gaspar also taught the Sabbath School lesson. I played the organ for church, we attended a potluck for which I had prepared food the previous day, and then Gaspar and I led a planning meeting. Our two college-student children had come home for the weekend with two of their friends, and after the meeting we went to the zoo with

them. When we returned home, I prepared supper for everybody, we had sundown worship, and then some other college-student friends joined us for Saturday-night games and socializing near the fireplace. It isn't hard to understand why I was more tired when our "day of rest" ended than I was when it started.

Many church families regularly experience Sabbaths like the one I just described, and church leaders may not be able to change much about their Sabbath ministry. Is this what God had in mind when He said, " 'Remember the Sabbath day by keeping it holy' " (Exodus 20:8, NIV)? Is there a way to reframe scenarios that aren't going to change? How can we serve God and keep His Sabbath in a way that doesn't exhaust us? Where are we now? What are the current questions about this topic?

Reality check

In filling out the survey I prepared for my dissertation, Adventists from all over the world shared their innermost feelings and questions about the Sabbath. To many of them, the Sabbath is a special joy and a delight. To others, it is an enigma, and they struggle about how to keep it holy. When asked why they kept the Sabbath, some Adventists who struggle with Sabbath keeping answered this way.

Needed rest so I don't work every day. I guess often I keep *Saturday* rather than *Sabbath*. (United States)

I don't really think I keep the Sabbath as God would like me to. (Portugal)

Because I was born into this religion. I didn't choose it. If I don't, I will burn in hell! (United States)

Because that is what God has asked us. I keep Sabbath the way I see fit, which might not always agree with other Adventists. (United States)

Because I know I should. In the past it has been much more of a blessing. Presently, it is sometimes a burden because of involvement. . . . I know I need to get myself back on track and focus on God. (Canada)

In reality I don't observe the Sabbath as I should, but I do it to do it. (United States)

Here are some answers to the question "What does Sabbath mean to you in your relationship with God?"

Right now, I'm not sure; Sabbath A.M. is such a hustle with children—arrive at church, get to Sabbath School, potty, feed, and play with the kids outside of church so they don't disturb anyone, and then go home ready to sleep. It sounds like I ignore Him, at least it feels that way. (Côte d'Ivoire)

Sadly enough, it is a burden for me because I cannot experience it freely. On other days, I have more inner peace and rest. I hope and pray that I can experience the Sabbath as a blessed and a nice day. (Austria)

Not enough. I see the Sabbath as a day for my relationship with God, but somehow this does not work yet (too many programs). (Germany)

Sabbath is a wonderful time for spiritual communication with God, but a pastor almost never has time for this. (Moldova)

I want my relationship with God to be stronger and closer, but I feel that because of my work the connection is not like it has to be. I would like to go to the worship each Sabbath and Friday too, but I am not always able to do this; that is why I feel some kind of guilt. (Russia)

For me it is an oasis even though the water may seem bitter at times. But I persist. (Mexico)

Well, it means another semi-boring day that is filled with meetings, missionary stories, and sleep. It doesn't really help my relationship with God. (United States)

Perhaps the Sabbath is a delight to you, and you don't relate to the above comments. Those presented in chapter 2 may better describe your

sentiments. On the other hand, maybe you have had dilemmas, frustration, and confusion as you have tried to keep the Lord's Day holy (Exodus 20:8). This book will help you to get past these problems.

Overview

Let's scan ahead to see where we're going. First, we'll need to take a look at the past to see how we got here. Chapter 1 deals with the development of Sabbath keeping within the Seventh-day Adventist Church in its early years. Has Sabbath keeping always been a source of conundrums for Adventists? How does our present Sabbath-keeping experience compare to that of the early Adventists? Why is the Sabbath such a big issue today? Why are we still asking the same questions?

In chapter 2, I present a brief overview of what's going on now in Adventist Sabbath keeping based on some of the major findings in my study.

Before we can get to guiding principles of Sabbath keeping, we need to examine our status in Christ. Chapter 3 answers the question as to what kind of spiritual condition you need to be in before advice on Sabbath-keeping principles will be meaningful. Only after we answer that will we be ready to look at how we can develop guidelines for Sabbath behavior.

Chapter 4 presents a pattern of understanding that can help us to displace a focus on rules and concentrate instead on God and His Sabbath-keeping principles.

In chapter 5, I begin to present specific principles for choosing Sabbath practices using a "*Vacation* With God and With His Family" metaphor. This chapter emphasizes preparation for the "Sabbath vacation."

Chapter 6 continues the study of biblical principles that clarify and expand the "vacation" aspect of Sabbath keeping.

An important focus of this "vacation rest time" is our worship of God and intimacy with Him. Chapters 7 and 8 provide biblical principles on this vertical aspect of Sabbath keeping, highlighting "Vacation *With God* and With His Family."

Fellowship with God's family—human beings (and pets, why not?)—is the horizontal focus of Sabbath keeping. In chapters 9 and 10 you will find biblical principles that emphasize nurturing human relationships on Sabbath: "Vacation With God and *With His Family.*"

Chapter 11 explores more deeply how to relate to some of the perplexities, misunderstandings, and uncertainties that you may encounter when you keep the Sabbath.

Finally, chapter 12 pulls it all together. There you will find additional advice on how to apply the biblical Sabbath-keeping principles to your life. This chapter also portrays entry into a new week after the Sabbath has passed. What souvenirs can we carry from Sabbath into the week that follows? This chapter directs our thoughts to our flight out of this old world to the land of eternal Sabbath.

Here's my prayer for the readers of this book:

> Teach me your ways, O LORD,
>   that I may *live* according to your truth!
> Grant me purity of heart,
>   that I may honor you.
> With all my heart I will praise you, O Lord, my God.
>   I will give glory to your name forever,
> for your love for me is very great (Psalm 86:11–13, NLT; emphasis added).

Now we need to begin our journey. Our first steps will take us back— back to the birth of the Adventist Church in the 1800s. We will notice the process and challenges in adopting the Sabbath into Adventist lifestyle.

Questions for Reflection and Discussion

1. Compare your Sabbath experience when you first became a Sabbath keeper with what it is now.
2. What Sabbath-keeping conundrums have you experienced?
3. What Sabbath delights have you enjoyed through the years?
4. What do you hope to learn from this book?

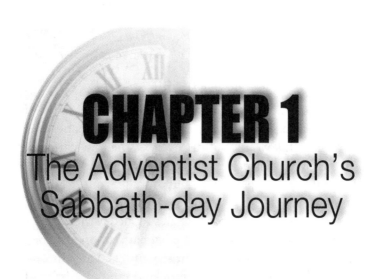

CHAPTER 1
The Adventist Church's Sabbath-day Journey

At a Seventh Day Baptist General Conference Session held in 1843, a resolution was passed, setting apart November 1 as a day of fasting and prayer that God would "arise and plead for his holy Sabbath." That prayer was soon answered through one of their members, Rachel Oakes.[1]

While celebrating the Lord's Supper on a Sunday in 1842, Frederick Wheeler, the pastor of a Millerite[2] congregation in Washington, New Hampshire, remarked that "all persons confessing communion with Christ in such a service should be ready to follow Him all the way, willing to obey God and keep His commandments." After the service, Rachel Oakes spoke to Pastor Wheeler. "I came near getting up in the meeting at that point," she said, "for I wanted to tell you that you would better set that communion table back and cover it with the cloth until you yourself were willing to keep all the commandments of God."[3]

Later, Pastor Wheeler said that Rachel's words cut him deeper than any that had ever been spoken to him. They became a turning point in his life, for he began to study the Bible to determine what the true Sabbath is and became convinced that he must keep the Sabbath of the fourth commandment.

By September 1844, there was sufficient agitation over the seventh day to prompt a two-part editorial in the *Midnight Cry,* a major Millerite publication. In February 1845, Thomas M. Preble, a Baptist Millerite preacher who had accepted the Sabbath in 1844, published his beliefs regarding the Sabbath in a piece known as the *Hope of Israel.* Preble expanded his explanation of the Sabbath a month later in a not-so-

subtle publication titled *A Tract, Showing That the Seventh Day Should Be Observed as the Sabbath, Instead of the First Day; "According to the Commandment."*

After reading Preble's *Hope of Israel* in April 1845, Joseph Bates, a former sea captain and a prominent figure among the early Adventists, was convicted that he must observe the seventh-day Sabbath. He soon began to proclaim his wonderful discovery. When he started across the bridge near his home on his return from visiting the Washington, New Hampshire, Sabbath keepers, a neighbor called out, "Hello, Brother Bates! What's the news?"

"The seventh day is the Sabbath!" Bates replied earnestly.[4]

Captain Bates was the father of the Sabbath among the people who were to form the Seventh-day Adventist Church. Early in 1846, Bates urged his Sabbath views on Ellen Harmon and James White (co-founders of the Adventist Church), who later married. They found Bates's strange teaching problematic and refused to accept it. Later, Ellen White wrote that she "did not feel its importance, and thought that he [Bates] erred in dwelling upon the fourth commandment more than upon the other nine."[5]

In August 1846, Joseph Bates published a tract titled *The Seventh-day Sabbath a Perpetual Sign.* About the time of their marriage, James and Ellen White received a copy of this forty-eight page tract. As they read the scriptural evidence presented, their confusion about and resistance to the seventh-day Sabbath dissolved, and they took their stand in support of it. "In the autumn of 1846 we began to observe the Bible Sabbath," Ellen White wrote, "and to teach and defend it."[6] At this time, about fifty Sabbath keepers were scattered throughout New England.

On the first Sabbath in April 1847, seven months after the Whites began keeping and teaching the seventh-day Sabbath, God gave Ellen a vision[7] stressing its importance. Thus, divine revelation confirmed the conclusions regarding the Sabbath that had been reached by earnest Bible study. Arthur White pointed out that "God unmistakably placed His seal of approval on their belief and teaching. This vital truth was not introduced through direct revelation, but was first seen through the study of His Word."[8]

Between 1848 and 1850, early Adventist leaders held some Sabbatarian conferences, calling together groups of ex-Millerites to teach them the truth they had learned regarding the Sabbath and other key doctrines. The number of Sabbatarians increased rapidly after 1850.

Cruising along—almost

Though the seventh-day Sabbath was becoming firmly established among early Adventists, the matter was not free from questions and differences of opinion. For quite some time the Adventist pioneers disagreed about when Sabbath days began and ended. Various individuals observed its beginning at various times—midnight, sunset, and 6:00 P.M. Some in Maine even observed the beginning and ending of Sabbath at sunrise, basing their practice on Matthew 28:1: "In the end of the sabbath, as it began to dawn toward the first day of the week . . ." (KJV).

For the better part of a decade, though, most Adventist Sabbath keepers observed Sabbath from 6:00 P.M. Friday to 6:00 P.M. Saturday. The father of Adventist Sabbath keeping, Joseph Bates, led out in promoting this six-to-six theory. He drew from the parable in Matthew 20:1–12, in which the workers were paid at "even" (verse 8, KJV). The parable says that some of these laborers began to work as late as the "eleventh hour," or 5:00 P.M., and worked for only one hour. "Even," then, must be 6:00 P.M. Bates also pointed out that at the equator—the middle of the earth—the sun sets at 6:00 P.M. James White supported Bates's opinion: "God has raised up Brother Bates to give this [Sabbath] truth. I should have more faith in his opinion than any other man's."[9]

God gave Ellen White a vision in which she heard an angel quote Leviticus 23:32: "From even unto even, shall ye celebrate your sabbath" (KJV). This vision cleared up the fallacy of the sunrise option for starting Sabbath; it was clear that Sabbath began at "even." But the vision didn't specify what "even" meant. So, the majority of believers continued to begin it at 6:00. P.M.

Then a deeper study of Scripture corrected this error. Converts to Adventism from among Seventh Day Baptists, and possibly others, who observed the commencement of Sabbath at sundown periodically spoke out about the error of the 6:00 P.M. position held by the majority of Adventists. Even James White admitted to not being fully satisfied with Bates's testimony favoring beginning Sabbath at 6 :00 P.M. He wrote, "The subject has troubled us, yet we have never found time to thoroughly investigate it."[10]

Finally, in the summer of 1855, James White requested that John N. Andrews give the matter of what time of day to start Sabbath a thorough investigation in Scripture. Andrews wrote an article in which he demonstrated from the Old and New Testaments that "even" meant sunset.[11] He presented his conclusions in a Sabbath morning Bible study

at the November 1855 General Conference Session in Battle Creek. Nearly all who were present at that conference accepted the sunset time and closed that Sabbath at sundown, even though they had started it at 6:00 P.M. the evening before.

However, two influential persons continued to hold firmly to the 6:00 P.M. position: Joseph Bates and Ellen White. So, this issue became divisive as the conference continued. Then God stepped in. He showed Ellen White in vision that the Sabbath begins and closes at sunset. This vision changed her mind. James White wrote, "This settled the matter with Brother Bates and others, and general harmony has since prevailed among us upon this point."[12] Uriah Smith, a prominent Adventist leader, spread the word that the Sabbath commences and ends at sunset.

Note that what God showed Ellen White in vision concerning the commencement of the Sabbath ran counter to her own views. Occasionally, she had a hard time accepting a newly clarified Bible teaching, but God sometimes chose to help her and others through visions that confirmed the results of earnest Bible study. Arthur White wrote that after the vision, "all could see that God was speaking, and that Ellen White was not merely repeating her personal, previously held views."[13]

Adventist Sabbath keeping through time

Periodically, articles in Adventist publications such as the *Review and Herald*[14] have addressed current Sabbath-keeping concerns. These articles reveal the trends in Adventist thinking regarding Sabbath keeping. In the remainder of this chapter we will take a quick overview of these trends.[15]

First half of the 1800s. The articles published between 1829 and 1849, before the *Review and Herald* began to be published, focused on topics such as the importance of keeping the true Sabbath, the error of Sunday keeping, the biblical basis of the seventh-day Sabbath, the history of the change of Sabbath observance from the seventh day to the first day, the keeping of *all* of God's commandments, and testimonies from or about people who had started keeping the Sabbath. Early Adventists were trying to establish their identity as keepers of the true Sabbath, so the question of *how* to keep the Sabbath was not at the forefront of their thoughts and writings. In fact, most of the early Adventists had been careful Sunday keepers under the influence of Puritanism and simply transferred their Sunday-keeping practices to the seventh-day Sabbath. Some of

these people were extremely strict regarding Sabbath keeping, even disfellowshiping some "lax" church members.

Accusations of Sabbath breaking were addressed occasionally in the *Review and Herald.* For example, in 1853, James White responded to a letter about Sabbath keepers in Vermont whom other members charged with cutting wood on the Sabbath and with making it a habit to do their visiting on that day. Some also accused these believers of traveling twenty to forty miles on the Sabbath to attend meetings. James White was unhappy about unauthenticated reports such as this and stressed the importance of not slandering fellow believers.

By the end of this half century, the Sabbath was so firmly established among Adventists that they considered it a normal part of their lives and referred to it often in their letters and diaries. The Sabbath activities they mentioned included attendance at meetings, preaching, resting, study, meditation, walking, visiting people, and attending funerals. (The funerals of James White, Andrew Farnsworth, and Ellen White were held on Sabbath.) Over all, the diaries of early Adventists testified of a sense of awe and of the presence of God pervading the Sabbath.

Last half of the 1800s. Many articles in Adventist publications of the last half of the 1800s focused on the sacredness of the Sabbath and the duty to perform acts of mercy. Isaiah 58:13 was much on the mind of Adventists at that time. They emphasized not "doing your own pleasure, . . . not doing your own ways . . . not speaking your own words" (NKJV). This trend shows that Adventists were beginning to focus more on the practice of Sabbath keeping. Some writers emphasized rules, some emphasized principles, and some included both. Here are some examples of Sabbath-keeping rules and principles that came up during that time.

- In 1849, James White discussed the biblical rule about kindling a fire on Sabbath.
- The very first series of Sabbath School lessons written by James White in 1852 stressed the principle that Sabbath is a holy time during which God's people are to set aside distractions and focus on Him. White shared some rules implied by that principle, such as that Sabbath keepers should avoid talking about worldly things on Sabbath.
- In 1854, the *Review and Herald* published an article written in 1813 by Seth Williston, a Sunday keeper, apparently endorsing his advice as applicable also to the seventh-day Sabbath. Williston's

article forbade riding in the fresh air, visiting friends, and excursions into nature.

- In 1854, Ellen White said parents shouldn't allow their children to wander about and play on the Sabbath either indoors or outdoors. This rule was apparently based on the principles of Sabbath sacredness and of the Sabbath being a time for families to spend quality time together.
- In 1857, James White addressed the matter of doing unnecessary cooking on the Sabbath.
- In 1871, contradicting Seth Williston's rules that forbade enjoying nature on Sabbath, Ellen White said that Sabbath wasn't meant to be a time of staying inside listening to long sermons and tedious, formal prayers. Instead, she said that all should have an opportunity to go outdoors. Children should spend time outdoors not in play but in their parents' company, enjoying the beautiful things that God has created. She based this on the principle that parents should make the Sabbath interesting and a delight.

The White family lived the principles of Sabbath keeping about which James and Ellen wrote. When they lived in Battle Creek, Adventist families sometimes met on Sabbath afternoons at the "White House." There they spent precious time talking over their Christian experiences, praying for each other and for God's work, and singing hymns. And whenever Ellen White had a quiet Sabbath afternoon to spend with her children, she would read to them. Sometimes she also invited their little neighborhood friends to enjoy the story hour. Ellen searched children's books and Sunday School journals for choice stories. Years later, her son Willie's wife gathered some of these stories, which then were published as a book called *Sabbath Readings for the Home Circle*.

When Willie White had a home of his own, he and his family lived out his mother's counsel about making the Sabbath "interesting and a delight." For example, when they were living in Basel, Switzerland, they would go on outings on Sabbath afternoons. On one of these outings, Willie's wife, Mary Kelsey White, and their daughter Ella (White Robinson) went for a walk with some of the mission workers to a cave that was said to be the home of a "petrified monk." Ella reported that the cave reverberated with moans and groans when the shabbily dressed wooden figure reached out its hand for a gift. Ella's curiosity got the best of her, and she slipped in behind the figure and found a decidedly unpet-

rified man who was turning a crank to extend the hand.

Usually, the mission workers spent Sabbath afternoons in church members' homes helping them find Bible answers to their many questions. Ella's parents generally took her with them on these visits, and often they were invited to stay for dinner.

Ella later wrote about a Sabbath in Battle Creek, Michigan, that she especially remembered. At the beginning of the day, their family had gathered around the heater in the front room to study their Sabbath School lesson. They noted that the presence of holy angels seemed very real to them that morning. A sick woman named Myrtle who was staying with them at the time was lying on the couch breathing heavily and suffering great pain. Ella's mother, Mary, said, "Children, let's pray for Myrtle. God loves to answer the prayers of children." Ella wrote that when they prayed, Myrtle was healed.

When Willie White and his daughters Ella and Mabel lived in Battle Creek after Mary died, he would spend the entire Sabbath afternoon with them. Because of his heavy responsibilities, they seldom saw him on weekdays, so they looked forward eagerly to Sabbaths when they could have him all to themselves for the entire afternoon.

On warm, sunny days, as soon as the Sabbath dinner dishes were stacked to await their washing after sundown, Willie and his daughters would gather blankets, pillows, paper, pencils, crayons, and a magnifying glass, and they would head for an oak grove near their house. There they would spread out their blankets and settle down for the afternoon. Sometimes the girls would gather leaves and examine them under the magnifying glass while their father read Jesus' words about God's care and the worry-free existence of nature. Willie usually brought with him on these little outings books about missionaries such as David Livingstone, William Carey, and Adoniram Judson. Before reading a story, he would ask Ella and Mabel to tell him the story he had read the previous Sabbath.

After Willie read the story, the girls might play missionary while their father rested. Then they would gather flowers or leaves, sometimes tracing them on paper and then coloring their tracings. Sometimes Willie would take them for a long walk in the woods, returning home by way of the Battle Creek Sanitarium, where the girls would leave the wildflowers they had gathered with patients sitting in wheelchairs or resting in hammocks on the lawn. These stories from the 1870s and 1880s show that, during that time, Adventist Church leaders stressed the principle of delightful spiritual togetherness.

After the 1888 General Conference, some Adventists writing about keeping Sabbath exhibited a clear, gospel-oriented tone. For example, G. D. Ballou built a biblical argument for associating the Sabbath with joy and celebration. He stressed that following this principle "takes away the Pharisaic rigor and Puritanic gloominess out of the Sabbath."[16]

In 1895, E. J. Waggoner emphasized the gospel-oriented Sabbath-keeping principle of trusting in God. He reminded his readers that God meant the Sabbath day to do more for us than merely to provide for our bodily recuperation. He requires that Sabbath keepers cease entirely from their own works so that they can have uninterrupted time to contemplate His works and learn the much-needed lesson of trust in Him. Waggoner said that as Sabbath keepers cease working at their livelihood, they are reminded that God supplies them not only with spiritual blessings but also with all temporal necessities.

While in Australia during the 1890s, Ellen White promoted the principle of active service for God on the Sabbath. On Sabbath afternoons, students would ride bicycles (yes, bicycles!) to homes scattered throughout the nearby villages and forests, where they would give Bible studies or conduct branch Sabbath Schools. Ella White Robinson reported that every week a group of Avondale students also rowed a boat four miles down Dora Creek to conduct Sabbath School and a church service in a cottage in a fishing village.[17]

From the early 1900s to the present. Adventist authors have continued to reflect Sabbath-keeping trends and to discuss Sabbath-keeping principles and rules. Here are some samples of Sabbath-keeping topics they covered between the early 1900s and 2001.

- Rules for Sabbath conversations (1910)
- The need to close camp meeting cafeterias and Adventist-owned restaurants on the Sabbath (1928)
- The need for more reverence in church (1938)
- The Sabbath as a holy, delightful day rather than a bleak day to be kept in a rigorous, puritanical way (1942)
- Principles to help decide whether or not Sabbath keepers should accept mail that has traveled on Sabbath (1946)
- The fact that *only* those who are converted can keep the Sabbath holy (1948)
- The importance of following principles—e.g., love for Jesus; laying aside personal affairs to make time for Jesus; Sabbath to be a

delight, a focus on God and the welfare of others—instead of a list of dos and don'ts (1955)

- Sabbath preparation and the Sabbath experience as coloring the entire week (1959)
- The problem of a professional firefighter who regularly takes shifts on Sabbath—the problem being that doing so makes it difficult to benefit from corporate worship, to lead one's family in making Sabbath a delight, etc. (1959)
- The danger of business as usual when Adventists work in non-Adventist hospitals on Sabbath (1961)
- The need for the church to be less judgmental about medical workers who must work on Sabbath, because they usually don't work on Sabbath because they want to, but because someone has to meet the needs of patients (1977)
- Suggestions for how women who have children can prepare for the Sabbath and experience the rest in Christ that the Sabbath offers (1980)
- Sabbath preparation including the settling of differences between members of a family or a church (1988)
- The point that we should emphasize principles rather than rules when teaching children to keep Sabbath—children must value something to consider it a delight (1989)
- How a person can keep the Sabbath when all alone (1990)
- The keeping of the Sabbath from the heart throughout the whole day, not just during the church service (2000)
- The biblical basis for deciding whether or not to make a practice of eating in restaurants on Sabbath; the conclusion that making a regular practice of eating in restaurants violates the holiness of the Sabbath (2001)
- The need for revival and reformation among Adventists regarding the observance of the Sabbath commandment (2001)

We've taken a peek at Sabbath keeping in Adventism's past. Perhaps you compared what you saw with your personal Sabbath-keeping experience. In some ways, it seems that it was easier to keep the Sabbath holy years ago. Why can't it be as easy now? Some of the things that our spiritual ancestors did indicate what we should do. But we can't base our Sabbath keeping on stories alone. We need universal, timeless biblical principles to guide us. Before we go there, however, it will be helpful to get a

better glimpse of the present. How do Seventh-day Adventists practice the Sabbath today—in *real* life? Let's take a look.

Questions for Reflection and Discussion

1. How does present-day Sabbath keeping differ from early Adventist Sabbath keeping? What similarities do you find?
2. How has reading the historical background of Adventism's journey into the Sabbath affected your perspective on Sabbath keeping?
3. How has this chapter made you feel?

Chapter 2
Good News, Bad News

I like sightseeing, and I particularly like views from high altitudes. Two of my favorite places are mountaintops and airplane windows. As I have had the rich experience of researching the issue of Sabbath-keeping practices and factors related to these practices among Seventh-day Adventists in fifty-one countries,[1] I feel as though I have been placed on a particularly good vantage point—as if I had taken an international flight and gained a perspective that would have been impossible to find otherwise. The views from the "airplane window," as well as the close-up "snapshots" after "landing" in various countries, have opened my eyes to present-day reality in Adventist Sabbath keeping. What I have seen is a mixed bag. There are reasons for concern about current Adventist Sabbath-keeping practices. There is also good news.

The good news

Some sections of my survey measured the degree of participation in certain Sabbath practices and attitudes. Other sections revealed how much a person agreed with beliefs about the Sabbath or with suggested motivations for Sabbath keeping. Those taking the survey answered some questions by marking a number to show their level of participation or their agreement with the item. The survey also had open-ended questions, which the responders answered by writing in their opinions. One open-ended question was "Why do you keep the Sabbath? Explain." Some of the replies thrilled my heart. I've grouped samples of them in various categories.

I found that many church members scattered throughout the countries represented in the survey emphasized the gospel, righteousness by faith, and their personal love relationship with God. Here is a sample of their answers.

Because I love my God and it [the Sabbath] is a day of the most intimacy with Jesus. (Réunion)

It really is a delight for me, a joy to my soul, and part of the saving grace. (Gambia)

I keep the Sabbath because God loves me and I want to be close to Him. I know He is my Redeemer! (Portugal)

I don't *observe* the Sabbath. I *celebrate* it because I love God and I want to live this Day fully with Him and in Him. (Switzerland)

The Creator is my Savior, Friend. He waits for me to visit; I can't miss it. (Russia)

Because I grew up keeping the Sabbath with parents who made sure it was fun and a blessing. At age 13 I made a commitment to God after learning the Good News of God's saving grace. The Sabbath reminds of that grace and of our blessed hope—a renewed earth, which will be a forever Sabbath. (United States)

Some answers revealed a balanced view of law and gospel.

Because I love God with all my heart and I want to obey His commandments. (Liberia)

To render worship to God, to observe all the Law, not in order to be saved but because I am saved by Christ. (France)

God commanded to keep the Sabbath, and we, because of love to Him, should do so. It is also a pleasure. (Moldova)

Due to Him working in me, He leads me to obey His law, and the Sabbath is also the sign that I am His. (Barbados)

It's a joy. It is a preparation here for heaven. It is obedience by faith alone. No other reason. (Venezuela)

Because God said to, and I love Him, and am showing my love and loyalty to Him and showing the world whose side I'm on. (United States)

Some Adventists answered the "Why do you keep the Sabbath?" question from a sociological or a quality-of-life standpoint. Their answers included rejoicing that the Sabbath helped them to feel more a part of God's family because it enhances fellowship. Others mentioned that they keep the Sabbath because it is a gift through which God supplies their physical, social, emotional, and spiritual needs, and the rest that Sabbath affords is a joy, a blessing, and a necessity.

The parts of my survey that required merely marking a number from 1 to 5 (or 6) gathered more good news about Adventist Sabbath-keeping beliefs, motivations, practices, and attitudes. The next several pages contain a summary of what I learned from the responses to these objective questions.

Surprising unity of belief across cultures

Before I started my study, I had certain preconceptions. I expected that Adventist Church members living in different places and cultures would have all kinds of different beliefs about Sabbath keeping. The survey revealed a surprising unity of belief regarding Sabbath observance among the Adventists who participated. The beliefs covered two dimensions: biblical guiding principles about nurturing a relationship with God—the vertical dimension—and biblical guiding principles about nurturing relationships with our fellow human beings—the horizontal dimension.

In my study, I measured how frequently Adventists practiced various types of Sabbath activities: spiritual nurturing activities, leisure activities, nonrestful activities, routine secular activities, and special relational activities. Even though the Adventists in the study showed a wide variety of involvement levels in these different areas, they appeared to have a general unity on certain Sabbath practices. For example, there was very little housecleaning, very little doing regular work, very little playing regular sports or going to ball games, very little nonemergency shopping.

The survey results showed that the various cultures differed most widely regarding Sabbath leisure activities, such as camping, boating, sex with spouse, etc.; relational activities, such as participation in fellowship; and special food and treats and other niceties, such as candles and flowers, etc.

A large proportion of the Adventists who took my survey are involved in spiritual nurturing activities on Sabbath. For example, 84 percent of the church members answered that they usually or always attend a church service; 79 percent regularly attend Sabbath School; 64 percent usually read or listen to the Bible, Christian literature, or sermons on Sabbath. High Sabbath School and church participation no doubt made the spiritual nurturing activities register as the strongest type of activities among those who took the survey. However, there were also other types of practices under "spiritual nurturing activities." The following were not as popular among Adventist Church members: preparation for Sabbath, family worship, service to others, and missionary work.

According to the survey results, relatively few Adventists do routine secular activities on Sabbath, such as doing regular work, 10 percent usually did this; watching or listening to secular TV/radio, 5 percent; eating out in restaurants, 4 percent; or shopping, 4 percent. Of all the Sabbath practices listed in the survey, Adventists participated in routine secular activities the least.

Few of those who completed my survey participated in the "nonrestful activities": cleaning house, 8 percent; playing regular sports or going to ball games, 4 percent; and attending public school, 4 percent.

Widespread commendable motivation for keeping Sabbath. When people become aware of scriptural truths, they will be motivated to some degree to apply those truths. My study measured four different kinds of motivation people have. I've labeled these motivations God-focused intrinsic motivation (meaning God-focused, internalized motivation based on "from the heart" religion—e.g., "I love God and His commandments with all my heart"); self-focused intrinsic motivation (related to self-centered or personal-gain motivations for Sabbath keeping, such as "Sabbath is fun and enjoyable; it helps me to have better health"); God-focused extrinsic motivation (externalized motivations for Sabbath keeping that are concerned with receiving God's blessing, keeping Sabbath to be saved; doing what God wants); and people-focused extrinsic motivation (people-focused external motivations for keeping Sabbath, such as people's expectations or "because I grew up that way").

About 85 to 90 percent of the study participants reported that God-focused intrinsic motivations are their reasons for keeping the Sabbath. Some 34 to 41 percent of those who took the survey mentioned people-focused motivations. I believe that certain aspects of all four motivations have their place in positive Sabbath keeping, but the God-focused intrinsic motivations appear to be more spiritually mature, demonstrating a deeper level of commitment, and a "with all my heart" love for God.

Low negative attitudes about Sabbath keeping. A low percentage of Adventists who participated in the study usually or almost always experienced the negative attitudes listed in the Sabbath Observance Exploratory Survey. Only 4 to 11 percent of the church members reported that the Sabbath is "usually" or "always" a burden and/or a stressor. These numbers demonstrate that Adventists generally appreciate and enjoy the Sabbath.

Sabbath is all about God—and relating to Him. Here's how some Adventists who obviously cherish their relationship with God responded to my open-ended survey question "What does Sabbath mean to you in your relationship with God?"

A special day of refreshment with God and His creation. A foretaste of reunion with Jesus. (Nigeria)

The Sabbath is a constant reminder for me that I have a God who not only created me but also redeemed me. (Liberia)

A time to part with the exterior world to be totally available to God. (France)

A sign of absolute and complete love, and salvation without works. (Switzerland)

It is a blessing—an intimate time—I rest with the Creator and He fills me with everything that He is. I wouldn't be able to live without the Sabbath! (Spain)

This is when I can spend some time with my favorite Person. (Ukraine)

My attitude about Sabbath serves as a barometer about my attitude toward God! (United States)

A refocus. It points me back to true north—God's throne of justice and mercy. (Bermuda)

The bad news

One Friday evening I was enjoying the Sabbath peace that had descended upon my home after a hectic week. In the midst of the quietness, the phone rang. Ivan, my college-student son, was on the other end. "Mom," he said, "I'm upset and disappointed. Jack[2] just called and asked me to go with him and some of my other friends to get some ice cream at a shop downtown. I told him that I would only go to places on Sabbath that will help me focus on God and that would help me get away from routine secular activities. That won't happen at an ice-cream shop.

"Mom, I don't want to lose his friendship, and I feel bad that I turned him down. Now he will label me as a 'holier than thou' sort of person. Did I do the right thing? Did I make a mountain out of a molehill? Sometimes it seems that I'm going against the flow most of the time."

Several months later, Ivan called again on a Friday night. Once more he was distraught. This time he had been invited to go to a secular concert that evening.

It seems that many Adventists are confused about Sabbath keeping. They universally agree on the time frame for Sabbath—sundown Friday night to sundown Saturday night. But sometimes they are confused about what to do within those sacred hours in their individual environments and cultures.

Even though my study found good news about Adventist Sabbath keeping, I was concerned about some things. The people who took the Sabbath Observance Exploratory Survey were not recent converts or fringe members. Forty percent of those who filled out the survey were church leaders. However, I noticed room for growth even among the "cream of the crop."

Other types of spiritual nurturing activities lacking. I mentioned that the majority of the Adventists in my study are involved in spiritual nurturing activities on Sabbath, especially attending church and going to Sabbath School. However, they are less involved in other directly spiritual nurturing practices. For example, only 62 percent prepare for Sabbath before sundown, 40 percent have family worship on Sabbath, 26 percent are involved in service to others, and 23 percent do missionary work. Do these findings suggest that many Adventists are part-time Sabbath keepers who

serve their time in Sabbath School and church and don't wholeheartedly celebrate the remainder of the Sabbath? Perhaps.

Maybe Adventists do fill the Sabbath hours before and after church with spiritually meaningful activities; after all, the survey didn't list all possibilities. However, Adventists seemed to have a rather low rate of participation in many of the activities listed in the survey that foster relationships and spiritual, emotional, and physical refreshment.

Involvement in spiritual nurturing activities related to stress. Adventists who were highly involved in spiritual nurturing activities tended to feel that rather than being boring, Sabbath is a happy, interesting day. However, the survey results showed that they had a relatively high stress level. It seems they were involved in too many Sabbath activities and didn't have enough time for family. The spiritually nurturing activities in which they were involved are appropriate for the Sabbath. But apparently those who filled out the survey were doing too much of a good thing or were doing these "Sabbath-appropriate" activities in a stressful manner. This raises a red flag because it conflicts with the purpose and spirit of the Sabbath. More on this later.

By the way, the Adventists in the study registered low participation in "leisure activities" on Sabbath. Either they didn't have time for these things on Sabbath, or perhaps they felt that the activities in this category are inappropriate for Sabbath. The low participation in leisure activities on the Sabbath may show that many Adventists are hesitant to have fun on the Sabbath and to enjoy any kind of leisure.

Sabbath is a stressor for church leaders. Even though not many Adventists who filled out the survey revealed negative attitudes about Sabbath, some negative attitudes do exist. One fact really stood out: Sabbath is a stressor for church leaders. This was one of the strongest findings in my study.

Often, Sabbath is a church leader's busiest day. Working in the service of God is compatible with the object of Sabbath keeping,[3] and preaching and leading out in Sabbath meetings can be spiritually beneficial. However, many church leaders find the Sabbath tiring rather than physically, emotionally, and spiritually refreshing. Here is what some of them wrote.

Sabbath is a wonderful time for spiritual communication with God, but a pastor almost never has time for this. (Moldova)

As a pastor, it [the Sabbath] is a day that I cannot completely appreciate in all of the fullness of my relationship with my Creator. (Venezuela)

I look forward to this special time with Him but I have to admit that as a Levite I feel under pressure with Friday vespers, Sabbath A.M. sermon, meetings Sabbath afternoon, and appointments Saturday night. (United States)

Room for improvement in relational activities. Slightly more than half, 54 percent, of the Adventists who were questioned do relationship-centered activities on Sabbath, such as having fellowship and relaxation time with family and friends. Forty-seven percent enjoy special Sabbath food at home or at potlucks or picnics; 23 percent do nature activities or take Sabbath walks or hikes; only 16 percent use Sabbath candles, flowers, or other special niceties. It seems that large numbers of those who participated in the study did not place making the Sabbath a delight (Isaiah 58:13) high in their priorities.

Some Adventists do routine secular or nonrestful activities on Sabbath. As I noted earlier, the Adventists in my study reported low involvement in routine secular activities on Sabbath—but some Adventists *are* involved in these things on Sabbath. For example, 14 percent admitted that they talk about any topic that comes into their heads on Sabbath; 10 percent do regular work; slightly more than 5 percent use secular media such as newspapers, TV, radio, or music; 4 percent do nonemergency shopping; and 4 percent eat out in restaurants.

As for "nonrestful activities," 13 percent reported that they attend church meetings or committees *all day* Sabbath; 8 percent study for Bible classes at their college or university; 8 percent clean house; 4 percent attend public schools and take exams; and 4 percent play or watch others play secular games and sports. Could this mean that some Adventists have a "business as usual" attitude about the Sabbath instead of a desire to set Sabbath time apart for special, focused, out-of-the-ordinary time with God?

Confusion on Sabbath keeping and righteousness by faith. Does Sabbath keeping contribute to our salvation? Seventy percent of those who filled out my survey said that it does. However, this may have been a matter of semantics. Maybe some of the people who filled out the survey meant that Sabbath keeping contributes to maintaining and nurturing the saved state that follows justification.

The survey item to which I refer says, "I keep the Sabbath because it contributes to my salvation." I intended this item to measure the extent to which Adventists believe that Sabbath keeping will save them. If the survey takers had that in mind when they answered the question, their

answers would be consistent with one of George Barna's findings in a survey that included Seventh-day Adventists. He found that 32 percent of Adventists believe that works *do not* earn salvation.[4] This figure seems to imply that nearly 70 percent believe works *do* earn salvation.

However, the respondents understood this survey question, the findings show that there is confusion on this issue. Adventist leaders and teachers must fervently clarify this in their teaching and writing. More reasons to straighten out confusion on this issue surfaced in the respondents' answers to "Why do you keep the Sabbath? Explain."

> Because God has said that I should keep the Sabbath in order to be saved. (Sierra Leone)

> In order to have eternal life. (Democratic Republic of the Congo)

> Because God commands to keep it in Exodus 20:8. His law is clear. If we don't keep it and we know it, we'll not go to heaven. (Colombia)

> Because I want to be obedient to God so when Jesus comes I can be saved. (Bermuda)

> Because I respect God and His day. I know that it is right. I believe in God and what He says is right. I want to be saved. (United States)

The negative attitudes toward Sabbath that the survey exposed show that some people in the Adventist Church, although not a majority, haven't understood the essence of righteousness by faith. They may be focusing primarily on keeping the right day, or they might be so busy with Sabbath activities that they become burdened and stressed. They might not be using the time to bask in the undistracted rest in Jesus that holy Sabbath time offers. For them, the Sabbath rest of faith might be turning into "the restlessness of works."[5]

Many Sunday keepers fully trust in Jesus for their salvation. They're keeping the wrong day for the right reason. Seventh-day Sabbath keepers who believe their Sabbath keeping will save them are keeping the right day for the wrong reason.

Cultural differences in Sabbath observance

Even though I was surprised at how similar Adventist Sabbath-keeping practices are in the fifty-one countries that I studied, I also noted there are some significant differences. Recently, I was reminded anew of this when I heard about an Adventist who moved from Germany to work at an Adventist institution in America. This man was irked at American Adventists for swimming in a lake on Sabbath. He decided not to participate with them in this "sin," choosing rather to keep the Sabbath in the way to which he was accustomed. So he got his soccer ball and kicked it around all Sabbath afternoon!

I'm all too aware of differences with Sabbath keeping because my son has told me about his Sabbath-keeping frustrations in college, because of tension and disagreement on this subject in some Adventist literature,[6] and because I have personally observed the church in several parts of the world. My experience overseas was an eye-opener and was what motivated me to do my study on international Sabbath keeping in the first place. This study gave me additional insights about cultural differences in Sabbath practices. Below is a boiled-down version of answers to a survey question that asked, "In addition to the practices listed above, what other practices, in your cultural setting, does your family participate in on the Sabbath?"

People from what was at the time of my survey the Africa–Indian Ocean Division (AID) often mentioned funerals, burials, and weddings as a regular part of their Sabbath observance. These services are formal tribal events. It appears that Sabbath has a tribal role for Adventists in SID. They tend to participate in large group activities. African society tends to be more openly religious and pre-secular.

The Adventists in the Euro-Africa Division (EUD) generally indicated that they did spiritually focused activities such as small-group Bible discussions, music activities, and so forth. The EUD is in a more secular society, and Adventists there seem to gravitate to smaller, relational groups in their Sabbath activities.

Euro-Asia Division (ESD—the former Soviet Union) Adventists indicated that they focused on fellowship with other Adventists on Sabbath. Many ESD Sabbath keepers are the only Adventists in their family, and they tend to take refuge with other Adventists during the Sabbath hours. Also, as in the EUD, the ESD has a rather secular cultural environment, and thus the Adventists there prefer a more informal, relational, small-group pattern of Sabbath observance.

On Sabbath, church members in the Inter-American Division (IAD) are largely involved in youth activities and giving Bible studies—which puts them in middle-sized groups. IAD Sabbath practices tend to be evangelistic. This territory is less secular than Europe or North America, but it is becoming increasingly secular.

North American Division (NAD) Adventists responded that their Sabbath practices focus on fellowship with family and friends. Thus, NAD Sabbath keeping is relational and small-group oriented. As in the ESD and EUD, the cultural environment of the NAD is relatively more secular than that of much of the rest of the world. Social researcher Monte Sahlin has concluded that the more secular the cultural context becomes, the more relational and small-group oriented people become. It appears that many Adventists in the NAD would rather retire to family and rest on Sabbath. Also, the NAD has a high-stress, fast-paced society that often results in people "collapsing" on Sabbath. They don't have a lot of energy to spend on creative Sabbath activities or in meetings and other group activities.

We must view cultural differences in Adventist Sabbath keeping in a balanced way. As we obey God by observing His Sabbath, we do so at the place in history and in the culture where we live. However, history and culture might condition us and distort our values. By appealing to culture, we could be guilty of giving ourselves license to participate in activities that are incompatible with Sabbath holiness. The main purpose of the Sabbath is to strengthen our bond with our God. Therefore, activities that strengthen this bond are acceptable. We need to remember that no one can rightly evaluate the personal motives of others. We should be slow to criticize our fellow Adventists who live in cultures other than our own and who engage in Sabbath activities that we might not sanction for ourselves.

So, are cultural differences in Sabbath keeping good news or bad news? These differences can be good news because when we become aware of them, we are compelled to rely on our personal relationship with Jesus and the guidance of His Holy Spirit to help us keep the Sabbath in our own culture. We will be driven to search His Word for divinely sanctioned principles to live by—principles that are valid for all cultures. When this happens, we will find ourselves saying No to certain distracting activities on Sabbath because of a bigger Yes—a close relationship with Jesus and His Word.

Questions for Reflection and Discussion

1. What Sabbath-keeping practices have you observed in cultures other than your own? In your own culture? Were they different than or similar to what you consider normal and acceptable? How did these similarities or differences make you feel?
2. Did you agree with the author's assessment of what constitutes good news and bad news about Adventist Sabbath practices? Why or why not?
3. What impact do the findings discussed in this chapter have on your Sabbath keeping?
4. What would you have done in the Friday-night quandaries that Ivan experienced? Why?

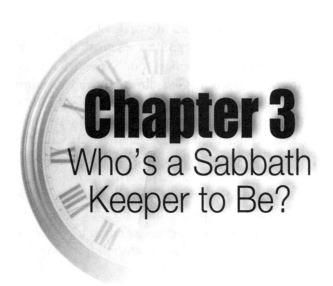

Chapter 3
Who's a Sabbath Keeper to Be?

Let me tell you about a church. Three or four families who had children created this church in a member's home more than twenty-five years ago. These families wanted a church with a casual and loving atmosphere. Children of all ages have always been an integral part of the congregation—the families even started a Pathfinder club[1] simultaneously with the church. They have always been welcome and have never been ignored or patronized. They participate in all aspects of the services, leading as well as sitting in the audience. This congregation built a gymnasium many years before they built the actual church—again, evidence that they were making the kids' needs their priority.

The church service precedes Sabbath School. This sequence is much more family friendly—the kids love to go to Sabbath School after church, the classes are always full, and no one cares if they run late. Sometimes kids stay in their classroom to finish a craft while the parents talk. And with this sequence, nearly everyone goes to Sabbath School.

One large Sabbath School class plans occasional Sabbath afternoon trips. They go to interesting places such as an extinct volcano, a cave, or to see wildflowers in the mountains. These trips are spiritually—and often literally—uplifting.

Prayer plays an important role in this church. Every Sabbath after the song service they take about five minutes to pass a microphone around so people can make prayer requests. These are written down, and then an elder prays for each request. Once in a while when something really major happens—such as a member leaving for Iraq or losing a family member in an

accident—the whole congregation stands in a circle all around the sanctuary and several people pray. It's a moving experience; sometimes tears flow.

Of course, this church has its challenges too. No church is perfect. But the point is that the atmosphere is God-directed. Sabbath mornings at this church are very uplifting because the focus is on God Himself. The members openly demonstrate that they have a personal relationship with Jesus Christ, their Savior and Lord. They are Adventist Christians who have met Jesus personally. Thus, they are experiencing the joy of salvation in their congregation and in their daily lives. Their joyful, love relationship with Jesus shapes and motivates what they do.

The culture of this particular church discourages members from judging people. It encourages, instead, acceptance and constructive love. When members drift away for a while, the church prays for them, and often they come back.

Sometimes members differ regarding Sabbath-keeping practices. But they don't judge each other. Most members of the congregation are well versed in God's ways, and they obey by God's grace. They are more interested in seeing how God works in people's lives, how He saves them from sin, than in judging people who don't see things exactly as they do. They have open minds and hearts that allow for continuing growth in spiritual life.

This book is about how to "do" Sabbath in real life. I've told you about my friend's church to illustrate that we need a love relationship with Jesus before we can truly keep His Sabbath—or follow any other Christian lifestyle practice. Before we can determine what a Sabbath keeper is to do, we must answer the question, who's a Sabbath keeper to be?

Result of a relationship

In the 1990s, when my family and I lived in Russia, we learned the Russian version of our names. My husband, Gaspar Francisco Colón, was Gaspar Hipolitovich to them. Our son, Ivan Christopher Colón, was Ivan Gasparovich. Our daughter, Sara-May Julia Colón, was Sara-May Gasparovna, and I, May-Ellen Marian Netten Colón, was May-Ellen Reginaldovna. Hipolitovich is Gaspar's *patronymic* name, based on his father's first name, Hipolito. Ivan's patronymic name, Gasparovich, is based on his father's first name, Gaspar. Women also carry their father's name but with an "ovna" ending, so Sara-May's patronymic name is Gasparovna, and mine is Reginaldovna.[2]

Russian patronymic names show to whom we belong, as well as who we are. In America and many other countries, people's last name, or family name, is their father's family name. In other words, our fathers are an important part of our identity—of who we are.

The most important name that we carry is *Christian.* Our identity is linked to God the Father, God the Holy Spirit, and God the Son—Jesus Christ (Ephesians 3:14–19). The Father's "whole family in heaven and on earth derives its name" from Him (Ephesians 3:14, 15, NIV). Since "all the fullness of the Godhead" dwells in Christ "bodily" (Colossians 2:9, NKJV),[3] we can also say that our identity is in Christ, the Father's other Self.

So, we should ask not only, Who am I? but also, Whose am I? If we are Christians, we belong to Christ. We are adopted as His sons or daughters (Ephesians 1:5). That makes us royalty, children of the King (Revelation 19:16). What we do flows out of who we are and to whom we belong. Our family name affects our behavior. "If anyone is in Christ, there is a new creation: everything old has passed away; see, everything has become new!" (2 Corinthians 5:17, NRSV).

Who is Christ?

We also must ask, who is Christ? He has many names and descriptions in Scripture. For example, He is our Creator, and He is love (John 1; 1 John 4:8). Whatever He does is bathed in love. In *Original Love,* Des Cummings comments that when Jesus made Adam in His likeness, He breathed into him the breath of life "as if kissing him into being."[4] After Jesus originated marriage with the creation of Eve, His love was implanted in the new couple. A wedding at the end of Creation week—what a grand finale! Is there any better symbol of love than a wedding?

The Creation story could have ended well with Adam and Eve's wedding on Friday night, but Jesus decided to take the next day off to be with the newly created couple. Because our Creator is love, He treasures relationships.[5] He didn't create anything on the seventh day other than time to relate to His new family members. Jesus created Sabbath to be a day for love—a day to celebrate His love in bringing humankind into existence, to celebrate love for each other.

Christ is our Re-creator—our Savior. When He lived on our earth in human flesh, He set out to restore and save both sin-wracked humanity and His special love day, the Sabbath. He intentionally performed

of His loving, healing miracles on the Sabbath (Matthew 12:9–15; Mark 1:21–28; Luke 4:38, 39; 13:10–17; 14:1–6; John 5:1–18; John 9). The religion of His day had turned His Sabbath into a day for law and legalism, even though Jesus had given it to people to be a day for love. Jesus' claim to be Lord of the Sabbath and His actions of love caused the Pharisees to plan for His death. Des Cummings states that "the twin towers of love in scripture are Calvary's cross and creation's Sabbath."[6]

Also, Christ is our Lord (2 Peter 3:18). If He is Lord of our lives, He will be in complete control of our thoughts, our practices—everything. We will love Him so much that we want it no other way. Our daily, hourly prayer will be, "Lord, control my mind, my words, and my actions." Christ prayed to His Father for all believers, " 'I in them and You in Me' " (John 17:23, NKJV). When Christ is in us, what comes out of us will be His doing lived out in our body. His life is in—or blends with—ours. Our life is in—or blends with—His.[7] "In him we might *become* the righteousness of God" (2 Corinthians 5:21, NIV; emphasis added). "When we submit ourselves to Christ, the heart is united with His heart, the will is merged in His will, the mind becomes one with His mind, . . . we live His life."[8] The late, renowned Methodist preacher William E. Sangster called this phenomenon the "we life."

The "we life"

Many years ago, an organist was performing a concert on an organ that required someone to manually pump air into it. Before the organist began each piece, he would say, "And now I will play for you . . ." and he would name the piece. Suddenly, the organ stopped, and try what he might, the flustered and embarrassed organist couldn't get a sound out of it. Then from behind the organ, a voice called out, "Let's have a little more 'we' in it!"

How can Christ be "in" us, and we "in" Christ? In other words, how can we actually experience the "we life"? Those words could be a mere theological platitude unless something in real life stands behind them.

The answer is that we each must have a personal encounter with God as Joseph did after he was sold into slavery by his hateful brothers. En route to Egypt, a very real encounter with God ended his uncontrolled grief and terror. After his thoughts turned to the God of his father Jacob, and all of the precious lessons he had learned in family worship came vividly before him, Joseph decided that the God of his fathers would be

his God. Then and there, he gave himself fully to the Lord, come what may. He would serve the Lord with an "undivided heart."[9] At that time, God moved into his heart and took full control. If Joseph had lived in the Christian age, he would have been able to say with Paul that Christ was in him (Galatians 2:20). Christ wants to be in us, too, to work within us as a hand controls and energizes the actions of a glove.

William Sangster called the blessed state of Christ being in us and our being in Christ "the doctrine of the divine indwelling." "In Christ" is oftentimes used as another way to describe salvation. Sangster explains that the apostle Paul considered this doctrine so crucial that he mentioned it 164 times in his thirteen letters![10] Paul said, "If any man be in Christ he is a new creature," (1 Corinthians 5:17, KJV), and "I am crucified with Christ" (Galatians 2:20, KJV). Paul seemed to be obsessed with this idea—a good obsession indeed!

I must make an important point here about the role of the Third Person of the Godhead in this process. Christ indwells people through the Holy Spirit. Preacher Gary Vest said, "We are all possessed—either by the Spirit of God or the spirit of the devil!" When we are possessed by the Holy Spirit, the "we life" becomes a reality (Ephesians 3:16–19;[11] John 14:16–26, especially verses 17, 20, 23). The Members of the Godhead are closely intertwined, and the Spirit has the role of making the indwelling of the Godhead actually happen in our lives.

Anglican writer William Law said, "A Christ not in us is a Christ not ours." A medical practitioner was wondering why one of his patients was not getting better. Then he discovered that the patient had bought the medicine but hadn't bothered to take it. After that, he typed on the labels of his medicines, "This will do you no good unless you take it!"

Once, after Sangster had preached a sermon on the topic "Christ in you and you in Christ," he went for a walk with his son along a seashore. As they walked, the boy said, "It is very hard to understand how we can be in Christ and Christ can be in us."

As Sangster was pondering how to explain such an abstract spiritual subject to a child, he saw a bottle on the beach. He half-filled the bottle with water, plugged its mouth with leaves, and flung it into the ocean. Then he said, "Now the bottle is in the sea, and the sea is in the bottle."

That line, "the bottle is in the sea, and the sea is in the bottle," tells us that when we become Christians, Christ must totally saturate our lives inside and out. How is it with you now? Have you met Him personally? Is every nook and cranny of your life immersed in Jesus? (Ephesians 1:22, 23).

If we are submerged in Jesus as the bottle is in the sea, if we have met Him personally, we will see spiritual disciplines and lifestyle in a new light. The principle of love will totally control us. For example, we're not likely to enjoy Bible reading or giving monetary love gifts and tithe until we meet Jesus personally. Nor are we likely to enjoy Sabbath keeping. Why would we want to spend a whole day with Someone we don't love?

Maintenance plan

We might ask ourselves how Christ can dwell in us permanently after our initial encounter with Him—after we've invited Him in. How can the mind of Jesus be in our mind? (Philippians 2:5). How can we abide in Christ, the True Vine? (John 15). How can we be transformed by the renewing of our mind? (Romans 12:2). How can we be changed " 'from the inside out' "? (Luke 3:16, *The Message*). How can we maintain and refresh the "we life"?

These things won't happen without the discipline of daily devotions seven days a week. They won't happen unless we fasten our eyes on Jesus—on Him hanging from the cross, where are displayed His bleeding wounds. It won't happen without our seeking to understand Him in His Book. It won't happen without our speaking to Him in prayer and "listening" for His guidance through the Bible, our conscience, our reason, and the church. It won't happen without our living it out in personal experience. It won't happen if we don't spend special, concentrated time with Him on the Sabbath.

The "we life" *will* happen if our daily, passionate heart cry is

Live out Thy life within me, O Jesus, King of kings!
Be Thou Thyself the answer to all my questionings;
Live out Thy life within me, in all things have Thy way!
I, the transparent medium Thy glory to display.

The temple has been yielded, and purified of sin;
Let Thy Shekinah glory now shine forth from within,
And all the earth keep silence, the body henceforth be
Thy silent, gentle servant, moved only as by Thee,

Its members every moment held subject to Thy call,
Ready to have Thee use them, or not be used at all,

Held without restless longing, or strain, or stress, or fret,
Or chafings at Thy dealings, or thoughts of vain regret.

But restful, calm, and pliant, from bend and bias free,
Awaiting Thy decision, when Thou hast need of me.
Live out Thy life within me, O Jesus, King of kings!
Be Thou the glorious answer to all my questionings.
(Frances Ridley Havergal, "Live Out Thy Life Within Me.")

"In Christ" and the Sabbath

Because Sabbath is about a relationship with Christ, we each can say, "Because I am in Christ, and Christ is in me, because my character has been transformed by His character, the Sabbath takes on a richer and more profound meaning for me."

In my dissertation, I summarized the meaning of the Sabbath as follows:

> The Sabbath is a holy gift of time created by God on the seventh day of creation week, given as a memorial to celebrate the power of His creation. Its sacred, delightful hours provide spiritual and physical rest and undistracted time to worship and focus on the Creator. It is "God with us" in a deeper sense than during the week. Not only does it point back to creation, but it represents redemption from sin and the future "God with us" at the second coming. It provides concentrated time for service to others and for healing. It has two dimensions: a vertical relationship focused on God and horizontal relationships with fellow human beings.[12]

When we have a profound relationship with Jesus and understand the meaning of the Sabbath, we can more easily find guiding principles to keep the Sabbath well. Here is a list of some guiding principles for living the Sabbath, which I have derived from my statement on the meaning of the Sabbath and is based on Scripture.

Guiding Principles for Sabbath Observance

Principle 1—Preparing. Sabbath keeping means preparing for this special day so we can enjoy its benefits (Hebrews 4:11; Exodus 16:28–30; Luke 23:54–56).

ciple 2—Resting. Sabbath keeping means resting from work, life's , and secular concerns and distractions—one of the purposes for which God gave us the gift of the Sabbath (Exodus 16:28, 29; 20:9, 10; 23:12; 34:21; Nehemiah 13:15–22; Jeremiah 17:27; Luke 23:54–56).

Principle 3—Renewing. Sabbath keeping means observing the day in a manner that renews us physically, emotionally, mentally, spiritually, and socially, since our loving Creator provided the Sabbath as a vacation for our welfare (Mark 2:27). This produces a sense of well-being that lowers stress (Matthew 11:29, 30).

Principle 4—Healing. Sabbath keeping means observing the day in such a way as to foster healing, relief, release, liberation, and refreshment. Any action that hurts ourselves or others is Sabbath breaking (Isaiah 58; Matthew 12:9–15; Mark 1:21–28; Luke 4:38, 39; 13:10–17; 14:1–6; John 5:1–18; John 9).

Principle 5—Celebrating. Sabbath keeping means celebrating the creation, or birthday, of the world (Genesis 2:1–3) and of our redemption (Deuteronomy 5:15), so its atmosphere should be one of joy and delight (Psalm 92; Isaiah 58:13).

Principle 6—Sanctifying. Sabbath keeping means keeping the Sabbath day holy—setting it apart for a special focus on God, His Word, and His agenda, to seek intimacy with Him, embrace Him wholly, and nurture a love relationship with Him that makes us holy (Exodus 20:8; 31:13; Isaiah 58:13; Ezekiel 20:12). This nurtures our "vertical" relationship—our relationship with God.

Principle 7—Remembering. Sabbath keeping means remembering, reflecting, and rejoicing about the creation of the world (Exodus 20:11), redemption from sin (Deuteronomy 5:15; Luke 4:16–19), and Christ's second coming and the creation of the new earth (Isaiah 66:22, 23).

Principle 8—Worshiping. Sabbath keeping means participating in corporate, focused worship of God with our church family (Leviticus 23:3; Isaiah 56:1–8; 66:22, 23; Mark 1:21; 3:1–4; Luke 4:16; 13:10; Hebrews 10:25; Revelation 14:7). This nurtures both our "vertical" and our "horizontal" relationships—those with God and with our fellow human beings.

Principle 9—Basking. Sabbath keeping means enjoying, studying, experiencing, and basking in the world God made rather than working at maintaining it (Psalms 92:4, 5; 111:2–4; Romans 1:20). At Creation, God was filled with satisfaction, "rejoicing in his whole world and delighting in mankind" (Proverbs 8:31, NIV).

Principle 10—Responding. Sabbath keeping is a joyful human response

to God's grace in obedience to His loving command to remember Him and His Sabbath gift (John 14:15). It is not meant to be a means of earning our salvation (Romans 3:20; Hebrews 4:9, 10). We respond to God's gift of rest by working for Him in His strength and for His glory (Exodus 20:8, 9; 2 Corinthians 9:8; Hebrews 13:20, 21).

Principle 11—Trusting. Sabbath keeping means trusting God to take care of what we leave undone during the hours of the Sabbath (Exodus 16:14–30; 20:10; Psalm 5:11, 12; Matthew 6:33). It means learning to depend on God rather than on ourselves.

Principle 12—Fellowshiping. Sabbath keeping means nurturing our relationships with family and friends (Mark 1:29–31; Luke 14:1). In the Sabbath, God provides time for focused fellowship with the whole family—even the family animals (Exodus 20:8–11). Sabbath and family go together (Genesis 1:1–2:25; Leviticus 19:3). This nurtures our "horizontal" relationships—those with our fellow human beings.

Principle 13—Affirming. Sabbath keeping means rightly representing the atmosphere of the Sabbath by a spirit of acceptance, love, and affirmation rather than a spirit of judgment and criticism (John 7:24).

Principle 14—Serving. Sabbath keeping means loving service to others and loving witness for God (Isaiah 58:7–10; Matthew 12:12; Mark 3:4; Luke 6:9; 13:12, 16).

Principle 15—Caring. Sabbath keeping means caring for physical needs on Sabbath; no creature—animal or human—should be allowed to suffer on this day (Exodus 23:12; Matthew 12:1–14; Mark 2:27).

Later in this book I will explain in more detail how these principles are based on God's character and how we can reflect His character in a real way as we live out these principles. I will also give practical ideas on how to apply these guiding principles—how to translate them into actual Sabbath keeping as we live the "we life."

The need for a "set apart" Sabbath day

Jesus set apart the seventh-day Sabbath especially to nurture His relationship with us: "God blessed the seventh day and made it *holy*" (Genesis 2:3, NIV; emphasis added). Holy means "set apart." Andrews University Professor Jacques Doukhan adds that in Hebrew, the word *holy* or *sanctified—qdsh—*means "set apart for a relationship" and is also used to describe marriage.

So, the seventh-day Sabbath is "set apart for a relationship"—"set

apart" from any other day or any other sabbath (Genesis 2:3; Exodus 20:8–11; 31:12–18; Leviticus 23:38; etc.); "set apart" to give us time to search for God and become more intimate with Him; "set apart" so that we will know that God is the Lord who makes us "holy" (Exodus 31:13)—or, in other words, who sets us apart to marry us!

This holy day provides opportune time to focus on Jesus, our divine Lover, and make ourselves more available to receive Him, be in Him, and He in us. Someone has said that when we *look* at Jesus—personally accepting Him—we are justified; when we *gaze* at Jesus, we are sanctified or made holy. Sabbath is for undistracted gazing.

When we receive the Sabbath refilling of "the mind of Christ," we will live out the meaning of the Sabbath in the coming week, for the Sabbath experience overflows into the other six days of the week. We must practice this attitude of trust all week. But God knew that we would need one special day set aside so we can undistractedly fill up with and bask in the Sabbath experience with the Lord of the Sabbath. Thus, He provided the Sabbath day as a special gift.

Some time ago I got into a discussion about the Sabbath with a Christian heating and air conditioning technician who was working in my house. He said that we don't need a specific Sabbath day to rest because we should have the Sabbath attitude and experience every day. As he left my house, he said, "I keep Sabbath every day." For some time I pondered what he said. I agree that we should have the Sabbath attitude and experience every day. A Seventh-day Adventist should also be a seven-day Adventist. Because we are children of God, focusing on Him, trusting Him, and depending on Him is a way of life—every day.

So why keep the seventh day special? On the Sabbath, we celebrate our seven-day relationship with our Lord. On that day we seek God and meet Him in a *special* way. This is a primary reason for the Sabbath. Also, God in His mercy has given this time as a special recharge and rest day each week. On this day we can stop our daily routine to be undistractedly refilled with "the mind [attitude] of Christ"—a spiritual pit stop in life's rat race. We would wear out if we allowed life to rush on without a decisive break. John Youngberg says that we need to take a break or we will break. We need to "come apart" or we will literally come apart emotionally and spiritually. Without a renewal day on a regular basis, our daily Sabbath attitude and experience could become depleted. As George White wrote,

wordswithoutspacemakenosense
wordswithout space makenosense
words without space make no sense
lifewithoutspacemakesnosense
lifewithout space makesnosense
life without space makes no sense
remember the sabbath[13]

Even the people who don't know about the Sabbath understand the importance of setting days aside to suspend work and remember special people or events. In the United States, people celebrate Martin Luther King Jr. Day, Mother's Day, Father's Day, Independence Day, Thanksgiving Day, Christmas Day, and more. These holidays come once a year. The Sabbath holiday (*holiday* means "holy day") comes every week to allow us to consistently remember and be refreshed in a special way by the most important Person in the universe. The Sabbath holiday commemorates the most important events ever to happen on planet Earth. It reminds us to look back at the creation of our world, to look up to the risen Christ, and to look forward to Jesus' coming and the new earth He will create. John Webster, professor at the La Sierra University School of Religion, concludes that keeping the Sabbath holiday is an act of remembering (Creation), celebrating (redemption), and hoping (for re-creation).

So what?

When we know who we really are and, consequently, what the Sabbath really means, we will long to experience the Sabbath to its fullest. Wonderful ideas are even more wonderful when we can apply them to real life. It's time to get practical about what has been said up to now. There has to be a way to deal with the challenges that some people have shared about Sabbath keeping. Why would God ask us to do something and then leave us out on a limb when it comes to carrying it out? Why would He give us a beautiful gift that we can't enjoy?

How should we then live out the Sabbath experience—the blessed gift that God gave for our happiness, a gift that humanity has been so reluctant to accept that God had to make it a command,[14] a mandated gift?[15] The answer is found in the One who gave the gift in the first place. We need to focus on the Creator God—the Gift-Giver—to find answers to

the quandaries that we humans have created as we have received and applied His Sabbath gift.

Chapter 4 will begin to explore a train of thought that will help Ivan with his Friday-night problems. It will help Kathy's aunt decide whether or not to allow her realtor to show her North Carolina property on Sabbath. It will provide you and me with a process for making personal Sabbath-keeping decisions that grow out of the "we life" with Jesus and are in line with the Gift-Giver's will.

Questions for Reflection and Discussion

1. How does your church compare with the church described at the beginning of this chapter? How does it differ? Why?
2. Evaluate your personal relationship with Christ and who you are. How does this affect the way in which you keep the Sabbath?
3. What does the Sabbath mean to you personally? How does this affect your Sabbath keeping?
4. How does the following text relate to this chapter: "God is love. Whoever lives in love lives in God, and God in him" (1 John 4:16, NIV)?
5. What do conversion experiences such as those recorded in Acts 2:37 and Acts 9:5, 6 have to do with what we do on the Sabbath?

Chapter 4
How's a Sabbath Keeper to Decide What to Do?

In *A Day to Remember,* George Vandeman told an old story about how traditions can take the place of common sense.[1] Here's how the story goes: Many years ago, a young Russian tsar took a walk in the royal gardens. On his walk, he noticed a palace guard standing with all his pomp and ceremony in a nearby field. The tsar asked the soldier what he was guarding. The soldier replied that he didn't know; he was standing in that particular spot only because orders called for a sentry there.

Curious, the young tsar looked up the historical records. He found that at one time Catherine the Great had acres and acres of rose gardens. She allowed the peasants to come and view the roses in her garden, but she ordered a sentry to stand guard over one particularly beautiful rosebush to prevent the peasants from taking clippings. The rosebush had long since disappeared, but no one had ever rescinded the order to guard it—so now a sentry was standing guard over a patch of weeds!

Some Sabbath keepers are like that Russian sentry. They don't have a clue about why they are following certain Sabbath practices. Now, it's true that we need to have dos and don'ts. But we need a reliable way to choose and to live them. We need to know which practices we should keep and which practices we should discard. Some church members, frustrated by the seeming difference in standards around the world, have even suggested that the General Conference should publish a list of dos and don'ts for the Sabbath.

In a *Cornerstone Connections* youth Sabbath School lesson, James Robertson shared some samples of the Sabbath-keeping rules the Jews had in

Jesus' day.[2] People were told that to observe the Sabbath properly, they must avoid tying or loosening a knot, lighting a fire or putting one out, eating an egg that had been laid on the Sabbath, writing or erasing more than two letters of the alphabet, spitting on the ground, carrying a handkerchief in one's pocket, carrying keys, and walking more than three-fifths of a mile.

The Jews were not alone in this approach to Sabbath keeping. Philip Yancey portrays the influence of Christian Sabbath (Sunday) keepers on the early legal code of Connecticut:

> No one shall run on the Sabbath Day, or walk in his garden, or elsewhere except reverently to and from meeting. No one shall travel, cook victuals, make beds, sweep house, cut hair, or shave on the Sabbath. If any man shall kiss his wife, or wife her husband on the Lord's Day, the party in fault shall be punished at the discretion of the court of magistrates.[3]

I attempted to start a list to honor the request of those who want a list of rules for keeping Sabbath. My friend Kathy Beagles added her ideas to mine. Here is what I have so far.

May-Ellen and Kathy's Unofficial List of Approved Sabbath Activities

During Sabbath hours, we and our children:

- May wade in water no higher than an inch below a modest skirt or pair of walking shorts
- May swing gently on swings if we do so slowly, low, and without pumping, breaking a sweat, or comparing the height we reach with that of other swingers
- May run in small spurts if done so for nature purposes and not for game-playing purposes (e.g., tag)
- May ride bikes if done in a comparable manner to taking a nature hike
- May kick a ball around if the activity isn't called soccer and score isn't kept
- May play tackle football as long as we recite Scripture when being ~~tack~~led—e.g., "Woe is me, for I am undone!" (Isaiah 6:5, JV)

- May eat in places where other people serve us as long as we pay for the meal outside the hours of the Sabbath
- May prepare meals on Sabbath as long as no single item cooks for longer than fifteen minutes (except for those items that bake in a self-timing oven while we are in church)
- May write checks as long as they are tithe and offering checks
- May talk about any subject as long as we say "God" or "Jesus" at least once in connection with each subject
- May sleep all Sabbath afternoon if we do so to avoid breaking the Sabbath

Although a little humorous, the above examples of Sabbath-keeping rules make a serious point. If rules are all we have, we could lose sight of the reason we keep Sabbath in the first place. It's also possible that the rules we deem appropriate might hinder someone else's personal relationship with Jesus. Sabbath keepers must learn to adapt their rules for practicing the Sabbath to their culture. How can we do this within the center of God's will?

For the guidance that can help us know how to "do" Sabbath whatever the time and place, we need a better source than a list of personal rules. The Bible is that better source; it provides the sure foundation for our living. If we come to regard its principles as unimportant or we allow them to disappear from our life, we will become confused about Sabbath keeping. King David's question is just as relevant today as it was when he first asked it: "If the foundations be destroyed, what can the righteous do?" (Psalm 11:3, KJV). Jesus reminded us that without a foundation, our "house"—our life—will collapse (Luke 6:49).

Foundations are biblical principles, absolutes, truths about God that are timeless and universal. It's high time that we rebuild the ancient ruins and raise up these age-old foundations in our personal lives (Isaiah 58:12). God has given us these biblical foundations to change our lives and not merely to increase our knowledge.

So, what are the divine foundations that can guide our lives?

First things first

If you want to fill a large jar with a mix of Ping-Pong balls, marbles, and rice, you would be wise to start with the larger items first—the Ping-Pong balls followed by the marbles and then the rice. If you fill it with rice first, you'll never get Ping-Pong balls or even marbles into it.

Similarly, as we search for guidance regarding Sabbath keeping, we need to begin with the "larger," more important matters: the *person* of God—the eternal qualities that make Him who He is—and then the *principles,* the timeless truths for all people, places, and situations. If we begin with the *precepts*—the rules that give specific directions on what we should do—we may never see beyond them to the larger matters. Mere rules may prevent us from knowing and appreciating God and His character. We might be tempted to give up without realizing that God wants to transform us into His image. So, we must begin with God—His person, His personality, His character.

When I lived in Africa, I noticed that I could distinguish members of certain tribes by unique marks on their bodies. In the same way, the qualities and behaviors that we exhibit are marks or signs that we belong either to God's kingdom or to the kingdom of the "rulers of the darkness of this world" (Ephesians 6:12, KJV). For example, loving acts are a mark of God's kingdom (John 13:35). Sabbath keeping is also a mark of His kingdom (Exodus 31:13). The key to developing such qualities in our lives is that we look beyond the kingdom rules to their Source—the King Himself.

God's character is love (1 John 4:7–9), so love becomes a way of life for us—a principle to live by, especially on Sabbath, the day set apart for love. Des Cummings says, "On the sixth day God created Adam and Eve, joined them in love, and called it marriage. On the seventh day God created a day for love, united them with Himself, and called it Sabbath."[4] If we apply this love principle to our lives, the rules that emerge won't be restrictive but simply tangible reminders of Someone you want to be like.

The test

Josh McDowell and Bob Hostetler present a pattern that illustrates a divine testing process. They call it the "test of truth." This test enables us to understand truth in a way that helps us to see past rules so that we can focus on God and His principles for happiness in life. They illustrate this "test of truth" with three lenses, which they identify with three *p*'s: precept (rule), principle, and person.[5]

When we "look" through these "lenses," we can discern the hidden truth and see what is right and what is wrong. We should view all of life and its many choices through these lenses. If we fail to use them all, our Sabbath keeping, and other Christian practices, may go out of focus.

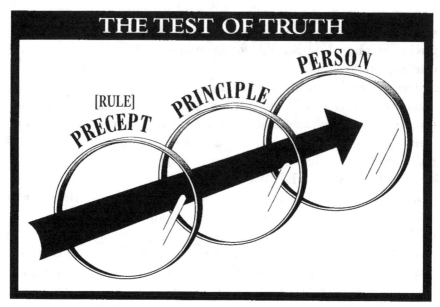

God's Word is filled with PRECEPTS—commands put there for our good. PRINCIPLES are the "whys" behind the precepts, and the PERSON behind the principles is God Himself. As we move from PRECEPT to PRINCIPLE, it leads to the very PERSON of God. It is through the Test of Truth that we compare our attitudes and actions to God's character and nature.

A closer look

Let's apply McDowell and Hostetler's three "lenses," the three *p*'s, to Sabbath keeping.

Lens 1—Precept. Precepts or rules are but the first step in understanding God's will for Christian living. For example, God was quite specific when He said that we should keep the seventh day, Saturday, as the Sabbath. He told us to do certain things to keep the Sabbath holy, such as to gather and prepare food before the Sabbath starts (Exodus 16:22, 23). And He forbade our doing certain things, such as regular food preparation and work activities (Exodus 16:24–30; 20:8–11). Like a parent telling a child to stay away from a busy highway, He issued specific commands, laws, and instructions in explicit terms.

The commands God gave us point to larger principles—principles that are, in fact, universal. Paul wrote that God's law "has become our tutor [literally, conductor or supervisor] to lead us to Christ, that we may be justified by faith" (Galatians 3:24, NASB). In Paul's day, there was a type of household servant called the *paidagogos*. This servant had

the duty of supervising the child's character development. Part of his job was to take the child to school each day. This person wasn't the child's teacher, but he was responsible for ensuring that the child was under the teacher's care.

God's laws have the same function as the household servant. They don't say only "Do this" and "Don't do that." No, they call us beyond the precepts—the specific rules—to principles that apply to everyone, everywhere, always. Ultimately, they point us to the God who expresses Himself through principles and precepts.

Lens 2—Principle. The *Random House Dictionary of the English Language* defines a principle as "a fundamental, primary, or general law or truth from which others are derived . . . something established as a standard or test, for measuring, regulating, or guiding conduct or practice." To theologian Nancy Vyhmeister, a principle is "a broad basic concept, permanent and unchangeable, a law that underlies rules, action, behavior."[6]

John Youngberg, my dissertation chairperson and mentor, shared with me this rhyme about principles:

> Rules are many,
> Principles are few.
> Rules may change,
> Principles never do.

A principle is larger than a rule or precept. A principle is a standard that may be applied to more than one type of situation. A principle helps to explain the *why* behind a command. For example, love is the principle behind God's command that we are to love our neighbors as ourselves (Matthew 22:37–39). Reverence for life is the principle behind God's command, "Thou shalt not kill" (Exodus 20:13, KJV). Honesty is the principle behind "Thou shalt not bear false witness" (Exodus 20:16, KJV). That we value our love relationship with God above all else is one of the principles behind "The seventh day is the sabbath of the LORD thy God: in it thou shalt not do any work" (Exodus 20:10, KJV).

The Bible has other principles that are foundational for today's Sabbath-keeping practices. These principles all stem from the overarching principle of love because the Sabbath is a day for love and for commitment to the One we love. In chapter 3, I listed several biblically based principles of Sabbath keeping that I arrived at during my doctoral study. These principles may exist at various levels of generality, but precepts can emerge from

them. All but three of these principles are general enough that our Sabbath keeping should reflect them to some degree every week. Our circumstances will determine whether or not we use the other three principles, numbers nine, twelve, and fourteen.

Obviously, we can't highlight every principle of Sabbath keeping every week or we would end the day of rest more tired than we started it! After all, the Sabbath lasts only twenty-four hours. In that time we can sample only some of the many joys God created for us when He gave us that day.

If we aim to discover the biblical principles behind the Sabbath rules, we will be better equipped to make sensible, God-guided choices for observing the Sabbath and living the Christian life in general. Still, principles are not the bottom line. There is yet another level beyond the principles to which both they and the precepts point.

Lens 3—Person. Practices or precepts (rules) are not right only because they reflect a principle; they are right because they come from God—they reflect His nature, His person. To live the Christian life and keep the Sabbath, we need to focus on God's nature, His attributes, His character.

For example, Exodus 34:6, 7 depicts God as the Lord, compassionate, gracious, slow to anger, abounding in love and faithfulness, forgiving, and just. First John 4:8 states that God is love. Jesus—God the Son—said that the Scriptures testify of Him (John 5:39). His life revealed the person and character of God. He inspired principles and precepts to live by. If we know the Person, we have a better idea of what the right choice looks like. True Sabbath keeping is about God, not only about us.

We shouldn't ask only "*What's* the point of this rule?" We should go deeper and ask "*Who's* the point of this rule?" When we live the Christian life, including the Sabbath, we must make choices from a strong, God-based foundation of truth, and we, His followers, must recognize Him as the basis—the origin—of all truth. "No one can lay any foundation other than the one already laid, which is [God, the Son] Jesus Christ" (1 Corinthians 3:11, NIV). God's laws flow out of who He is.

The apostle Paul saw the law as "the embodiment of knowledge and truth" (Romans 2:20, NIV). In Psalm 19:7–9, David described God's law as perfect, sure, right, radiant, pure, and righteous. The law has these qualities because these qualities belong to the Lawgiver—God Himself. Ellen White referenced a similar idea when she stated that God's law "is a transcript of His own character, and it is the standard of all character."[7] McDowell and Hostetler conclude that when an action is right, it is so because God is like that.

So, hatred is wrong because God is love; stealing is wrong because God is just; and lying is wrong because God is true. Applying this lens to Sabbath keeping, hurting someone's feelings or person on the Sabbath is wrong because God is a healer—God the Son deliberately healed on the Sabbath. As I noted in a previous chapter, He performed seven healing miracles on that day of the week. John Brunt emphasized that these miracles illustrate God's character and portray the principle that His day is for healing, not for hurting.[8]

As we shall see in the following chapters, our Sabbath-keeping rules should be based on principles that reflect our Ruler, Jesus Christ. After all, Sabbath is all about *Him*!

Jesus permeates the fourth commandment. Biblical scholar George Rice points out that in the Bible, the word *LORD* in large and small capital letters corresponds to God's name, YAHWEH, or "I AM." Jesus said that He is the "I AM"—for instance He said, " 'Before Abraham was, I AM' " (John 8:58, NKJV). In other words, Jesus is this YAHWEH. The fourth commandment reads, " 'The seventh day is the Sabbath of the LORD. . . . For in six days the LORD made the heavens and the earth, the sea, and all that is in them, and rested the seventh day. Therefore the LORD blessed the Sabbath day and hallowed it' " (Exodus 20:10, 11, NKJV). Sabbath is all about *Him*—Jesus, the LORD, the I AM. Speaking of Jesus, God the Son, one Sabbath keeper exclaimed, "Sabbath is my SONday!"

In line for seven hours

Early in June 2004, I had an experience that illustrated for me this concept of *precepts* based on *principles* that in turn are based on a *person*. President Ronald Reagan had just died, and his body was lying in state at the U.S. Capitol rotunda. The powers that be in Washington established rules—*precepts*—that if people wished to pay final respect to President Reagan personally, they must come to the Capitol on certain days, during certain hours, and wait in line to file by his flag-draped casket. The *principle* behind these rules was to show respect to President Reagan, a *person* who had been respectful of the people he governed.

My husband and I decided to take part in this experience. On Friday, June 11, we arrived at the Capitol at 12:30 A.M., and instantly realized that we would be there for a very long time. To make a long story short, after standing in line with tens of thousands of other patriotic souls for

seven hours, we finally entered the Capitol rotunda and viewed Reagan's guarded, flag-draped casket.

Why did we stay awake and stand in line all night to pass by President Reagan as he lay in state? Why did we willingly follow the rules to experience this historic event? It was all about the *person* of Ronald Reagan. As we waited in line, we weren't focusing on the drudgery of it all but on the *who* of it all.

The Person upon whom we focus on the Sabbath is so much more than a president. He is not dead and lying in state—He is alive! And not only is He alive—He is Love and altogether lovely. He is caring, almighty, Creator, Redeemer, Healer . . . the list could go on forever, for I will never be able to totally fathom or describe the person and character of God (Job 11:7). Sabbath is *all* about Him!

Applying the concept

We can clearly separate some Sabbath choices into right verses wrong. For example, it is clearly right to refrain from secular work on the Sabbath, and wrong to do secular work on the Sabbath (Exodus 20:10). It is also right to avoid commercial transactions on the Sabbath (Nehemiah 13:15–22). But sometimes we are confronted with options that are more difficult to decide; issues that appear to be right versus right.[9] For instance, Isaiah 58:13 tells us God intends the Sabbath to be a delight. Since it's permissible to enjoy delightful food and fellowship on the Sabbath with minimal Sabbath-day effort, does that mean it's permissible to eat out at restaurants on the Sabbath?

If we are living the "we life" that gives us the mind of Christ, that mind will enable us to "test and approve what God's will is—his good, pleasing and perfect will" (Romans 12:2, NIV). The "test of truth"— precept, principle, and person—gives us a biblical and practical blueprint for understanding moral absolutes. However, it doesn't offer a quick fix. We shouldn't think of the three *p*'s "test of truth" as a machine that enables us to feed the problem in one end, turn a crank, and pick up our answer at the other end. But this thought process will put us on the road to more sensible, principled Sabbath keeping. It will help us in many types of situations if we use it within a genuine love relationship with God.

We also need to ask Jesus for the "eyesalve" that He offers (Revelation 3:18), so that we will be able to "see" what is the best thing to do when

we encounter Sabbath quandaries. "The eyesalve is that wisdom and grace which enables us to discern between the evil and the good, and to detect sin under any guise."[10]

Sabbath keeping is something that grows along with the rest of our spiritual growth, and must be guided by the Holy Spirit, the Counselor who guides us into all truth (John 16:13). "Take on . . . a God-fashioned life, a life renewed from the inside and working itself into your conduct as God accurately reproduces his character in you" (Ephesians 4:23, 24, *The Message*).

In subsequent chapters we will explore more closely how the three *p*'s apply to questions about Sabbath keeping, such as those mentioned above. In the meantime, what about the predicament described in the introduction to this book—that of Kathy's aunt regarding whether or not to allow her property to be shown on Sabbath? Can the three *p*'s "truth lenses" help her see how to resolve her problem?

To show or not to show

We left Kathy starting to share with her aunt the train of thought that she was learning to use for herself in thinking through issues such as this one. In Kathy's own words,[11] here is what she shared with her aunt:

> Every precept should be based on a principle, and every principle should arise from something in the personhood of God— who He is, His character—for us to seek to emulate and/or worship. So I began to talk through this situation in that context. The *precept* was that even 'the stranger that is within thy gates' was not to work. By precept alone, a person wanting to be circumspect would ask that no one view the house on Sabbath with an interest in purchasing it. Rational thinkers, however, could come up with plausible reasons to explain away "work," "stranger," and "gate." So, on to the *principle* of the matter.
>
> The principles, in my thinking, are that we are to trust Christ as Creator, Lord, and Savior, and to obey His Sabbath commands, *precepts,* as a pledge that we love, trust, and worship Him. But how was this bringing us closer to a helpful rationale for this particular decision? On to the *personhood* aspect of the paradigm.
>
> What truth about God did this precept and this principle lead us to? God the Son trusted in His Father during His earthly

ministry. In Gethsemane and on the cross, He modeled complete trust and submission to His Father's will. As Lord of our lives, He asks us to trust and obey Him. Even if we do not know how something will work out or why He asks us to do something, we submit freely and obediently to His Lordship and care. To me, that is why we would choose not to let someone show our house on Sabbath. If there were any doubt about whether or not it was OK to let it be shown on Sabbath, I would want to err on the side of trust and obedience and not let any stranger "work" within my "gates," trusting God to bring about the appropriate sale at the appropriate time.

In this particular situation, I believe trust was at the crux of the quandary. Did my aunt really trust God to sell her house for her in His good time whether or not she took every opportunity that came her way to help sell it?

My aunt probably would have decided to take the conservative approach whether or not I had worked through this train of thought aloud with her. But for me it was an eye-opener even though I was not the one with the question. My first reaction had been, I sadly admit, *Here we go nitpicking again. The real issues at stake in Sabbath keeping are so big that we shouldn't spend time quibbling over whether or not we are "doing business" in one situation or another.* I was right—but in a completely different way than I at first imagined and with a different conclusion than I at first expected. I must admit that it felt good to think something through and to have a deep, about-God reason for deciding whether or not to do something on Sabbath. It felt good to not be deciding merely to adhere to the list of rules with which I felt I could rationally live. It felt good to have Sabbath keeping finally be about God and not just about me.

Kathy's aunt did eventually sell this property plus another one despite not letting it be shown on the Sabbath.

If we run this real estate situation through the "test of truth," this is how this process might look:

Precept	**Principle**	**Person**
Show trust/ obedience to God by not allowing the "stranger who is within your gates" to work.	Trusting/ obeying God.	Jesus is a model of trust/obedience.

Questions for Reflection and Discussion

1. What characteristics of Jesus' person are reflected in the Sabbath?
2. Apply the precept-principle-person pattern to real or imaginary Sabbath-keeping situations. Write down the precept, the Bible-based principle, and the Divine Personhood characteristic you would use to help you decide what to do.
3. Evaluate Kathy's conclusion about whether or not her aunt should allow her property to be shown on Sabbath while she was not present. What would you have done? Why?
4. Read the following statement and discuss how it relates to the three *p*'s: "Christ's true followers will be in conformity to the mind and will and character of God, and the far-reaching principles of the law will be demonstrated in humanity" (Ellen G. White, *Review and Herald,* March 9, 1897).

Chapter 5
Vacation With God and With His Family—Part 1

I love to go on vacation with my family. It is a precious time every year that I plan for and prepare for and that I bask in when it finally comes. Our vacation in 2003 was especially memorable. We wanted to do something special to celebrate the completion of my doctoral work, so we decided to visit the Bahamas.

My husband, Gaspar, and our two children, Ivan and Sara-May, boarded the Discovery Cruise Line's ship from Fort Lauderdale, Florida, and we docked in Freeport, Grand Bahama, several hours later. We settled into Island Palm Resort Hotel and figured out how we would spend the next four days. There was never a dull moment. One day we kayaked to a very small island that is a national park—Peterson Cay National Park. We snorkeled all the way around that island. We enjoyed having close encounters with all manner of big, colorful tropical fish; Ivan and Sara-May saw a barracuda. After having lunch on the island, we kayaked back to Grand Bahama.

On another day, we rented motor scooters and went exploring on Grand Bahama. We stopped at marketplaces and bought colorful Bahamian souvenirs and gifts, and we "scooted" to various beaches and indulged in the water and sun. I felt as though I were several decades younger as I clung tightly to Gaspar while he tried to keep up with Ivan and Sara-May.

This vacation will always stand out in my memory as a time of celebration, joy, and love. It reminds me of the Sabbath, because the Sabbath is a time to celebrate what God has done for us. It is like a vacation with God and His family.

Since I have had the privilege of working for the Adventist Church for several years, I have worked my way up to four weeks of vacation per year. I consider that a big deal. However, one day I realized something even more exciting—there are fifty-two Sabbaths per year. That makes *seven and a half weeks of Sabbath time—seven and a half weeks of vacation time with God and His family!*

In the next chapters we'll focus on the how-to's of Sabbath keeping. We'll consider in more detail a sampling of specific biblical principles for living the "we life" on Sabbath. In this chapter we'll focus on the *resting—*vacation—aspect of Sabbath keeping.

The examined life

When we go on vacation, we usually do some planning and packing. We are intentional in preparing for it ahead of time so we can relax and enjoy the actual vacation. And, of course, we consider the culture and environment of the destination as we plan and pack.

Let's say we're taking a dream vacation to the Bahamas or Europe or some other faraway land. When we go to the airport, transportation safety personnel puts us and our bags through a screening process, for nobody wants any bags or suicide bombers to blow up on a plane. Similarly, before we begin our Sabbath vacation, "screeners" check our identity and the "baggage"—the motivations and plans—that we are bringing. This pre-Sabbath screening will influence how we plan and pack for our trip.

David prayed, "Test me, O LORD, and try me, / examine my heart and my mind" (Psalm 26:2, NIV). In *The Message* version, this verse reads, "Examine me, GOD, from head to foot, / order your battery of tests." So, with the psalmist, we'll ask God to check both our mind *and* our heart. May He find not only lots of information in our head but also transformation in our heart and life.

Paul continued this theme by advising us to "test all things; hold fast what is good" (1 Thessalonians 5:21, NKJV). "Examine yourselves to see whether you are in the faith; test yourselves" (2 Corinthians 13:5, NIV). The unexamined Sabbath experience is the least satisfying and might be downright hazardous to our spiritual growth. God has provided the Bible to serve as an effective screener for determining what practices and motivations to bring into the Sabbath hours. "All scripture is inspired by God and is useful for teaching, for reproof, for correction, and for training in righteousness, so that everyone who belongs to God may be proficient,

equipped for every good work" (2 Timothy 3:16, 17, NRSV). This Scripture is "the only true guide in all matters of faith and practice."[1]

So, we show up at Principle International Airport (PIA) en route to the Sabbath. Our Sabbath plans and the motives behind our Sabbath-keeping practices are with us. We meet up with three security points at PIA: a check-in counter, the luggage-screening point, and the people-screening point.

At our first stop, we weigh our baggage and check it in. Machines will screen these bags later. We must also show our passport or photo identification (ID) to an official of this airport before we can go to the boarding gate. Our ID must be "in Christ," or we won't be allowed to board the plane to our Sabbath vacation (John 3:18). Why? We must be associated with Christ in order to continue our journey into the Sabbath experience of resting in Him (Matthew 11:28). Even though the Sabbath was made for all humanity (Mark 2:27), it is only meaningful for those who, by God's grace, are saved, born-again Christians—those who are "in Christ." We seek to experience the Sabbath because we are saved—not in order to be saved. If we try to enter the Sabbath rest experience without becoming saved, committed Christians, we won't arrive (Hebrews 3:11, 18, 19; 4:3).

After we pass the personal identity check, we meet the divine Security Officer with His luggage-screening machine. We place our carry-on "Sabbath plans" luggage on the conveyer belt, and it goes through the X-ray machine, which sees right through it. The Security Officer uses the Bible as His X-ray luggage screener. The Bible contains principles to help us decide which Sabbath-keeping plans we will ultimately take on our flight to the Sabbath (hence *Principle* International Airport). This Bible-principles screener detects if the carry-on "Sabbath plans" luggage is consistent with biblical Sabbath-keeping principles. Whatever luggage the Officer and His X-ray machine deem appropriate for our Sabbath vacation, we may take on our flight.

The screener detects plans or practices that are inappropriate for the trip. The Officer confiscates any such items. In a real airport, items that might be acceptable elsewhere—knives, flammables, etc.—are forbidden on flights. Similarly, when we're beginning our Sabbath vacation flight, we may have to give up plans and practices that are acceptable on any other day. We say No to them because of a bigger Yes—we are going on a vacation with God and we don't want to be distracted.

The people screener

There is another Security Officer at PIA. This One operates a people screener. This Officer goes a step beyond the luggage screener. He checks to be sure that people aren't carrying dangerous items on their persons. I heard recently that someone has developed an airport screening machine that sees through people's clothes. In our imaginary Principle International Airport, there is such a screening machine. The divine Security Officer uses His machine, also known as the Word of God, to see beyond the outward appearance (1 Samuel 16:7). "The word of God is living and active. Sharper than any double-edged sword, it penetrates even to dividing soul and spirit, joints and marrow; it judges the thoughts and attitudes of the heart. Nothing in all creation is hidden from God's sight. Everything is uncovered and laid bare before the eyes of him to whom we must give account" (Hebrews 4:12, 13, NIV; see also Revelation 1:16; Ephesians 6:17; Isaiah 55:11).

Jesus, the Word of God, examines the hidden motives for our Sabbath behaviors and practices. (Of course, nothing is hidden from Him any other day either.) He notes our response to questions, such as the following: Do we love God and His commandments with all our heart? Are we keeping God's Sabbath commandment from the heart? Do we crave spending quantity and quality time with God on Sabbath? Do we get satisfaction from following Jesus all the way? Do we cherish our relationship with God and want to nurture it on His day? Or are we keeping Sabbath mainly for personal advantage, such as because it is fun, relaxing, or promotes better health? (There is nothing wrong with personal-advantage reasons for keeping Sabbath, as long as these are not our only reasons for keeping it.) Do we keep the Sabbath mainly to gain a blessing from God? Do we keep it to earn salvation? Do we keep it mainly because we grew up that way or because people expect us to do so?[2]

Our thoughts, motives, and attitudes produce our outward behaviors and practices. Jesus, the Word, and His written Word examine our hidden motives *and* our resulting outward practices, so we can also apply Hebrews 4:12, 13 to our imaginary luggage screener. These verses really fit here, for Hebrews 4 is about entering into God's rest, symbolized by the Sabbath. God and His "screeners" help His children to have the best possible Sabbath vacation as they enter into His Sabbath rest.

What happens if God's screener finds some hidden contraband—a wrong motive or a forbidden Sabbath plan? He sees that it would be harmful to us and others if He lets them through. If we ask, He will create

in us a clean heart and will renew a right spirit within us (Psalm 51:10). By His grace and in His strength, we will discard our wrong practices, knowing that "it is God who works in [us] to will and to act according to his good purpose" (Philippians 2:13, NIV).

You may wonder how God can be the Security Officer at PIA and also the One whom we'll be visiting when we reach our Sabbath destination. The Sabbath experience is all about God. He shows up in many roles throughout it. Yes, the Members of the Godhead serve as Security Officers at PIA, and They are also the focus of fellowship when we arrive at the Sabbath. The versatile divine characters in our little story remind me of the many roles of Jesus in Scripture: He is the Good Shepherd (John 10:11) and the Lamb (John 1:29). He is the Priest (Hebrews 4:14, 15) and the Sacrifice (Hebrews 9:26). He is our Judge (Acts 17:31) and our Lawyer (1 John 2:1). Can you think of some others?

It's OK!

In real airports, I have noticed that people who successfully pass the identity check don't seem to mind having their luggage or their person screened. It makes them feel secure. When our identity is "in Christ," this will also be the case at Principle International Airport. In our spiritual imagination, we will be willing to let God, the divine Security Officer, put our "practices-plans" luggage and personal motivations through the Word of God screener. Like David, we will want God to examine our heart and our mind (Psalm 26:2.) This examination will help us to see whether we are in the faith (2 Corinthians 13:5). Moreover, if we regularly allow Him to examine our Sabbath-keeping motivations and practices, we will be more critical of ourselves and less critical of others. This is in harmony with the spirit of the Sabbath.

When our identity is in Christ—when He is in us and we are in Him—the Bible-principle screeners are actually in our hearts. We will have internalized them (Deuteronomy 6:6; Psalm 119:11.) When we allow God and His Word to screen our Sabbath motivations and practices, biblical principles will prevent us from making mistakes. Screening safeguards us against unhappiness, inappropriate behaviors, and other people's judgment. Thus, Sabbath becomes more worry-free and enjoyable. Of course, we should experience biblical screening of our lives every other day too.

If all things are relative and not clearly defined in our lives, we'll be constantly debating and deciding. This could be the reason there is so

much debate regarding how to keep Sabbath. In *How Good People Make Tough Choices*,[3] Rushworth Kidder points out that sports referees typically require clear out-of-bounds lines on playing fields and courts rather than only a crumbled shirt tossed to mark each corner. These officials don't require the lines because they are out-of-control nitpickers. They do so because they don't want the game to be overwhelmed by a mass of petty squabbles about whose foot was where. When clear boundaries are in place, the players can use the energy that otherwise would be given to debates to focus instead on playing and enjoying the game.

When we observe God's Sabbath, clear guidelines prevent us from bringing into this day our own works and squabbles so that we can truly enter into God's rest. Marva Dawn reminds us that "to develop the habit of Sabbath keeping requires some intentionality on our part, but ultimately it sets us free from any sort of legalism."[4]

In real life, even if we are "in Christ," our growth into biblically sound Sabbath-keeping practices takes place gradually. Recognizing his own personal weaknesses, spiritual giant Paul admitted, "Not that I have already obtained all this, or have already been made perfect, but I press on to take hold of that for which Christ Jesus took hold of me" (Philippians 3:12, NIV). This implies that even when Christ is in us, there is room for spiritual improvement until we are glorified at His second advent. "When a person comes to Christ, s/he is not completely transformed; that is, there remains an element of his [or her] redemption that is yet to come. . . . We see through a glass darkly in this present life (1 Corinthians 13:12)."[5]

Our environment may also create difficulties with Sabbath observance. When my family and I lived in Russia, many female Sabbath keepers were married to men who were not Sabbath keepers. These women had a difficult time keeping the Sabbath holy when at home. Some of them would spend the entire Sabbath day in another Sabbath keeper's apartment so they could be free from distractions. This scenario is not limited to Russia. In chapter 9, I will address how to keep Sabbath when your spouse and other close family members are not Sabbath keepers.

Regarding our struggles with Sabbath-keeping practices, Dorothy Bass commented, "We are practicing—pun intended. Like a novice learning to play a musical instrument, we may be off-key at times. It may be years before we are in harmony, and we will never get it perfect. But that need not stop us."[6]

Jesus—the Son of God, the One who supervises the screening—sympathizes with our weaknesses and situations because He "has been

tempted in every way, just as we are—yet was without sin" (Hebrews 4:15, NIV). We can approach Him with confidence and "receive mercy and find grace to help us in our time of need" (verse 16, NIV). He will enable us to keep His Sabbath and truly rest in Him, for "all His biddings are enablings."[7] He will teach us how to "pack" our "luggage"—taking charge of our motivations, attitudes, and plans for the Sabbath experience. (See chapter 3.)

Teach me your way, O Lord,
    and I will walk in your truth;
give me an undivided heart (Psalm 86:11, NIV).

How can a young man keep his way pure?
    By living according to your word.
I seek you with all my heart;
    do not let me stray from your commands.
I have hidden your word in my heart
    that I might not sin against you.
Praise be to you, O Lord;
    teach me your decrees (Psalm 119:9–12, NIV).

When we have learned these lessons at the feet of our Creator, our attitudes, motivations, desires, plans, and practices will be consistent with His character. Sabbath keeping will come from the heart. We will enjoy the Sabbath from the inside out, for Christ will be in our "undivided heart" and we will be "in Christ." Our Sabbath practices will be in line with His will. What we do will flow out of who we are in Christ. This Sabbath experience is the greatest teaching tool of the gospel. It's "the brightest of billboards proclaiming Calvary's freedom."[8]

The luggage and people screeners specifications

When I bought a printer for my computer, a user's manual came with it. The manual contained a section titled "Printer Specifications" that listed the features of my new printer. The luggage screener and the people screener in our imaginary Principle International Airport are built to specifications that enable them to scan for certain items.

I mentioned on page 70 some of the screening items, the personal motivations, that the people screener checks. The luggage screener is designed

to use biblical guiding principles that help "travelers" decide what practices to take into Sabbath time. They're universal—meant for all people, at all times, in all places—and are based on God's personal character (see chapter 4). The whole Bible testifies of Jesus and His character (John 5:39). Thus, the specifications that determine what the Principle International Airport Bible screener will pass and what it will reject are based on the character of God.

Now let's take a closer look at specific biblically based Sabbath-keeping principles. I emphasize the phrase *biblically based* because the main presuppositions of this book are (1) that the Bible is our sole guide for faith and practice, its teachings provide the norm by which we are to evaluate corporate and individual behavior, and (2) that all Scripture testifies of Jesus and gives us a glimpse of His character.

The remainder of this chapter and all the chapters that follow will examine more closely the biblically based guiding principles against which the screener checks the Sabbath practices of the travelers. I used these principles in my international survey. I will also present the characteristic of God's Person on which each guiding principle is based.

After I present each guiding principle and discuss its biblical basis, I will share some suggestions and examples for applying that principle. These ideas will reflect my culture; you will need to think of ways to live out the principles in your situation and culture. I'm providing the sample ideas to prime your pump. You can take it from there. We must each individually learn to apply biblical principles to real life. A list of rules that someone else has thought out won't serve us well in the long run.

Sometimes we will struggle with how to act in certain situations even though the principle itself is very clear. Thus, at each step of the way we must plead to God the Holy Spirit for guidance in what to do in each situation. Living biblically, living as Christians, is about relating to and depending on God—for Sabbath keeping is all about Him. Following *His* biblical principles under the guidance of *His* Holy Spirit, we can discover answers to the question, What does Sabbath look like, feel like, taste like, and sound like?

For the purposes of this book, I will group the fifteen biblical guiding principles listed in chapter 3 into three parts that stem from the phrase "Vacation / with God / and with His family." Part 1 will cover "vacation" principles, part 2 will cover "with God" principles, and part 3 will cover "with His family" principles. I will explain each of the principles in these three categories in the remainder of this book.

The first guiding principle fits under the "vacation" aspect of Sabbath keeping—which is about preparing for out vacation day with God.

Principle 1

Characteristic of the Personhood of God on which principle 1 is based. God is a preparer. He prepared the beautiful Garden of Eden and the plan of salvation before He created humankind and the Sabbath (Genesis 1–2; Proverbs 8:27–31; 1 Peter 1:20). He has prepared an inheritance for the redeemed, the kingdom prepared since Creation (Matthew 25:34). He has prepared a place for us—a custom-made home in heaven (John 14:1–3). He will prepare the Holy City as a bride adorned for her husband (Revelation 21:2).

Principle 1—Preparing. Sabbath keeping means preparing for this special day so we can enjoy its benefits (Hebrews 4:11; Exodus 16:28–30; Luke 23:54–56).

Understanding the biblical basis of principle 1. As I mentioned earlier, when we go on a vacation we usually do some planning and packing. We are intentional in preparing for it so that we can relax and enjoy the time off. And as we plan and pack, we consider the destination culture. These ideas apply to our weekly Sabbath vacation with God as well. The planning and packing for the imaginary Principle International Airport screening process corresponds with preparation for the Sabbath.

In Jewish thinking, preparing for the Sabbath is as sacred an activity as is praying. Jewish women are exempted from certain prayers because they have already "prayed" by preparing their family for the Sabbath. The Jews call the Sabbath a queen. The arrival of the Sabbath is the arrival of royalty. Prepare accordingly.

God systematically planned and carried out His work during Creation week, setting the stage for the glorious celebration of it all on the seventh-day Sabbath. In his book *Original Love,* Des Cummings admitted that he and his wife began to realize that in regard to the Sabbath, they were acting more like evolutionists than creationists because a fundamental assumption of creationism is the planning the Creator did. God did nothing by accident. Cummings said that in contrast, too often he and his wife were like evolutionists waiting for a "holy accident" to happen. When Sabbath accidentally went well, they were happy, and when it didn't, they were disappointed. However, the seventh day of Creation was not the result of a "holy accident" in which God waited

to see what would happen on that day. Rather, He carefully planned for it in advance.

The principle of preparation for the Sabbath appears again in the story of the children of Israel's journey to the Promised Land. When God sent them manna, He commanded them to gather a double amount to meet their needs on the Sabbath (Exodus 16:28–30). The principle of Sabbath preparation was still in operation on the weekend that Jesus died for humankind's re-creation. Referring to Good Friday, scripture says that "it was Preparation Day, and the Sabbath was about to begin" (Luke 23:54, NIV). Also, God has been following the principle of preparation as He prepares for His family's homecoming in heaven (John 14:1-3).

In his book *52 Sabbath Activities for Teen Groups*,[9] Don Pate explains that many Jews don't use the phrase "keeping Sabbath." Instead, they say that they "make Sabbath." "Making Sabbath" has a more creative ring than "keeping Sabbath." Instead of a mentality of limitation, there is a mentality of expansion and creativity. God took this stance when the Godhead joyfully and lovingly created the world for His human children. What would our Sabbaths be like if we joyfully and lovingly planned ahead to make each one special for Jesus and for those around us? Let's find out!

Acting on principle 1. Even though Friday is the special preparation day for the Sabbath, we should prepare for the Sabbath all through the week. "On Friday let the preparation for the Sabbath be *completed.*"[10] We should "remember the Sabbath day" all week because we want "to keep it holy" when it comes. The whole week pivots around that special day. Martha Zimmerman[11] portrays this idea in the simple diagram on the next page.

Intentionality is a magic word in living this weekly rhythm of the sacred. Paraphrasing a suggestion of Karen Mains, as we get ready to "observe," we can say to ourselves, "I'll make this coming Sabbath special for You, Jesus, by . . ." We can also get ready to "remember" after the Sabbath is over by saying to ourselves, "Jesus, here's what I'll carry in my heart from this last Sabbath into the new week."[12] Then we plan to make that happen.

To help us in our planning, we used a form with blanks to fill in for meals and activities throughout the Sabbath—for Friday evening and Sabbath morning, afternoon, and evening. (See the "Our Sabbath Plan" form on page 194 in appendix A.) We found this form very helpful when our children were growing up. Early each week, sometimes during family

Sabbath

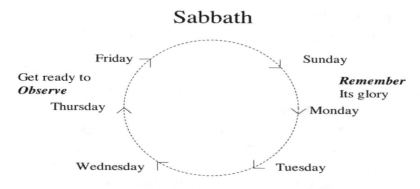

worship, our family would discuss our plans for the following Sabbath. Ivan and Sara-May would make the suggestions and would record our decisions on the form. My husband, Gaspar, and I shared biblical principles for Sabbath observance with our children to guide them as they made their suggestions. We then would post the form on our refrigerator, where we could see it all week. This would build up excitement and anticipation for the coming Sabbath. We found that when parents and children plan Sabbath together and build up anticipation for that special day, there is less chance that the children will complain about Sabbath being an unhappy "don't" day.

Make a family project of carrying out those plans, and prepare for as many of them as possible during the week so that Friday afternoon doesn't become a whirlwind. Depending on their ages, the children can help prepare the Sabbath meals, prepare their Sabbath clothes, polish shoes, clean the house, yard, car, and so forth. We want all these things done before our heavenly Royal Guest arrives at sundown—so nothing will distract us from Him. We'd do no less for an earthly guest. The parents of one family used to set the atmosphere for their children by reminding them that "the King is coming!"

Families with little children can do a "Sabbath countdown" all week to help foster excitement and anticipation. Tell the children every morning, "Today is (Monday). There are (five) more days to Sabbath."

I've found that it also helps to prepare the environment in my home so when the special day arrives, everyone remembers that it has come. For example, you can put away secular magazines and papers. Karen Burton Mains even prepared a little hanger for her TV that reads "Preempted for Spiritual Prime Time."[13]

An hour's cushion

Even if we lay Sabbath plans early in the week, the clock seems to tick faster on Friday afternoon than on other days. Sometimes sundown arrives before we're ready to welcome Jesus into our home for His Sabbath visit. I have on my refrigerator a paper clock with movable hands that can be set to mark the time of sundown each Friday.[14] I usually reset it early each week as a daily reminder. This refrigerator clock also fits into our imaginary airport scenario, for we must be at the Principle International Airport *on time* for our journey into the Sabbath. To guard the edges of the Sabbath, we actually "board the plane" one hour before Sabbath to be sure we're on time for our sundown appointment with Jesus. I have learned the hard way that I must be intentional about guarding the edges of the Sabbath, or I won't be ready for departure into the best experience of the week. In *A Love Song for the Sabbath*, Richard Davidson reminds us that the holy Sabbath is wholly for the Lord—*all of it,* even the edges.[15]

I have never planned not to be ready for Sabbath. I have always felt that it is important to be ready by whenever sundown occurs on Friday evening. But I used to try to squeeze in as much of my agenda as possible before that time. And all too often, I haven't left enough of a margin of error for the all too frequent Friday afternoon surprises.

One particular Friday comes to mind when the slippery slope of this mind-set especially came into play. I was rushing to get my Friday to-do list accomplished before sundown at 6:38 P.M. My husband, Gaspar, had the tasks "mail letters at post office and get gas in car" on his Friday list. At 6:20 P.M., he hadn't yet done these tasks.

I said, "Honey, the mail isn't urgent, and our other car has plenty of gas for Sabbath, so don't try to do all that now." But Gaspar thought he could get it all done before sundown. However, he got stuck in a big traffic jam and he didn't return home until almost an hour later, so he wasn't around to welcome Jesus when He arrived for His Sabbath visit in our home. I allowed myself to become upset, which isn't Sabbath behavior, and our Sabbath beginning was not happy.

After that experience, we resolved to allow for a larger margin of error in our calculations of how long something might take to do. We decided that to avoid "skidding" into the Sabbath, we would allow for "braking" time.

When I'm on time for divine appointments with Jesus, I'm showing Him respect. These appointments might be sundown Friday, Sabbath School, Sabbath worship service, or daily private devotions. That's why

I set the reminder clock on our refrigerator to one hour before sundown. This practice of aiming to be ready for Sabbath one hour before sundown has helped us to be ready to welcome Jesus peacefully when He comes to our home for His weekly Sabbath visit. Thus, when our family gathers around the piano for sundown worship, we are not still recovering from coming to a screeching halt when Sabbath began. I'd rather not greet Jesus when He joins us for worship with "Hap-*[pant]*-py *[pant]* Sab-*[pant]*-bath *[pant]*, Je-*[pant]*-sus *[pant]*. *Phew!*" I'm still working on this issue, and I'm noticing that each step in this direction enhances Sabbath peace.

There is another necessary part of preparation for Sabbath. We each must settle all differences we have with members of our family or our church. "Let all bitterness and wrath and malice be expelled from the soul. In a humble spirit, 'confess your faults one to another, and pray one for another, that ye may be healed.' James 5:16."[16] If all differences in our families or churches were never more than a week old, would there be any divided families or churches?

One particular Friday evening I sensed that Sabbath peace had not yet descended upon our home. During the week, I had said something to Gaspar that was judgmental and unkind. I knew that I must make it right before we could enjoy Sabbath together. During sundown worship I confessed to him that I was wrong, and asked his forgiveness, which he freely gave. At that moment, Sabbath truly began for us. Sabbath peace had come at last.

For more suggestions on Sabbath preparation and other aspects of "Sabbath making," see "Ideas for Celebrating Sabbath in Your Family" in appendix A. You will also find many practical ideas in resources such as John and Millie Youngberg's *Family Sabbath Traditions to Bless Your Heart and Home* (Nampa, Idaho: Pacific Press®, 2001); Karen Holford's *100 Creative Activities for Sabbath* (Nampa, Idaho: Pacific Press®, 2006); Ellen G. White, *Child Guidance* (Washington, D.C.: Review and Herald®, 1982), 527–537; Ellen G. White, *Education* (Oakland, Calif.: Pacific Press®, 1903), 250–252; and Ellen G. White, *Testimonies for the Church* ((Mountain View, Calif.: Pacific Press®, 1948), 6:353–368. (I've included sample counsels from the latter three books in appendix B.)

You might be thinking, *Wow! Preparing for the Sabbath is a lot of work, and I'm already too busy.* During some seasons of your life, you may need to lay very simple plans for Sabbath, but simple can still be special. Happy Sabbath making!

Questions for Reflection and Discussion

1. Decide whether you agree or disagree with the following statement and state the reason for your response: The six working days are preparation for the Sabbath, and the Sabbath is preparation for the six working days.

2. A story is told of two students at an Adventist college who were shooting guns on the Sabbath. When the dean asked them what they were doing, they answered, "We're guarding the edges of the Sabbath." How do *you* guard the edges of the Sabbath?

3. Using the "Our Sabbath Plan" form in appendix A, plan next Sabbath with your family or by yourself if you're alone.

4. Give some examples of ways that simple Sabbath activities can still be special.

Chapter 6
Vacation With God and With His Family — Part 2

When I lived in Russia, I heard a story about a man who had a close relationship with Jesus. I never learned his name, so I'll call him Vladimir. He was a wholehearted Sabbath keeper. No matter what the circumstances, he consistently focused on God every Sabbath. His ox kept the Sabbath too!

The year was 1948, and the place was Siberia, in a *gulag*, or labor camp, in the heart of the Soviet Union. Communist authorities sent people to these camps to be punished with hard labor for breaking the laws of the land.

The authorities had sentenced Vladimir to twenty-five years in a *gulag*. Then, to make an already terrible situation worse, they began to punish him because he wouldn't work on God's holy Sabbath day. Every time he refused to work on a Sabbath, he was sentenced to stand for ten days in a three-by-four-foot jail cell with only bread and water to eat. He would get out on a Wednesday, and on the next Sabbath he would be sent back to solitary confinement for another ten days.

After Vladimir had suffered a year of this, a general came to inspect the camp. He saw Vladimir in the miserable cell and asked, "Who is he?"

A jailer replied, "Oh, he's a lazy, stubborn man," but Vladimir countered, "Sir, I am neither lazy nor stubborn. I am a believer in God. As a sign of my loyalty to Him, I rest on Saturday. However, I am prepared to work twice as much on Friday in order to have Saturday off."

The general said, "Very well. You will supply the water for the thousand prisoners in this camp. You must fill the reservoir with well water from outside the *gulag*."

The officials provided an ox to help Vladimir do his water duty, and for ten long years the two prisoners—the man who loved Jesus and His Sabbath and the ox—worked together. Every Friday, Vladimir and the ox did twice as much work as usual. And every Sabbath they rested.

After ten years, the jailer decided that Vladimir should be released because he was such a good worker. However, the ox remained a prisoner and helped the next man who had to carry water for the prisoners in the camp. However, when the next Saturday came, the ox absolutely refused to move, and nothing could change its mind. This happened every Saturday, until finally, the exasperated jailer told the new water hauler, "You will *never* change that ox's behavior. The Sabbath keeper has made the ox into a Sabbath keeper, and Sabbath keepers are very, very stubborn!"

This story serves well as an introduction to guiding principles 2 through 5, which I will discuss in this chapter. Like principle 1, all of them fit the "vacation" aspect of Sabbath keeping. They speak to our laying aside the burdens of life and taking a revitalizing break.

Principle 2

Characteristic of the Personhood of God on which principle 2 is based. God is the epitome of rest. "My soul finds rest in God alone" (Psalm 62:1, NIV). Through Jesus, God offers rest to all who come to Him (Matthew 11:28). Jesus Himself rested on the Sabbath after He worked all week creating the earth (Genesis 2:1).

Principle 2—Resting. Sabbath keeping means resting from work, life's burdens, and secular concerns and distractions—one of the purposes for which God gave us the gift of the Sabbath (Exodus 16:28, 29; 20:9, 10; 23:12; 34:21; Nehemiah 13:15–22; Jeremiah 17:27; Luke 23:54–56).

Understanding the biblical basis of principle 2. We start with the most obvious aspect of Sabbath—resting from physical work. " 'Six days you shall labor and do all your work [working six days is part of the Sabbath rest commandment], but the seventh day is the Sabbath of the LORD your God. In it you shall do no work: you, nor your son, nor your daughter, nor your manservant, nor your maidservant, nor your cattle, nor your stranger who is within your gates' " (Exodus 20:9, 10, NKJV). Even the family animals (and *gulag* animals) deserve a rest.

The Sabbath "day off" serves the six working days. If we truly observe the Sabbath as a day of rest, we will accomplish more on the six workdays.

Dwight L. Moody argued that a person can do more in six days than in seven. In 1941, during World War II, Winston Churchill counseled his nation that if they were to win the war, it would be by their staying power. For this reason, they must have one holiday per week and a one-week holiday per year. During the French Revolution, France experimented with a ten-day, or metric, week. The results were disastrous. People can't work ten days without rest.

In *Catch Your Breath,* Don Postema reminds us that being active all the time is like exhaling all the time. We must take time to inhale too. That's part of the rhythm of staying alive. Sabbath is for catching our breath—for inhaling deeply to stay alive physically and spiritually.[1]

The Sabbath commandment says that our Creator finished creating on the sixth day. He made the Sabbath by resting on the seventh day. He didn't rest at the end of Creation week because He was tired, but because He expects us to rest. Mark Buchanan proposes a good definition for Sabbath keeping: "Imitating God so that we stop trying to be God."[2]

Here are some other biblical references that link Sabbath with rest from work and from other secular concerns and distractions:

- Rest from gathering manna (Exodus 16:28, 29)
- Rest for everyone—including servants, strangers, and even animals (Exodus 23:12)
- Rest even during plowing and harvesttime (Exodus 34:21)
- Rest from treading winepresses, bringing in sheaves, loading transport, and selling provisions and other goods (Nehemiah 13:15–22)
- Rest from carrying burdens (Jeremiah 17:27)
- After Friday preparation, rest "according to the commandment" (Luke 23:54–56, NKJV)

Rest is the chief biblical characteristic of Sabbath keeping. According to an ancient interpretation, we are to rest even from the thought of labor.[3] Similarly, Ellen White wrote, "Before the Sabbath begins, the mind as well as the body should be withdrawn from worldly business."[4]

If we become excessively vigilant about our Sabbath keeping, we won't truly rest. If instead we energetically focus on Jesus, we'll be able to relax and enjoy resting in Him. Instead of being under the gun, we'll be open to His grace and instruction.

The book of Deuteronomy explains that the Israelites were to keep the Sabbath in part because they had gone four hundred years without a vacation. Regular time off is great news for a slave! When the Israelites entered the Promised Land, God even asked them to be sure their land observed a Sabbath every seven years. " 'For six years sow your fields, and for six years prune your vineyards and gather their crops. But in the seventh year the land is to have a sabbath of rest, a sabbath to the LORD. Do not sow your fields or prune your vineyards. Do not reap what grows of itself or harvest the grapes of your untended vines. The land is to have a year of rest' " (Leviticus 25:3–5, NIV). God is so considerate to everyone and everything He has created!

Just before Jesus' disciples were accused of Sabbath breaking for plucking grain and eating it, Jesus made a call to spiritual rest. He said, " 'Come to me, all you who are weary and burdened, and I will give you rest' " (Matthew 11:28, NIV). We'll consider spiritual rest—resting in Jesus from our own works—again in chapter 8, under guiding principle 11.

Acting on principle 2. Sabbath liberates us from the need to be finished.[5] Even though we haven't finished all our phone calls, projects, and other secular concerns, we stop at sundown Friday because it is time to stop. And we don't have to feel the least bit guilty for doing so! Stopping when it is time to stop also means that we abandon any Sabbath-preparation chores that we haven't finished before sundown. It is even better to stop a while before sundown so that we won't need to skid into Sabbath and collapse when sundown comes.

As I said in the previous chapter, I've found it helpful to aim to be ready an hour before Sabbath begins. I don't always succeed, but at least that is my aim. When I do so, I'm more relaxed when I welcome Jesus into my home for His appointment with my family.

Look at it this way: this Sabbath privilege of a guilt-free laying aside of our daily cares and responsibilities is a guilt-free gift from our caring Creator. A document on Sabbath observance voted by the 1990 Seventh-day Adventist General Conference Session reminds us that we shouldn't allow even good works, such as "missionary" manual labor, to obscure the chief biblical characteristic of Sabbath observance—rest. So, it's better to schedule community outreach that involves manual labor for a day other than the Sabbath. Of course, emergencies are a legitimate exception.

God gave us Sabbath rest as a basic human right. (It's also a basic animal right—Exodus 20:10; 23:12.) Because of our tendency to forget this

privilege of rest, God found it necessary to issue a commandment regarding it. And it is a *commandment*—not a polite invitation.[6] Tilden Edwards calls Sabbath time a "mandated gift."[7]

During the Sabbath, we shouldn't emphasize efficiency. We should set aside any pressure to be productive. Sabbath keeping is more a matter of attitude than activity. Some people might call Sabbath keeping a waste of time, but we will have greater productivity during the remainder of the week if we will rest on the Sabbath. British reports on the productivity of airplane factories during World War II reveal that workers who took time off produced more than those who didn't.[8] (What does this imply for pastors, for whom the Sabbath is often the busiest day? We'll get to that later in this chapter.)

Putting into practice the principle of rest from work and other secular concerns and distractions on the Sabbath, Nehemiah forbade routine buying and selling at the gate of the newly rebuilt Jerusalem (Nehemiah 13:15–22). In these end times, as we prepare to live in the New Jerusalem, we also should avoid routine secular and commercial activities on Sabbath. This helps us to avoid things that would distract us from the blessings the Sabbath offers.

When we avoid commercial activities, we also remind ourselves that during the sacred hours of the Sabbath there are no distinctions between rich and poor, advantaged or disadvantaged. There is no distinction between those who can buy and those who cannot—all are equally dependent on God. Samuele Bacchiocchi notes that Sabbath is a demonstration of the social justice that God wants everyone to experience every day of the week.[9]

Buying meals in restaurants on Sabbath seems similar to the actions of the Israelites when they tried to gather manna on that day. God wanted them to prepare their Sabbath nourishment on the sixth day. He wanted them to depend on Him to take care of them over the Sabbath.

Generally, when we do commercial activities such as shopping and eating out at restaurants, we are doing business as usual. Through Isaiah, God calls His people to " 'keep your feet from breaking the Sabbath / and from doing as you please [or doing business as usual] on my holy day' " (Isaiah 58:13, NIV). Anyway, it's nice to have a break from the stress of regular buying and selling on at least one day a week. It's a blessing to be able to focus instead on buying the metaphorical gold refined in the fire, the white clothes of Christ's righteousness, and the salve to put on our eyes so we can see (Revelation 3:18).

Though a nap on Sabbath afternoon (preferably not during church) is appropriate, Sabbath *rest* doesn't mean merely sleeping or being lazy or idle. God doesn't mind our resting when we're exhausted. However, when we have visitors in our home, we normally wouldn't sleep during their entire visit unless we were ill. Sleeping and ignoring our guests would be rude. On Sabbath, royalty—the divine King—is visiting us. We certainly shouldn't ignore our royal Visitor.

What's the difference between the Sabbath as a day of rest and a day of idleness? In our resting, we should cultivate "attentive leisure"[10] before God. We can experience attentive leisure in a church worship service. But if we regularly attend church meetings all day Sabbath, we will trigger fatigue. Another way to be leisurely attentive to God is to spend time with Him and His Word in a quiet nature setting. Or we can stay inside and listen to or perform Sabbath music or read a spiritually uplifting book. On Sabbath, we intentionally enter God's presence so that we can fall into His arms and under His influence. Sabbath is a day to set aside our routine "doing" so that we can bask in "being" God's children. We are human "beings," not merely human "doings."

Principle 3

Characteristic of the Personhood of God on which principle 3 is based. God is a restorer of our being—"He restores my soul" (Psalm 23:3, NIV). He exudes renewal (Psalm 103:5; Matthew 11:29, 30; Isaiah 40:31; 2 Corinthians 4:16).

Principle 3—Renewing. Sabbath keeping means observing the day in a manner that renews us physically, emotionally, mentally, spiritually, and socially (Mark 2:27). This produces a sense of well-being that lowers stress (Matthew 11:29, 30).

Understanding the biblical basis of principle 3. " 'The Sabbath was made for man, not man for the Sabbath' " (Mark 2:27, NIV). It is a gift for us from a loving God, not a day taken away from us by a demanding God. It is to be a blessing, not a burden. Not only are we to rest from our regular weekday burdens, but we must do our Sabbath activities in a way that minimizes stress. God designed that we allow Sabbath to restore us. So, if we're more tired and stressed when the Sabbath ends than we were when it started, something is definitely wrong with our Sabbath keeping.

We should seek not only physical renewal but also emotional and spiritual renewal. Sabbath gives us the opportunity to position ourselves so

that God can make us "lie down in green pastures" and lead us "beside quiet waters" (Psalm 23:2, 3, NIV). He can't restore our souls (verse 3) if we are constantly in a stressful mode on Sabbath. God created the Sabbath to give us a break so that all the days of our lives won't run together into one continuous, stressful grind. Sabbath time "beside quiet waters" provides both quality and quantity time for us each to be restored and filled with God so that we can give Him out to others.

Remember, God gives humanity fifty-two Sabbaths, or seven and a half weeks, of vacation time each year. During that time Sabbath keepers can find rest and peace for their souls, for the Lord of the Sabbath's yoke is easy, and His burden is light (Matthew 11:29, 30). When we take His yoke upon us, we are "pulling" together with Him and adjusting to His pace and step.

A group of Jews experienced the renewal that Sabbath brings while they were crammed into a train on the way to a Nazi concentration camp. An old Jewish woman had taken two Sabbath candles with her. When she brought them out, Sabbath peace descended on the suffering group, transforming a miserable situation. Sabbath can renew and transform us and those around us wherever we are.

Acting on principle 3. We need to celebrate Sabbath in a way that doesn't exhaust and stress us. If your life is very stressful and frenetic during the week and you attempt to find several additional hours to prepare for the Sabbath, this preparation can become drudgery. In that case, keep your preparation as simple as possible. We should adjust our Sabbath activities to our individual situations and resources. Sabbath keeping doesn't need to involve elaborate activities; it can be simple.

At this stage of my life, my husband and I are in a whirl of constant activity and obligations. (Ironically, trying to finish this book about Sabbath rest is a part of my whirlwind.) No one has to remind us to avoid wasting our time with entertainment, for we can't seem to find the time for it anyway. It seems that we are constantly exhaling with no time to inhale. Sometimes my husband and I welcome the Sabbath simply by watching the sunset. We sit together in silence—resting, relaxing, and enjoying God's and each other's company after a tiring week.

If you are a new Sabbath keeper, you should choose to begin your Sabbath keeping simply and not try to do everything at once. Incorporate Sabbath-keeping practices slowly, layer by layer, as appropriate to your circumstances—first into personal life, then into couple life, then into family life, and finally into your relationship with people in the church and in the outside world.

As I said in chapter 4, we shouldn't attempt to do everything Sabbath encompasses every week. After all, the Sabbath lasts only twenty-four hours. In that time, we can sample only some of the many joys God created for our enjoyment on that day. If we try to do too many Sabbath-appropriate activities in any one Sabbath, we'll not really rest and we will become stressed. We may not be able to do principles 9, 12, and 14 every Sabbath. However, we must follow the remaining guiding principles, or we wouldn't have a Sabbath experience.

Perhaps you might want to prepare a monthly plan for your Sabbath afternoons to bring balance into your Sabbath life. Your monthly plan might look like the following:

- On one Sabbath per month, the focus will be on Christian hospitality. (If you have children at home, be sure your plan involves them.)
- One Sabbath per month can be service-oriented—visiting the elderly, the sick, etc.
- Reserve one Sabbath per month for a picnic. Go out into nature. Become involved. Look at leaves, pick berries, look for birds. Give each child a bag, jar, etc. (See Eileen Lantry's *A Family Guide to Sabbath Nature Activities.*)
- Keep one Sabbath per month for just your family as a "fall-apart day." Take a nap and then do something special with your spouse and/or children.

The Adventists who took part in my international study were very involved with spiritual nurturing activities. These activities included Sabbath preparation, attending Sabbath School and church, worship, prayer, attending other church-sponsored meetings on Sabbath, music activities, preaching, leading out in meetings, helping those in need, missionary work, preparing religious material, fasting, and so forth. However, the greater their involvement in these activities, the more stressed they were. As I pointed out in chapter 2, such Sabbath activities are in keeping with biblical principles, but if we do too much of even good things or do them in a stressful manner, we are out of sync with the purpose and spirit of the Sabbath. We need to adopt a Sabbath mind-set that promotes joyful worship and spiritual renewal—basking in the Sabbath presence of the Prince of Peace. Dorothy Bass has noted that a growing number of worshipers go to church without their watches to foster this unstressful mind-set. In

fact, many Jews do not carry timepieces on Shabbat.[11] Of course, there needs to be a balance between allowing worship services to go on forever and a mind-set that unduly calculates and rushes the worshiper's special time with God.

Karen Mains believes that the purpose of Sabbath rest is not only to provide physical and emotional rest and renewal but also to give us time for fellowship. Sabbath is "a delightful space on the weekly calendar reserved for being better acquainted with ourselves, others, and God; it is a time for good talk, holy laughter, serious ideas, and shared intimacies between Creator and creature."[12] The result will be replenished, quieted, nurtured, and caressed souls.

You may remember that Adventists in my study showed a low level of participation in leisure activities on the Sabbath. Perhaps this reveals that many Adventists are hesitant to have fun on Sabbath and enjoy any kind of leisure for reasons that I discussed in chapter 2. We can have fun and leisure within the framework of keeping the Sabbath holy. For example, whenever possible, my husband and I go to our special Sabbath afternoon place on a beautiful public reservoir out in nature. Sometimes friends come with us. From March to December, our two canoes are there waiting for us. We indulge in the holy fun of sitting out in the middle of the lake and watch the water birds play around us or busy beavers do their thing. Sometimes we have friends and family with us. We talk. We laugh. We bask in the beautiful, God-given environment around us. Often, we take a lunch or supper to enjoy on the bank of the lake. If we time it right, we have sundown worship in the middle of the lake or from our blanket on the edge.

At this point, I will again bring up the issue based on one of the strongest findings in my international study: Adventist Church leaders experience higher stress on Sabbath than laity does. If you are a church leader, when Sabbath arrives, you may have laid down your secular burdens, but often Sabbath is your busiest and most stressful day. Yes, serving God on Sabbath is in harmony with Scripture. Nevertheless, you as a leader need to find a way to lower your stress in the process of doing it. I include myself in this mandate, so I'll use "we" from now on. If we regularly have church meetings all day Sabbath, when will we have a chance to enjoy a stress-relieving Sabbath-day's blessing—on the only day that God has especially blessed?

Each church leader will need to work this out individually—and the watchword is *intentionality*. With God's help, we need to decide what

works best in our individual situation. Since stressful Sabbaths are often the default setting for church leaders, only intentional measures will turn this around.

Some church leaders say, "I'll have my rest day on another day of the week since I can't rest on Sabbath." Another day may give us a type of rest, but one cannot have a true Sabbath rest and blessing on any day other than the Sabbath, for the seventh-day Sabbath is the only day that God has blessed for this purpose.

What can a pastor or other church leader do? Bruce Moyer shared with me how he managed to "de-stress" himself on Sabbath when he was a pastor. He informed his church members that he would alternate Sabbaths. He would be available for church activities on two Sabbath afternoons a month—his "church Sabbaths." (When possible, his family would join him in the church activities on those afternoons.) He would reserve the other Sabbath afternoons for spending time with his family. Another pastor told his church that for the first two hours after sundown on Friday, he intended to have undivided time with his family.

Once when my husband and I were in pastoral ministry and our children were young, after we sang "Sabbath Is a Happy Day," our children told us that Sabbath was *not* a happy day for them. That was a wake-up call. We vowed that even though our Sabbath afternoons were busy with church responsibilities, we would seek to carve out a block of quality time with them on Sabbaths. Sometimes we did very simple things, such as going to the local park and sitting on a blanket with them on the grass or feeding the ducks. And, of course, the more time the better. Again, it's all about intentionality.

If you are a church leader, you're probably saying to yourself, "Hectic Sabbaths are part of my work as a church leader and that's not going to change!" We must find ways to reframe this situation. As church leaders, we need to begin by asking ourselves, who is the force behind my ministry? Ministering will wear us down if we try to do it in our own strength. If we have a particularly busy Sabbath scheduled, we should try to find at least a few minutes during that day to have special time with God and with our family.

Oswald Chambers concluded that when we serve God from human effort, the result is exhaustion. But when we are empowered by the Holy Spirit, He revitalizes us, and we are at peace.[13] Isaiah 26:3 promises that God will keep in perfect peace those whose minds stay on Him because they trust in Him.

It may not be wrong to be physically tired at the end of the Sabbath. But spiritual exhaustion at the Sabbath's close is an indication that we received our energy supply from ourselves and not from God. If we are constantly physically exhausted, we will eventually become spiritually exhausted. If we are physically exhausted, we will be too tired to pray, read the Word, and replenish our spiritual supply so that we will have something to give. The physical and the spiritual are related.

When an occasional Sabbath is unavoidably exhausting, we need to be sure that the rhythm of our week is such that we replenish the overdraft on our energy account before long. Too many Sabbaths that are exhausting could eventually lead to spiritual weakness.

As the director of the General Conference stewardship department, Ben Maxson had a hectic schedule of traveling and training. He recommends that busy church leaders be intentional about "Sabbathing" during Sabbath hours. He also suggests that busy leaders plan periodic personal spiritual retreats for quiet study, prayer, and meditation—preferably in a special place. (This is not to be confused with downtime.)

My husband and I have found that it's best to do the bulk of our sermon preparation during the week so that on Sabbath our preaching is merely the "overflow" of what we have experienced all week. Even though sermon preparation is a spiritual activity, I have found that heavy sermon preparation on Sabbath can be another stressor I can do without.

There is another issue in Sabbath stress that is relevant for leaders and laity alike: why must we do all our ministry on the Sabbath? *Searching for God, the Stress Reliever, is the most important reason for Sabbath.*

Lay members of the church should not make Sabbath the only day on which they do ministry and outreach. They should be unselfish enough to spend some of "their" time during the week doing ministry. As members of God's family, we build our whole life—not just the Sabbath—around ministry. It is compatible with the Sabbath, but we shouldn't limit it to that day.

Even though as church leaders we may not always be able to change how we minister on the Sabbath, we can, by God's grace, choose to receive our strength for ministry from Jesus. We can intentionally choose to come to Him during the Sabbath hours to bask in His special Sabbath rest. We need to be as intentional about our Sabbath rest as we are about working for God in other duties. The Lord of the Sabbath is saying to us, "Come unto Me on the Sabbath, all you pastors and other church leaders who serve Me on My holy day and are weary and heavy laden, and I will give you rest."

Principle 4

Characteristic of the Personhood of God on which principle 4 is based.
God is a healer (Exodus 15:26; Psalms 103:3; 147:3; Matthew 4:23; Acts
10:38). He has "healing in His wings" (Malachi 4:2, NKJV). God the
Son announced that His mission is to restore sight to the blind and to
release the oppressed (Isaiah 61; Luke 4:18, 19).

Principle 4—Healing. Sabbath keeping means observing the day in
such a way as to foster healing, relief, release, liberation, and refreshment.
Any action that hurts ourselves or others is Sabbath breaking (Isaiah 58;
Matthew 12:9–15; Mark 1:21–28; Luke 4:38, 39; 13:10–17; 14:1–6;
John 5:1–18; John 9).

Understanding the biblical basis of principle 4. Jesus followed the principle of healing on the Sabbath, as confirmed by the seven miracles of
healing He performed on the Sabbath (Matthew 12:9–15; Mark 1:21–28;
Luke 4:38, 39; 13:10–17; 14:1–6; John 5:1–18; 9:1–41). Except for the
healing of Simon Peter's mother-in-law, Jesus deliberately chose to heal
the afflicted ones—He did so without even being asked. In *A Day for
Healing,* John Brunt points out that in all the other healing miracles recorded in the Gospels (excluding resurrections and some exorcisms), the
ill person, a relative, or friend requested the healing.[14] In other words,
Jesus deliberately set up these healing situations on the Sabbath. He
healed cases that weren't acute, that could wait until the Sabbath ended.
Sabbath scholar Jo Ann Davidson comments that He could have saved
Himself a lot of trouble if He had waited, for the Jewish leaders were
looking for excuses to kill Him.[15] The Healer took advantage of each situation to show that *the Sabbath is about healing, about restoring to wholeness.* The people He healed must have especially loved the Sabbath after
what Jesus did for them on that day.

After Jesus healed the man at the pool of Bethesda on Sabbath, He told
the Jews who criticized Him for the healing, " 'My Father is always at his
work to this very day, and I, too, am working' " (John 5:17, NIV). We can
see God's work on the Sabbath in births, sunshine, rain, the growth of
crops, the continued turning of the earth, and continuance of life in general, as well as in His Son's healing ministry. If God stopped working to
sustain life on Sabbath, the day would not be Sabbath. It would be death
and hell. The Bible doesn't say that when God rested from His work of
creating the world, He rested from His work of sustaining it too.

As Sabbath keepers, we can join with God in the work of healing and
improving the quality of life of those around us. "God's holy rest day was

made for man, and acts of mercy are in perfect harmony with its intent. God does not desire His creatures to suffer an hour's pain that may be relieved upon the Sabbath or any other day."[16]

We often associate the word *shalom* with the Sabbath. *Shalom* can mean "health" as well as "peace." John Brunt has pointed out that in the New Testament the word translated "heal" can also mean "save." Jesus and salvation stand at the heart of His Sabbath. For the Christian, Sabbath is a day of healing and a day for salvation. It symbolizes release from hurt and oppression. Brunt suggests that we ask ourselves at the end of each Sabbath, "Has this day contributed to the special fellowship with Christ that brings healing and life?"[17]

Acting on principle 4. Sometimes I have taken time off so I could heal from an illness or surgery or recover from fatigue. God gives us the Sabbath vacation to foster healing for ourselves and those around us. Setting aside our usual busyness during the Sabbath, we can become more involved in the healing of others and ourselves. This happens when we intentionally focus on promoting physical, emotional, and spiritual healing.

Since the principle that we are discussing shows that the Sabbath is a day for healing, what rules would reflect that principle? We might say that we will build up our health by indulging in healing spiritual retreats during the Sabbath—times when we can be alone with God. We will contribute to the health of other members of our family by enabling them to do the same. During the Sabbath we will intentionally reconnect with our family to heal tensions that may have developed. During the Sabbath we will make a point of not being critical or judgmental. During the Sabbath we will seek to reduce suffering in the world by visiting the physically, emotionally, or spiritually sick; helping the needy; relieving suffering; encouraging the discouraged; becoming involved with the needs of the community in a way that is consistent with other Sabbath principles.

However, as I've said previously, we shouldn't become so involved in service that we are stressed out. Stress doesn't promote healing. Balance is important.

The spirit of the Sabbath encourages us to build people up instead of showing a judgmental spirit that hurts them. Taking a rule-book approach to preserving the sanctity of the Sabbath can result in our developing a critical spirit toward those who break Sabbath-keeping rules. A critical, judgmental spirit breaks people down—and thus breaks the Sabbath. We should keep the Sabbath carefully, following biblical principles, but we should do so with a humble, noncritical spirit.

A close relationship with Jesus, the Healer, helps us to rise above our natural way of looking at people. It will enable us to accept them unconditionally. It's as if He gives us magic eyeglasses of love and respect through which to see people. We are to point them to Jesus, the Balm in Gilead, so that they can be healed, renewed, refreshed, released, transformed, and converted. He loves them just the way they are, but He doesn't want them to stay that way. Any Sabbath experience that fosters healing encounters with Jesus is part of living out the principle of making the Sabbath a healing experience.

When emergencies arise during Sabbath hours, we may need to ask ourselves, "Will delay in responding to this situation increase the harm?" If it will, we should do what is necessary to prevent the harm in that situation.

Principle 5

Characteristic of the Personhood of God on which principle 5 is based. God celebrates and rejoices. He celebrated Creation (Genesis 2:1–3; Proverbs 8:27–31). He rejoices when people come to Him (Deuteronomy 30:9; Isaiah 62:5; Zephaniah 3:17; Luke 15). He will celebrate at the marriage supper of the Lamb (Revelation 19:7–9). He is a source of joy (Psalm 43:4). Speaking of God, David said, "In Your presence is fullness of joy; / At Your right hand are pleasures forevermore" (Psalm 16:11, NKJV). " 'You will find your joy in the LORD' " (Isaiah 58:14).

Principle 5—Celebrating. Sabbath keeping means celebrating the Creation, or birthday, of the world (Genesis 2:1–3) and of our redemption (Deuteronomy 5:15), so its atmosphere should be one of joy and delight (Psalm 92; Isaiah 58:13).

Understanding the biblical basis of principle 5: In *Making Sabbath Special,* Céleste Perrino-Walker paints a word picture of an announcer counting down on Sabbath evening as sundown approaches: " '10, 9, 8, 7, 6, 5, 4, 3, 2, 1! We have lift-off!' And you shoot out of the bonds of tiresome inactivity to do something fun before the whole weekend is shot."[18]

God says, " 'Remember the Sabbath day, to keep it holy,' " but He doesn't say, "Remember the Sabbath day to keep it *gloomy*"! There are plenty of reasons to celebrate joyfully on the Sabbath. When I think of celebrating, the first thing that comes to my mind is birthdays. The Sabbath is the birthday of the world. It is set in a framework of celebration, joy, and delight. In *A Day to Remember,* George Vandeman linked the spirit of celebration to the Sabbath by referring to God's powerful ques-

tion to Job: "Where wast thou when I laid the foundations of the earth? . . . When the morning stars sang together, and all the sons of God shouted for joy?" (Job 38:4–7, KJV). Vandeman wrote of "the majestic, thundering voice of the Creator. Worlds flung into space. Suns set aflame. Electrons set to dancing. And back of it all the stars singing. The music of the spheres. The sons of God shouting praise to their Creator!"[19] That is celebration!

A marriage is another event that calls for celebration, joy, and delight. The Sabbath also partakes of that theme. Genesis 2:18–24 records the first wedding of a man and a woman, which was celebrated on the sixth day of Creation week. A few hours later, on the first Sabbath, God celebrated another wedding—His wedding with humankind! All the Sabbaths since that first Sabbath have been a weekly anniversary of that wedding between God and humankind. God knows the human tendency to forget anniversaries, so He gave a commandment that tells us to "remember" to celebrate! Some have suggested that the celebration of the Sabbath is a forerunner of "the marriage supper of the Lamb" (Revelation 19:7–9), when God celebrates His marriage to His people and their redemption from bondage to sin.

Psalm 92, the Sabbath psalm, is resplendent with celebration, joy, and delight. Sabbath is portrayed as a time of exultation. Not a trace of gloom can be found in it. Clearly, God wants our Sabbath vacations to have an atmosphere of celebration.

Often Isaiah 58:13 is quoted in bossy tones: " 'If you turn away your foot from the Sabbath / From doing your pleasure on *My holy day* . . .' " (NIV). However, as the verse continues, God says He wants us to " 'call the Sabbath a delight.' " The Hebrew *oneg,* translated here as "delight," literally means "exquisite delight." Old Testament scholar Richard Davidson has pointed out that in the one other place the word is found in the Old Testament, it describes a royal palace.[20] It is as if the King of the universe is inviting His people to His Sabbath palace for a regal, all-day spiritual feast and fellowship vacation. This is no ordinary delight. Why? Psalm 16:11 says, "In thy presence is fulness of joy; at thy right hand there are pleasures for evermore" (KJV). And Psalm 37:4 tells us to "delight yourself in the LORD" (NIV).

Acting on principle 5. When Dwight L. Moody was a boy, he and his brothers used to shout for joy when the Sabbath ended because for them it was the worst day in the week. Learning from the negative Sabbath experiences of his childhood, he advocated his belief that Sabbath "can be

made the brightest day in the week. Every child ought to be reared so that he shall be able to say that he would rather have the other six days weeded out of his memory than the Sabbath of his childhood."[21]

According to noted Jewish scholar Abraham Joshua Heschel, it is a sin to be sad on the Sabbath day. After Sabbath meals, the Jews recite a prayer that "there be no sadness or trouble in the day of our rest."[22] In *Family Sabbath Celebration,* John and Millie Youngberg remind us that if we do not make Sabbath a happy day for our children, they may choose to outgrow the fourth commandment as they outgrow childhood.[23]

The book *Fit Forever: One-a-Day Devotionals for Body, Mind, and Spirit* contains a story by Jan Kuzma.[24] While Jan was growing up in Nazi-occupied Poland, his father found ways to make Sabbath a delight for his family despite the obstacles. It was illegal to hold religious meetings, but people would meet to worship anyway, gathering at the home of one of the church members. Jan's family would carry gifts and flowers, pretending to be attending a party. The congregation would speak the words of hymns, fearing that the neighbors would report them if they sang.

After a special Sabbath lunch, his father would take the family to a lovely park overlooking the Vistula River, or they would enjoy the sandy shore of Lake Lansk. Jan always associated his childhood memories of delightful Sabbaths with his father, for that was the day he spent with his family. When Jan learned English, he was delighted to discover that the word *abba*—the Aramaic term for "Daddy"—was in the middle of the word *Sabbath*. Jan concludes, "No wonder Sabbath is a delight!"

How can we promote celebration on the Sabbath? While the Sabbath is a day for holy delight, this doesn't mean we should celebrate it like a regular party day. After John and Millie Youngberg presented a Jewish-style Sabbath celebration in the Cayman Islands, a boy there told them the experience was "like having a sacred party" to celebrate the birthday of the world. Actually, we can learn something from the way the Jews celebrate the Sabbath. Because they consider the Sabbath to be the queen of the week, the wife, the queen of the home, they proclaim the beginning of the Sabbath by lighting special Sabbath candles some forty minutes before the actual setting of the sun in order to safeguard the edges of the Sabbath. (Since the candle lighting is considered "work," it must be done before sunset.) This ceremony is known as *Kabbalat Shabbat.*

Before lighting the candles, the wife prays a special Sabbath prayer. The two candles represent Creation and Redemption. The candles re-

mind the worshipers of God's words, "Let there be light," on the first day of Creation. Jo Ann Davidson told me the explanation Jews give as to why they light candles at sundown: "You can light a whole roomful of candles from one candle, and that candle is just at bright as ever. So the first Sabbath has lit many Sabbaths since then, and it is just as bright as ever!"

After the candles are lit, the father blesses the children and his wife. They share special Sabbath wine and braided challah bread, and the Sabbath meal, the choicest food of all the week, follows this special celebration. Before each course, someone says, "For the honor of the Sabbath!" During the meal the family sings joyful table hymns that reflect the celebration aspect of the Sabbath.

This Jewish-style Sabbath celebration can tickle our imagination and illustrate the atmosphere of celebration that characterizes the Sabbath. In a way that fits our individual situations and cultures, we can make Friday evenings special. That might mean having a special Friday-night meal served on special dishes. Perhaps it will include other special features, such as flowers, candles, music, and a special worship activity like Bible charades. When my children were young, I'm not sure who enjoyed these Friday evenings more, my husband, Gaspar, and I or our children—except the Friday night when we were acting out the story of Ananias and Sapphira. "Sapphira," Sara-May, dropped dead on Gaspar's foot, and he was limping for days!

Leviticus 24:8 says, " 'This bread is to be set out before the LORD regularly, Sabbath after Sabbath, on behalf of the Israelites, as a lasting covenant' " (NIV). This verse reminds us that traditional Sabbath objects, such as special bread, children's Sabbath toys, and Sabbath candles encourage us to step back and remember *why* this time is special. You might even occasionally serve a Sabbath birthday cake inscribed with the words "Happy Birthday, Earth!"

For years, my family has used a "blessing book" during Friday evening worship. We write down something that has happened in our lives during the past week that we consider a blessing, along with the date that it occurred. Then we celebrate by praising God in prayer for this blessing. It is a celebration in itself to read these blessings later on.

For my family, Sabbath morning was a time to capture this celebration. As our children were growing up, we always had sweet rolls as part of Sabbath breakfast. To avoid having to wash many dishes before leaving for church, we used paper plates and cups. On each paper plate, our

daughter, Sara-May, would make drawings and write messages, such as "Happy Sabbath, Dad!" and "Jesus loves you, Ivan!" This spirit of celebration can continue into Sabbath School and church services, Sabbath dinner, afternoon activities, and the closing of Sabbath.

It is also fun to try celebrating Sabbath with experiences that delight all five senses. For example, enjoy the Sabbath with a few of the following:

- *Sight:* Flowers, special dishes, candles
- *Hearing:* Music sung or played by family members or played on the home stereo system, nature sounds
- *Taste:* Special food, favorite foods
- *Touch:* Clean sheets, backrubs
- *Smell:* Bread baking on Friday afternoon, incense or other room fragrances

What ideas do you have?

Make Sabbath delightful in your current situation. During some seasons of your life, you may need to lay rather simple plans for Sabbath. But simple can still be special. May God help us to make our Sabbaths a delightful celebration "so interesting to our families that its weekly return will be hailed with joy."[25]

I invite you to celebrate what God has done for you by taking a vacation with Him and His family this Sabbath. Come away! Enjoy quality time with Him. The main idea is that Sabbath should be in a class by itself, more special, joyful, and delightful than any other day of the week—a holy holiday![26]

We have covered basic guiding principles for living the "vacation" aspect of Sabbath keeping. In the next two chapters we will look at some principles and their practical applications that address the "with God" part of the Sabbath experience.

Questions for Reflection and Discussion

1. Recall a delightful Sabbath that you have experienced. What did you do that Sabbath? Who were you with? Where were you?
2. How does Amos 8:5 apply to your Sabbath keeping?
3. Which do you prefer: sundown Friday night or sundown Saturday night? Why? Have you ever thought or said, "Another Sabbath is behind us. Good! We don't have to face that again for a whole week, and am I relieved!"? If so, what can you do to change your attitude?
4. What other practices can you suggest that are based on principles 2–5?

Chapter 7
Vacation *With God* and With His Family—Part 1

Two college students met and fell in love. They wanted to spend the Thanksgiving holiday together, however, the young man's parents were planning to take their family to Puerto Rico during Thanksgiving, and they insisted that he join them. So, the young woman went to Maine to spend Thanksgiving with her mom and aunt.

When the young man arrived home in New York, his parents told him they had cancelled the Puerto Rico trip. At that, he sequestered himself in a corner, feeling sad and sorry for himself. All he could think about was his desire to be in Maine with his girlfriend. Eventually, his mom couldn't stand it any longer and asked him what she could do to make him feel better. To make a long story short, she put him on a plane to Maine.

Before the young man boarded the plane, he called his girlfriend's aunt and schemed with her to surprise his girlfriend. When eventually the young woman saw him, she gasped, "What are you doing here? *What are you doing here?* WHAT ARE YOU DOING HERE?" as she cried tears of joy. I remember this special surprise very well for I was the young woman and my husband, Gaspar, was the young man.

It was love that compelled Gaspar and me to spend that Thanksgiving together. We just had to be with each other as often as possible and for as long as possible. The little encounters during our busy weeks in college were nice but not enough. We longed for long blocks of time that would allow us to set our regular routine aside and spend more focused time with each other. Thanksgiving vacation provided that kind of time. So

did the Sabbaths that we spent together. All the special time together eventually led to our wedding on June 4, 1972.

Richard Davidson says that God longs to enjoy a love relationship with us more intimate than anything that human lovers experience. God loves us so deeply that He can't wait a year or even a month for special time with us. Thus, He decided to set aside a whole day every week—a Sabbath—for an all-day date with us, His beloved. On that special day He and we can enjoy intimate fellowship beyond compare.

To make a special date happen, lovers must set apart a special, definite time. Who would want to miss that appointment by arriving on the wrong day? Or who would want to arrive late on the right day? Not only should we start our special "date" with God on time on His holy day, but we should be wholly there—with all our heart.

In *Keeping the Sabbath Wholly,* Lutheran evangelical writer Marva Dawn recommends that we exercise "deliberate intentionality"[1] in our Sabbath keeping. We need to do this because we don't naturally focus on God. I know this is true because my mind wanders easily during worship services. Deliberate intentionality will help us to live out the principles the Bible-principles screener uses at our imaginary airport. We practice deliberate intentionality at Christmas time and when celebrating the birthday of a loved one. Why not transfer this focus to the One we love most of all—Jesus—and to His special day?

We will discuss principles 6, 7, and 8 in this chapter, focusing on the *with God* part of keeping the Sabbath. The seventh-day Sabbath is not about a day; it's about a Person! It's all about *Him!*

Principle 6

Characteristic of the Personhood of God on which principle 6 is based. God is holy (Leviticus 11:44; 19:2), personal and loving (1 John 4:8), and He seeks intimacy and special time with His family (John 15:15; Revelation 3:20). He sanctifies, or makes holy, the Sabbath and His people (Genesis 2:3; Exodus 20:11; 31:13).

Principle 6—Sanctifying. Sabbath keeping means keeping the Sabbath day holy—setting it apart for a special focus on God, His Word, and His agenda, to seek intimacy with Him, embrace Him wholly, and nurture a love relationship with Him that makes us holy (Exodus 20:8; 31:13; Isaiah 58:13; Ezekiel 20:12). This nurtures our "vertical" relationship—our relationship with God.

Understanding the biblical basis of principle 6. Sabbath is a very holy subject. When I direct my full attention to the Sabbath, I feel I am on holy ground as did Moses at the burning bush. We are to " 'remember the Sabbath day by keeping it holy' " (Exodus 20:8, NIV) because God sanctified it; He made it holy. Not only is the day holy but the Lord of the Sabbath is also holy. Because the Sabbath connects us with a holy God, on that day we focus on Him and His character instead of on ourselves and our usual activities.

Isaiah 58:13 reminds us that we should not simply do as we please on the Sabbath. Instead, we're to honor God and His holy day by not going our own way and doing our own business. God presents this advice in the context of taking the focus off ourselves and directing it to Him and the needs of others. When we set aside our agenda on Sabbath, we clear the way for God to share His agenda with us.

God asks us to observe the Sabbath because it is holy to us and holy to Him (Exodus 31:14, 15). Some leaders set up requirements for other people that they don't follow themselves. God practices what He preaches. He proclaims the Sabbath to be holy to us and holy to Him. He asks us to rest, and He rests. *Holy* means "sanctified," "set apart," or "wholly for the Lord."[2] "Holiness is wholeness for God; it is the entire surrender of heart and life to the indwelling of the principles of heaven."[3]

In *Sabbath Reflections,* James Wibberding points out that the Hebrew verb "to sanctify" is the same word from which the noun "sanctuary" comes.[4] The Sabbath is the day for sanctification because on that day we spend special time with God, just as the sanctuary is the place for being sanctified because God is with us there. So God offers us holiness, or sanctification, in time and place. The Sabbath and the sanctuary focus on "God with us"—a central teaching in Scripture.

Old Testament scholar Jacques Doukhan reminds us that in Levitical law, the Sabbath is the only celebration day that is not annual and the time of which does not depend on natural or astronomical cycles. The justification for the Sabbath is essentially religious, and faith is the only reason for observing it.[5] Since the origin and significance of the Sabbath is distinctively religious, during its hours we focus on God instead of on ourselves or secular matters.

Some Christians include the seventh-day Sabbath among ceremonial sabbaths—annual festivals such as Passover, the Feast of Tabernacles, and the Day of Atonement. They say the seventh-day Sabbath was among the ceremonial sabbaths that were nailed to the Cross, which

were "a shadow of the things that were to come" (Colossians 2:14, 17, NIV). But we must maintain a clear distinction between ceremonial sabbaths and the Sabbath that was created at the end of Creation week, before the Fall. Ceremonial sabbaths pointed *forward* to Jesus' sacrifice for our sins. The seventh-day Creation Sabbath points *back* to Creation as an eternal memorial.

"The LORD said to Moses, 'Give the Israelites instructions regarding the LORD's appointed festivals, the days when all of you will be summoned to worship me. You may work for six days each week, but on the seventh day all work must come to a complete stop. It is the LORD's Sabbath day of complete rest, a holy day to assemble for worship. It must be observed wherever you live. *In addition to the Sabbath*, the LORD has established festivals, the holy occasions to be observed at the proper time each year' " (Leviticus 23:1–4, NLT; emphasis added). The Lord's seventh-day Sabbath is "set apart" not only from the other six days of the week but also from all the other sabbaths recorded in Scripture.

When God created the first human beings at the beginning of time, He created them the day before the Sabbath so they could begin their lives with a spiritual, relational experience. The Sabbath provided special bonding time with Him, just as newborn babies have special bonding time with their mothers just after birth. This bonding time continues during other special moments in children's lives, such as when they cuddle up to their mother just before bedtime. Dawn Jakovac, the mother of a toddler, calls the Sabbath God's "cuddle time."[6] The Sabbath command is the most intimate and personal of all the commandments. It is "a golden clasp that unites God and His people."[7]

The Sabbath is holy, God is holy, and He wants us to be holy. He said, "Sanctify yourselves therefore, and be ye holy: for I am the LORD your God" (Leviticus 20:7, KJV).

"Sanctify yourselves"? How is that possible? And what does keeping the Sabbath have to do with bringing about personal sanctification or holiness?

The Sabbath day contains no magical quality that automatically transmits holiness. Rather, God makes the Sabbath holy by gracing it with His presence. When we have intimate communion with God, we actually partake of His holiness. When we spend time in someone's presence, we unconsciously absorb some of their qualities. Because the hours of the Sabbath are filled with such intimate fellowship, we put ourselves in a position to receive a good dose of God's holiness. However, we must

remember that we are not the source of this holiness—God is. Thus, the Sabbath becomes the sign, the embodiment of the entire life of sanctification.[8]

A couple of Bible scholars drive this point home. In *Jubilee of the World,* Charles Scriven points out that when we truly keep the Sabbath, the other days of the week "become opportunities to *embody* what the Sabbath stands for, to give strong bones and warm flesh to mere words."[9] And Abraham Joshua Heschel reminds us that "who we are depends on what the Sabbath is to us."[10]

Moreover, Sabbath is a sign that *God* is the One who sanctifies us. " 'You must observe my Sabbaths. This will be a sign between me and you for the generations to come, so that you may know that I am the LORD, who makes you holy' " (Exodus 31:13, NIV). The New King James Version translates that last clause " 'I am the LORD who sanctifies you.' " (See also Ezekiel 20:12.)

On our own, we cannot make ourselves holy by keeping the Sabbath (or, for that matter, by doing any other good thing). *God* makes us holy when we choose to put ourselves in a position where He can make it happen. The Sabbath is a sign that we are God-dependent. May all glory go to Him, for Sabbath is all about *Him*!

Qadesh, the Hebrew word behind the concept of holiness or sanctification in Exodus 31:13 and Ezekiel 20:12, is also used for marriage. Doukhan points out that this word means "set apart for a relationship," "to betroth," "to pledge marriage," "to marry." It is conjugal terminology.

If that is the case, Exodus 31:13 can mean "Observe my Sabbaths. This will be a sign between me and you for the generations to come, so that you may know that I am the LORD, who sets you apart to *marry* you"! Can you grasp what that really means? Adam and Eve were created and married on the sixth day of Creation. The seventh-day Sabbath was their honeymoon. But their relationship was part of a love triangle, for they had special bonding time with God too. On that first Sabbath, humanity and God were wed. (In other places in Scripture, God explicitly says that He is our Husband—see Isaiah 54:5; Jeremiah 3:14.) Each Sabbath since then has been a kind of wedding "anniversary" date with our Divine Lover. God didn't want to celebrate this "marriage" only once a year or even once a month. He scheduled a *weekly* celebration!

Sabbath is all about *Him*—about Him wanting to be with you and me! He's crazy about us and wants to spend quality time with us on that special date day. I am amazed that the Creator who made and runs the universe

has this kind of time for us. When we don't allow Him to do that, He is hurt—and so are we, even though we may not realize it. On our Sabbath date with Him, do we have eyes only for Him?

Acting on principle 6. What does it mean to be married? It means that I commit all of myself to my spouse and I honor that commitment in season and out of season. In Exodus 31:13, God makes that kind of a commitment to His bride—us. And when we sanctify, or set apart, time to be with Him, we're doing the same thing. We're pledging to commit all of ourselves to that time and to our heavenly Spouse with whom we spend that time. Then we must honor that commitment whether or not doing so is convenient.[11]

When Sabbath time arrives in our homes, Jesus comes with the Sabbath. He is Immanuel—"God with us"! So when the sun sets, don't say only "Sabbath is here." Say also "Jesus is here! Welcome, Jesus, to our home."

Regarding the matter of intimacy with God, I am more of a struggler than an expert. I desperately need the Sabbath as a special prime time that recurs regularly to jump-start my intimacy with God. Slowing down on Sabbath so that I can focus on and bask in this intimacy with God is a struggle for me because I tend to be a type A person. Maybe that is why I felt called to write this book—what I write is for me. And as my fingers click on the keyboard and the chapters take shape, I pray that the Lord of the Sabbath will help me to grow and change.

Just as our houses didn't become ours overnight, so optimal Sabbath keeping and intimacy with God won't happen overnight. But it will happen eventually if we lay aside other plans and distractions and let Him help us focus on Him.

I appreciate Richard Davidson's explanation of how to focus on God on the Sabbath.[12] He says the holy Sabbath is "wholly for the Lord" in at least three ways. First, we are to keep the *whole* Sabbath holy. As I explained in chapter 5, *all of it* is wholly for Him—even its edges. To me, that means that Isaiah 58:13 is not only about keeping the church service holy, but the whole Sabbath day. Sabbath doesn't end when church is over. "The Sabbath school and the meeting for worship occupy only a part of the Sabbath. The portion remaining to the family may be made the most sacred and precious season of all the Sabbath hours. Much of this time parents should spend with their children."[13]

Occasionally, my husband and I enjoy Friday night or Sabbath afternoon get-togethers in which we focus on God with family and friends. (I

wish it were possible to do this more often than occasionally.) Our get-to-gethers are not highly organized. We share our joys and sorrows, sing some songs, pray, read from the Bible or another spiritual book, and play soft Sabbath music in the background during our fellowship. We try to be a spiritual support and accountability group to each other regarding our discipleship, our daily walk with Jesus. There's something special about being together during the Sabbath hours. We have a different attitude about everything, and the fellowship is extra sweet.

As I said, God can fulfill His promise to make us holy when we choose to empty ourselves of ourselves and to put ourselves in a position so it can happen. During all its hours, the Sabbath affords us undistracted time to intentionally be where God can be found—in church, in His Word, in nature, in places of witness and service—branch Sabbath Schools, hospitals, prisons, etc.

A word of caution: sometimes we can get so busy in church, in nature, or in witnessing and service that we might not give the written Word of God its proper share of time in our Sabbath schedule. Our Sabbath experience is lacking until we've made time to learn from God by studying His Word personally. And "the Bible should never be studied without prayer,"[14] so, on Sabbath, don't forget to pray, for Sabbath is the best time for this sanctifying experience.

Second, we Sabbath keepers are "wholly for Him"—*all of us,* including our children. When our children are with us, we should include them in our Sabbath activities, "devising means to impart proper instruction . . . and interesting them in spiritual things."[15] In so doing, we can make the Sabbath a happy, holy holiday for our children, showing them that they are important to us by spending time with them and that God is important by focusing on Him together with them.

When my children were small, my husband and I would naturally gravitate toward socializing with the adults when we were with other families for Sabbath afternoon dinner and fellowship. But even though it was tempting not to do so, at least one of us tried to break away from the adults to sit and relate to our children and any other children who were there. Sometimes one of us would go outside with the children while the adults talked, or we'd stay inside and look at a Sabbath-type book together or play Bible or nature games.

At times we neglected this, for we craved adult interaction. I found it easy to be indifferent to where our children were or what they were doing. But when my husband and I remembered to spend time with them, the

joy that we gave them bounced back to us. And when we spent time with them, they were less tempted to play as they would on an ordinary weekday.

Ellen White provided wise counsel to motivate parents to spend time with their children on Sabbath: "Parents, above everything take care of your children upon the Sabbath. Do not suffer them to violate God's holy day by playing in the house or out-of-doors. You may just as well break the Sabbath yourselves as to let your children do it, and when you suffer your children to wander about and suffer them to play upon the Sabbath, God looks upon you as Sabbathbreakers."[16]

If we are married, our spouses also deserve prime time on Sabbath— whether or not they are Sabbath keepers. The weekdays tend to separate us. The Sabbath should bring us back together. We will deal more with this issue in chapter 9.

Our Jewish friends have a ceremony to close Sabbath that includes a "Saturday night candle" (*Havdalah* candle). This candle has several wicks twisted together. The lighting of this candle symbolically says that the Sabbath has brought the members of the family together once again. Sabbath also brings our entire heavenly family together with all our earthly family. It's all about *Him*—about Him wanting to be with us!

Richard Davidson's third point is that we are wholly God's *all the time*, even outside the Sabbath hours. If we are wholly for ourselves during the week, we cannot be wholly for the Lord on the Sabbath! As I explained in chapter 5, the whole week pivots around the Sabbath day. That day is the embodiment of a wholehearted daily relationship with Jesus.

God offers His presence in a special way on the Sabbath, when we are free from secular distraction. But He is also available every day to walk with us in our secular occupations. Every menial task can take on a sacred aspect when we draw strength and wisdom from His abiding presence. On Sabbath we can celebrate these daily sacred moments. Sabbath provides quality *and* quantity time with Jesus. We need both regularly. During the week, life comes at us fast, and our time with Him is often rushed. During the Sabbath, we stop our regular routine and distractions and focus on celebrating our seven-day relationship with our Lord.

I often journal my weekday happenings, prayers, and biblical insights. Occasionally, on Sabbath I look through my daily prayer journal and praise God for the times during the week when He has brought me through a difficult situation or brought me special joy. I also enjoy looking through our family "blessing book" on Friday evenings. (See chapter 6.) When our

children were home, we often played "I spy" during Friday sundown worship—looking for examples of how God had blessed us during the past week.

Not only do we celebrate on Sabbath the previous week's sacred moments, but the sacred time on Sabbath brings inspiration to the days in the new week. On Sabbath we develop and strengthen attitudes of love and caring for God, our family, and the world He loves so that we can better live out these attitudes during the new week. Abraham Joshua Heschel summed it up well: "The Sabbath is the inspirer, the other days the inspired."[17] When I am a Seventh-day Adventist Sabbath keeper, I become a seven-day Adventist! As the Christmas spirit extends beyond the actual day, so the Sabbath spirit extends beyond the actual day.

Once when I was mixing some orange juice, it occurred to me that Sabbath is like orange juice concentrate. We receive a concentrated dose of Jesus as we spend undistracted time with Him on Sabbath. When we go through the new week, we mix the "Sabbath concentrate" into our routine work and other activities. When we mix water with orange juice concentrate, we can still taste the orange flavor. When we mix the weekday routine with the "Sabbath concentrate," the weekdays take on the flavor of the Sabbath. So, all week long we can enjoy the essence of our Sabbath time with Jesus!

Other Sabbath issues

Fasting on Sabbath. Some people fast from food on Sabbath to improve their focus on spiritual things. Perhaps this is appropriate at times, but if we fast in a rigid manner every Sabbath, we may compromise the celebration aspect of this special day. By refusing to condemn His disciples for picking and eating grain on Sabbath, it seems that Jesus was helping them stay focused on the joy of that day. Unmet needs might keep us from enjoying and delighting in our Sabbath experience with Him.

Ellen White dealt with the Sabbath food issue in a very balanced way:

> We should not provide for the Sabbath a more liberal supply or a greater variety of food than for other days. Instead of this the food should be more simple, and less should be eaten, in order that the mind may be clear and vigorous to comprehend spiritual things. Overeating befogs the brain. The most precious words

may be heard and not appreciated, because the mind is confused by an improper diet. By overeating on the Sabbath, many have done more than they think to dishonor God.

While cooking upon the Sabbath should be avoided, it is not necessary to eat cold food. In cold weather let the food prepared the day before be heated. And let the meals, though simple, be palatable and attractive. Provide something that will be regarded as a treat, something the family do not have every day.[18]

In a broader sense, Sabbath is a fasting day. On Sabbath we refrain from our usual weekday secular activities so that we can better focus on Jesus.

Accountability time. Sabbath also regularly calls us to be accountable. Ellen White stresses the need to reckon with our souls each Sabbath "to see whether the week that has ended has brought spiritual gain or loss."[19]

The Sabbath as "set apart." We set apart—"sanctify"—our food, our clothes, and our plans pertaining to Sabbath before its sacred hours begin. The story in Exodus 16 of setting apart a double portion of manna for Sabbath illustrates this principle. It's interesting that this setting apart idea even shows up in 1 Corinthians 16:1, 2. There Paul asked the Corinthians to set aside their offerings on the first day of the week—a day other than the Sabbath. The issue is not only rest but preparing—setting apart ahead of time. Sometimes situations arise on Friday or Sabbath over which we have no control. When that happens, we shouldn't feel guilty because, for instance, we eat a meal in a restaurant. But we shouldn't let exceptions become the norm.

Principle 7

Characteristic of the Personhood of God on which principle 7 is based. God remembers and reflects on important happenings. For example, He paused to reflect on His accomplishments at Creation (Genesis 1:4, 9, 12, 18, 21, 25, 31; 2:2, 3; Exodus 20:11). He remembers His covenants with humanity (Genesis 9:15, 16; Leviticus 26:42, 45).

Principle 7—Remembering. Sabbath keeping means remembering, reflecting, and rejoicing about the creation of the world (Exodus 20:11), redemption from sin (Deuteronomy 5:15; Luke 4:16–19), and Christ's second coming and the creation of the new earth (Isaiah 66:22, 23).

Understanding the biblical basis of principle 7. " 'For in six days the LORD made the heavens and the earth, the sea, and all that is in them, but he rested on the seventh day. Therefore the LORD blessed the Sabbath day and made it holy' " (Exodus 20:11, NIV). "By the seventh day God had finished the work he had been doing; so on the seventh day he rested from all his work. And God blessed the seventh day and made it holy, because on it he rested from all the work of creating that he had done" (Genesis 2:2, NIV).

I am indebted to several scholars and writers for their insights on principle 7. In what follows, I will share with you a sample of their Bible-based insights interspersed with my own.

Jacques Doukhan points out that the Sabbath teaches that Creation is a historical event with a beginning and an end. As the last day of the Creation week, then, the Sabbath draws attention to the end of the work of creation. The idea of a finished creation is incompatible with the idea of evolution. The Sabbath is a reminder that Creation is a historical event that started *and ended* in the past. Evolution, on the other hand, teaches that creation has always been ongoing and is still in progress.[20]

Evangelist Mark Finley reminds us that the Sabbath is more than just a doctrine that new believers must adopt. Instead, it is our identity in an age in which the theory of evolution predominates. When we understand that the Sabbath celebrates our creation in God's image, we realize who we are. This awesome realization gives self-worth and meaning to our lives.

Ellen White reminds us that Sabbath is a memorial day—a memorial of God's creative power. God has not set apart any other day in the week for this purpose. No one can change this day in any way, for what it commemorates can't be altered.[21]

Deuteronomy 5:15 presents redemption from slavery as a reason for keeping the Sabbath: " 'Remember that you were slaves in Egypt and that the LORD your God brought you out of there with a mighty hand and an outstretched arm. Therefore the LORD your God has commanded you to observe the Sabbath day' " (NIV). Slaves freed so they didn't have to work for their former masters any longer—what could be better than that! In the Sabbath commandment, God gave the Jews a way to make freedom a part of their lives forever. Thank God, He has given this gift of freedom to spiritual Israel as well. Dorothy Bass comments that slaves can't skip a day of work, but free people can![22]

When God delivered the Jews from slavery, He also foreshadowed the ultimate redemption from sin accomplished by Jesus' death on the cross.

In *Divine Rest for Human Restlessness,* Samuele Bacchiocchi reminds us that early in Jesus' earthly walk on a path that would lead ultimately to the cross, He stood up in a Nazareth synagogue on Sabbath and read Isaiah 61:1, 2 as part of the inaugural address of His redemptive mission:

> "The Spirit of the Lord is upon me,
> because he has anointed me to preach good news to the poor.
> He has sent me to proclaim release to the captives
> and recovering of sight to the blind,
> to set at liberty those who are oppressed" (Luke 4:18, RSV; see also Isaiah 58:6).[23]

We can also relate the seven acts of healing Christ performed on Sabbath to His redemptive mission.

When Jesus said " 'It is finished' " before He died on the cross, He had completed a stage of humanity's redemption. (The book of Hebrews shows that *application* of this finished work is still in process in the sanctuary in heaven.) Jesus kept the Sabbath even when He died—He rested in the tomb on the Sabbath (Luke 23:53–55) just as He rested after He finished creating at the beginning of time. So, we keep the Sabbath because Jesus has redeemed us. We keep the Sabbath because we are saved, not in order to be saved.

Jacques Doukhan links the Sabbath to the Second Coming and the glorious future as reflected in Isaiah 66:22, 23: " 'As the new heavens and the new earth that I make will endure before me,' declares the Lord, 'so will your name and descendants endure. From one New Moon to another and from one Sabbath to another, all mankind will come and bow down before me,' says the Lord" (NIV). Doukhan declares that the Sabbath not only looks back and remembers humanity's roots in Creation, but it is also eschatological—it points forward to humanity's re-creation, our final, complete restoration.[24]

Seventh-day Adventists might be interested to know that the very name of our denomination brings eschatological insight. Doukhan points out that the *seventh-day* Sabbath is actually the first *eschaton,* or ending; it marks both the end of the week and the end of the creation of the heavens and the earth. And the *seventh-day* Sabbath is called the day of the Lord (Exodus 20:10; Deuteronomy 5:14). The word *Adventist* refers to Christ's second advent, which is also called the "Day of the Lord" (Isaiah 13:9; Joel

2:31; 1 Thessalonians 5:2; 2 Peter 3:12). Thus, the name *Seventh-day Adventist* begins with the completion of Creation on the Sabbath (the day of the Lord) and ends with Christ's second advent (the Day of the Lord).[25]

All that is interesting, but there's more! On the Sabbath day of the Lord and on Christ's second advent "Day of the Lord," the Lord comes to us (compare "God with us"). In addition, the Sabbath relates the remembrance of Creation to the hope of the Second Coming (re-creation, restoration of the original creation).[26]

Nancy Van Pelt connects the Sabbath to the second coming of Jesus by suggesting that observing the Sabbath is actually a weekly rehearsal of preparation for that event.[27] Suddenly, "be ye also ready" (Matthew 24:44, KJV) has a wider meaning.

Thus, observing the Sabbath regularly reminds us of the three major milestones in salvation history: Creation, Redemption, and Christ's second coming. In so doing, it regularly corrects our perspective. It reminds us from whence we came, why we are here, and where we are going. "The value of the Sabbath as a means of education is beyond estimate"[28] toward these ends.

Acting on principle 7. " '*Remember* the Sabbath day by keeping it holy' " (Exodus 20:8, NIV; emphasis added). The Sabbath is a "holy day," not a "holiday" to be observed in the manner in which we keep most modern holidays. But we easily forget that. The Sabbath is a holiday with God—a time to celebrate the fact that He created us and our world and then redeemed us so that we can live in His house forever. We need to be reminded regularly of the One who has provided our past, present, and future. We must remember *Him*, not just His Sabbath day. That day should provide special, undistracted time with Him, and we should not leave Him out of our conversation and activities. Why would we ever want to forget the One who promises that He never forgets us (Isaiah 49:15)?

In an article in the *Adventist Review*, Jim Nix pointed out that our church is losing the concept of holiness in time. He regrets that many Adventists forget this and go to the mall on Friday night or Sabbath afternoons, regularly eat out in restaurants, attend sporting events, and run in marathons. He concludes that if this trend continues, the Sabbath will become for Adventists what Sunday has become for most other Protestants.[29]

I don't think that many Sabbath keepers deliberately try to forget that the Sabbath is meant for focused intimacy with God and for special time to remember, reflect, and rejoice, regarding His creative and re-

deeming power and Christ's second coming. But it happens. It is our default setting.

Remembering the concepts of holiness in time and of focusing on Creation, Redemption, and Christ's second coming will definitely affect our activities and conversations on Sabbath. During its sacred hours, we often need to ask ourselves, "Does this activity or this conversation lead me to concentrate on myself and on the activity, or does it direct my thoughts to God?"

Sabbath conversation presents some of us with a special challenge. I admit that I sometimes forget to focus my Sabbath conversation on issues that relate to God—not " 'speaking idle words' " (Isaiah 58:13, NIV). And when I am in a group, it is sometimes a challenge to do this without being obnoxious. I find it very natural to talk about what has been on my mind all week. If I tie my daily situations to God's activity in them, that's one thing. But if my main focus is on me and my own interests and I leave God entirely out of the conversation, that's something else entirely. It takes deliberate intentionality to get myself onto another track—one in which I not only quit my weekday work but also my weekday words.[30]

When I have guests over for dinner, I try to find out ahead of time what their interests are so that our table conversation can be of interest to them and they will feel at home. Do you and I take into consideration that God is One of our Sabbath dinner guests—for Sabbath is all about Him? Does He feel at home and comfortable at our table or wherever we find ourselves? Sometimes I put an extra chair at my Sabbath dinner table to remind myself and everyone present that Jesus is with us too, and we wouldn't want to leave Him out of our conversations.

What can we do to make God feel at home with us? What might make Him smile? We can intentionally think of topics ahead of time that will help keep the conversation focused on spiritual themes. We might hide a scripture promise under each plate so that our guests can enjoy a treat from God's Word. Or we might place small cards inscribed "WIGD?" next to each person's dinner plate. Then at the meal we can explain that "WIGD?" stands for "What Is God Doing?" and invite each person to share what God is doing in his or her life.

Philippians 4:8 gives us a good list of things to think on any day of the week and especially on Sabbath: "Whatsoever things are true, whatsoever things are honest, whatsoever things are just, whatsoever things are pure, whatsoever things are lovely, whatsoever things are of good

report; if there be any virtue, and if there be any praise, think on these things" (KJV). I have started a list of Sabbath-afternoon conversation starters to help us remember the One who is the reason for the Sabbath. This is a "whatsoever things" list for Sabbath afternoons. Some starters are more appropriate for adults, and some will work for adults or children.

Conversation Starters for Sabbath Fellowship

- Tell us about your spiritual journey.
- WIGD? (What is God doing in your life?)
- Tell us how you became a Christian.
- Share with us how God saved a friend or relative from a destructive lifestyle.
- Tell us about where you have served the Lord through the years.
- Tell us about your mission service.
- Tell us about a witnessing experience you've had this week.
- Tell us about a vacation you spent in a nature spot. What did you learn about God's creative power?
- How did you meet your spouse?
- What are your grown children doing now?
- What do you want to be when you grow up? Why?
- What is the most valuable advice your parents gave you?
- What is your biggest wish?
- In what ways are you unique?
- What adult do you admire the most? Why?
- Who is your best friend? Why?
- If you could offer your friends just one bit of advice, what would it be?
- The world is very interesting lately because _____.
- What do you think of the news?
- This week I read _____ in _____ (a book or the Bible). What do you think about what you read?
- What questions would you like to ask God when you get to heaven?
- What will your home in heaven be like?
- What are you thankful for this week?
- What spiritual topic would you like to discuss?
- What other conversation ideas do you have?[31]

When I go out in nature, I see things that help me to remember, reflect, and rejoice about Creation, Redemption, the Second Coming, and the new earth. I am amazed by the intricacies of flowers, by the way the earth renews itself after a rainstorm or a forest fire, and by the realization that after Jesus remakes our earth, I will walk through woods that have no dead flowers, trees, or animals. Only beauty and vibrant, eternal life will be everywhere. What ideas do you have that help you to remember the Sabbath and what it really means?

Principle 8

Characteristic of the Personhood of God on which principle 8 is based. God desires corporate worship (Isaiah 66:22, 23). Jesus attended and led out in worship services while on earth (Luke 4:16).

Principle 8—Worshiping. Sabbath keeping means participating in corporate, focused worship of God with our church family (Leviticus 23:3; Isaiah 56:1–8; 66:22, 23; Mark 1:21; 3:1–4; Luke 4:16; 13:10; Hebrews 10:25; Revelation 14:7). This nurtures both our "vertical" and our "horizontal" relationships—those with God and with our fellow human beings.

Understanding the biblical basis of principle 8. The principle behind Exodus 20:8–11 is the decluttering of the seventh day of each week so that we can worship God regularly and intimately. We worship God intimately when we are alone or in a group by intentionally turning toward the Son of God in heaven as a flower turns toward the sun in the sky.

Worship (worthship) means to attribute worth or worthiness to a person whom we reverence and hold in high regard. God's worthiness and our unworthiness stand in stark contrast when we get a glimpse of who He really is. One day while Isaiah was in the temple, he saw "the Lord seated on a throne, high and exalted, and the train of his robe filled the temple" (Isaiah 6:1, NIV). The six-winged seraphs above Him called out,

"Holy, holy, holy is the LORD Almighty;
the whole earth is full of his glory" (verse 3, NIV).

Isaiah was smitten with his unworthiness and God's worthiness, and he cried, " 'Woe to me! . . . I am ruined! For I am a man of unclean lips, and I live among people of unclean lips, and my eyes have seen the King, the LORD Almighty' " (verse 5, NIV).

When we worship, we connect with the One who fills our void, who gives us personal worth and confidence. Isaiah experienced this when he worshiped in God's presence. When we realize that our worth is based on the fact that God created and redeemed us, we respond with genuine gratitude, praise, and worship.

The New International Version translators labeled Psalm 92 as "A psalm. A song. For the Sabbath day." Praise, worship, and joy overflow from every line, indicating that Sabbath is a time for us to unite in worship to God. Verses 1 and 4 exuberantly proclaim,

> It is good to praise the LORD
>   and make music to your name, O Most High. . . .
>   I sing for joy at the work of your hands.

Music is very much apart of our corporate worship of our God.

Isaiah 56:1–8 sends a divine message to all people to keep the Sabbath " 'without desecrating it' " and to worship God. Jesus modeled this Sabbath activity by going to the synagogue each Sabbath "as was his custom" (Luke 4:16, NIV; see also Mark 1:21; 3:1–4; Luke 13:10). Leviticus 23:3 proclaims the Sabbath a " 'day of sacred assembly' " (NIV).

Revelation 14:7 is an end-time call to all people to show loyalty to the Creator and to worship Him, the Lord of the Sabbath: " 'Worship him who made the heavens, the earth, the sea and the springs of water' " (NIV). Corporate worship strengthens faith in these end times: "Let us not give up meeting together, as some are in the habit of doing, but let us encourage one another—and all the more as you see the Day approaching" (Hebrews 10:25, NIV).

Isaiah 66:22, 23 states that the Sabbath that started at Creation will continue into eternity. It will be a time for a corporate Sabbath worship experience in the new earth: " 'As the new heavens and the new earth that I make will endure before me,' declares the Lord, 'so will your name and descendants endure. From one New Moon to another and from one Sabbath to another, all mankind will come and bow down before me,' says the Lord" (NIV).[32]

Acting on principle 8. It's pretty clear we are to go to worship services on Sabbath! We're to be there not only bodily but also mentally, emotionally, and spiritually. We're to go there emptied of our week and of ourselves. And we're to respect God by being there on time.

Even though the people around us in the sanctuary are important and

the fellowship is wonderful, the main point of the worship service is the Lord of the Sabbath. When we are in the congregation, we must rivet our thoughts on Him. Whether we are preaching, doing special music, or leading worship in other ways, what we do is about Him, not about us.

During the worship service I like to imagine that God and His throne are in the front of the sanctuary. I make-believe that I am looking at Him throughout the service. Sometimes I sit in the pew and tell Him why I love Him and thank Him for what He has done for me and with me during the past week.

Sometimes families experience stress and unhappy feelings toward each other when they prepare to go to church on Sabbath morning. Some have confessed that they fight on the way to church and try to get their faces to switch from frowns to smiles as they enter the church parking lot. How can we avoid that scenario?

My family isn't perfect, so we've had to take deliberate measures to keep the pre-church atmosphere happy. I put on happy Sabbath music and sometimes sacred music videos to create a positive atmosphere that will prepare our hearts and minds for worship. We try to rise early enough on Sabbath morning so that we don't feel unduly rushed; we have our Sabbath clothes chosen and ready on Friday; and we have a simple breakfast that doesn't use many dishes. (We found that it is best to dress young children *after* breakfast!) When our children were small, we would review their Sabbath School memory verses while we ate breakfast. Sometimes we would listen to *Your Story Hour* or other Sabbath tapes while we ate. And we would pray for a Sabbath blessing and that we would be ready to truly worship Jesus at church.

Since we go to church to honor, praise, and worship the King of the universe, we should give some thought to our personal appearance. If we were going to meet an earthly ruler or someone else we admire and highly respect, we would likely wear our best clothes. Everything about Sabbath is holy—set apart. Therefore, we should put aside our everyday clothes and wear our best clothes to the Sabbath worship service—"neat and trim, though without adornment."[33] Everyone, rich and poor, can choose their "best" clothes.

It is very special to worship God in church, sitting together as a family. With Isaiah, parents can come before God and say, " 'Here am I, and the children the LORD has given me' " (Isaiah 8:18, NIV). When I was growing up, I could never do that completely. My father was not a Sabbath keeper. He never attended church with my mother, brother, and me. The

families of church leaders can't always worship together either. But they should do so whenever they can.

Parents should do all they can to make the worship experience a happy, meaningful time. For young children, sermons might as well be preached in a foreign language, so bring Sabbath books and quiet activities that can occupy that time. But even young children can participate in prayer and singing, so use those books and other activities only during the sermon. You might want to find out what hymns will be sung during the coming worship service and sing them with your children during the week so they will enjoy singing them with the rest of the congregation.

Older children can benefit from the sermon. Have them listen for and write down key words that the preacher uses and look up the Bible texts. One parent showed me a "sermon report sheet" with a place for the child to write the name of the preacher, the scripture reading, the title of the sermon, interesting points from the key texts and quotations, "God's message to me," and even a place to indicate that they shook the speaker's hand and thanked him or her. Another parent gives her children points for each section of a similar form that they fill out.

Some families with children deliberately sit in the front of the congregation to minimize distractions and so that they can be closer to what's happening up front. Other suggestions that I believe are wise: Avoid using the mother's room during church except for emergencies. Cover your child's mouth on the way out if they are crying. Don't give children food during the church service.

Parents can encourage their children to learn to worship God and appreciate the church worship service by having family worship during the week. This special family time provides the opportunity to sing, to pray, and to share feelings and meaningful ideas from God's Word at the children's level. Donna Habenicht reminds parents to make family worship *short, simple,* and *sweet.* If your family worship fosters good attitudes in your children, these attitudes can carry over into the Sabbath worship hour.

Occasionally, you and your family might choose to spend time with God in nature during the Sabbath instead of going to the regular church worship service. When I'm on a trip with family and/or friends during Sabbath, we still have a worship service. We sing worship songs, study a Bible passage together, focus on a nature object lesson or some interesting nature facts, and share what God is doing in our lives. We continue the worship experience when we take a hike by encouraging everyone to look for spiritual object lessons in what we see.

Music that praises God plays an important role in Sabbath worship. It calls forth our emotions as well as our intellect. Often, tears come to my eyes when I focus on the words of the hymns I'm singing. Sometimes they are tears of repentance, and sometimes tears of joy. We shouldn't hold back holy emotions as we uninhibitedly lift our hearts and voices to our Creator in Sabbath music. Such musical expression is our highest joy and pleasure—another way to make Sabbath a delight.

> It is good to praise the LORD
> > and make music to your name, O Most High,
> to proclaim your love in the morning
> > and your faithfulness at night,
> to the music of the ten-stringed lyre [guitar]
> > and the melody of the harp [or piano].
> For you make me glad by your deeds, O LORD;
> > I sing for joy at the works of your hands.
> How great are your works, O LORD,
> > how profound your thoughts! (Psalm 92:1–5, NIV).

Questions for Reflection and Discussion

1. How does your attitude toward the Sabbath relate to your attitude toward God?
2. Does your attendance at the Sabbath morning worship service awaken in you a hunger and thirst for God that continues throughout the week? If not, why not?
3. Comment on the meaning of the following statement: "Had the Sabbath been universally kept . . . there would never have been an idolater, an atheist, or an infidel."[34] (Suggestion: read what was left out at the ellipsis.)
4. Think about your most recent Sabbath. Did your activities bring you closer to Jesus? Did they honor Him?
5. What other practices would you suggest that are based on principles 6 through 8?

Chapter 8
Vacation *With God* and With His Family—Part 2

In 1976, my husband, Gaspar, and I had an unforgettable adventure. We went backpacking with some friends into the Grand Canyon. Laden with heavy backpacks, we descended from the top of the canyon at Hualapai Hilltop. As we trekked down narrow switchbacks into the canyon, we met other hikers and mule trains. We laughed as we watched the mules' big ears move in rhythm with their walking.

When we reached the American Indian village of Supai, we bought a few supplies at the general store. After reviving ourselves a bit there, we hiked two more miles to the Havasupai campsite, where we weren't one bit sad to lay down our burdens and set up camp. As we looked around, we felt dwarfed by the orange cliffs soaring above us. We wandered over to beautiful Havasu Falls and enjoyed a refreshing swim in the pool of blue-green water below the falls.

We were still at the Havasupai campground when Sabbath arrived. That week our sundown worship differed from the usual. To welcome the Sabbath in a special way, we took a walk together to a secluded place in full view of the cliffs. There we sang worship songs together. I'll never forget it—our songs echoed off the orange-tinted canyon walls around us. We would sing a few measures of a song and then we would hear those same measures again as we continued with the song. We were singing rounds with the canyon walls! What an exciting way to start the Sabbath! I can honestly say that was one of the most memorable Sabbaths I have ever experienced. Our next biblical principle encourages us to bask in nature on the Sabbath.

Principle 9

Characteristic of the Personhood of God on which principle 9 is based. God is the Creator, and He appreciates His creation—He considered it all "very good" (Genesis 1:31, NIV).

Principle 9—Basking. Sabbath keeping means enjoying, experiencing, and basking in the world God made rather than working at maintaining it (Psalms 92:4, 5; 111:2–4; compare Romans 1:20).

Understanding the biblical basis of principle 9. Jesus is the Lord of the Sabbath because He is the Lord of creation. When we go out in nature on Sabbath, we personally experience what the Sabbath celebrates—God's amazing handiwork. When He finished creating the world in all of its glory, He pronounced it "very good." If God declares something very good, it is very good indeed—amazing beyond description! Such an accomplishment is well worth celebrating, and that is what God did. "Thus the heavens and the earth were completed in all their vast array. By the seventh day God had finished the work he had been doing; so on the seventh day he rested from all his work. And God blessed the seventh day and made it holy, because on it he rested from all the work of creating that he had done" (Genesis 2:1–3, NIV).

God was able to make mother earth in six days—" 'the heavens and the earth, the sea, and all that is in them, but he rested on the seventh day' " (Exodus 20:11, NIV). He was so delighted with His masterpiece that He created a day for Himself and all living things to step back and enjoy it all. (Yes, Sabbath is for animals too—see Exodus 20:10.) The Creation stories in Genesis 1 and 2 and the one in Proverbs 8:22–31 all suggest that God had much to enjoy when the heavens and earth were completed in "their vast array" (Genesis 2:1, NIV).

Human beings and God's other creatures can join Him in honoring His work. We can use all of our senses to bask in it all. But this takes a block of time—quantity as well as quality time. That's why we have the Sabbath.

The psalmist declared, "The works of the LORD are great, / Studied by all who have pleasure in them" (Psalm 111:2, NKJV). Verse 4 says, "He has made His wonderful works to be remembered" (NKJV). Literally, that reads, "He made a memorial [or "remembrance" or "mention"] for his wonderful works."[1] That memorial is the Sabbath—the day God made for basking in nature.

Psalm 92:4, the Sabbath psalm, reads,

For You, LORD, have made me glad through Your work;
I will triumph in the works of Your hands (NKJV).

Basking in nature on Sabbath will cause us to not only enjoy and study nature but also to triumph! Why? Because God's attributes and glory are better understood by the things that He made (Psalm 19:1; Romans 1:20). If we would but look at His creation, we would see abundant evidence of His goodness and love. Don't miss it!

Acting on principle 9. Scripture makes it clear that we miss a lot if we don't get out into nature. Ellen G. White highly recommended that we use Sabbath time to do nature activities, especially if we have children in our home.[2] We can have lots of Sabbath-appropriate fun with our families when we spend time with them outside rather than allowing them to run wild and play as they do on weekdays. Most children love adult attention, and they love experiencing nature. So spending time with them in the out-of-doors is a winning combination.

One of my favorite summer Sabbath activities is picnicking out in nature. There we don't need to use a CD player to supply dinner music; the birds provide it for us with a live performance. Sometimes we use our canoe to reach an isolated picnic site. We spread a blanket on the ground and eat our meal. When we're through, we enjoy staying there and reading stories. Blue herons and other waterbirds keep us entertained. We use our binoculars and bird book to spot and identify new birds.

The sky is the limit for family nature activities on Sabbath. They need not be elaborate. However, we must remember to keep the focus on God in whatever we do. When we plan a Sabbath nature activity, or any other Sabbath activity, we should be able to say Yes to the question "Will this activity lead me to focus on God?" In other words, during the Sabbath, the focus is off us and whatever activities we pursue.

In *Adventist Hot Potatoes,* Martin Webber tells a story about two church leaders who met one Sabbath afternoon on a seashore.[3] One had binoculars strung around his neck, and the other was carrying snorkeling paraphernalia. Binocular Man chastised Snorkel Man for intending to snorkel on Sabbath. As he entered the water, Snorkel Man replied, "I'm going fish watching. You're going bird watching. Happy Sabbath!"

If we were to go surfing, we would most likely focus on ourselves, our enjoyment, and the activity. But if we were to go fish watching—to go into the water to look at the beautiful and interesting fish, shells, coral, etc.—we could quite easily keep our focus on God's handiwork.

Another Sabbath pastime I enjoy is simply lying on a blanket and using my imagination while viewing cloud formations. I seem to see all manner of animals and other creatures up there, and I'm reminded anew that

the heavens declare the glory of God;
the skies proclaim the work of his hands (Psalm 19:1, NIV).

When we lived in Africa, we would sometimes spend a weekend with other families at the seashore. We'd stay in little straw huts called *piotes*, have Sabbath School on the sand, and make sand Bible story scenes. What holy fun we had! Our family also has many pleasant memories of going to a zoo on Sabbath afternoon. Abidjan, Côte d'Ivoire, West Africa, had an enjoyable zoo with all manner of animals.

You might want to take your children out in the woods or by the seashore and give them each a bag or a jar to gather "pieces of nature," such as sticks, flowers, rocks, leaves, sand, and so forth. Have them use what they've gathered to make Bible story scenes and then try to guess what each other's scene is. In my family, we also extended this idea to general spiritual lessons. We would gather materials from nature, and then at sundown worship we would share what we found and explain what spiritual lessons our finds illustrated. Your family might also enjoy searching in nature for items that represent each day of Creation week.

The book *Child Guidance* points out that the wonderful works of creation teach children to see expressions of God's love. Also, when we study the laws of nature we are reminded that all living things are governed by nature's laws. Through nature's object lessons we can teach children to obey God's law.[4]

There are many books that contain great ideas for Sabbath nature activities. Among the older books are those by Eileen E. Lantry, *A Family Guide to Sabbath Nature Activities* (Mountain View, Calif.: Pacific Press®, 1980); Glen Robinson, *52 Things to Do on Sabbath* (Hagerstown, Md.: Review and Herald®, 1983); and Gerita Garver Liebelt, *From Dilemma to Delight: Creative Ideas for Happy Sabbaths* (Hagerstown, Md.: Review and Herald®, 1986). Two more recently published books are Don Pate's *52 Sabbath Activities for Teen Groups: A Resource of Proven, Surefire, Guaranteed-Fun Ideas That Make Sabbaths Unforgettable for Youth* (Hagerstown, Md.: Review and Herald®, 1995) and Karen Holford's *100 Creative Activities for Sabbath* (Nampa, Idaho: Pacific Press®,

2006). Sabbath afternoon is also a great time to work on Pathfinder Adventist Youth (AY) nature honors.

Sometimes I don't do anything structured when I'm outside. Just lying on a hammock or walking in the woods—alone or with someone— yields plenty of Sabbath fun. There's no reason in God's still-beautiful world why Sabbath can't be enjoyable!

Principle 10

Characteristic of the Personhood of God on which principle 10 is based. Love motivated Jesus' keeping of His Father's commandments (John 15:10).

Principle 10—Responding. Sabbath keeping is a joyful human response to God's grace in obedience to His loving command to remember Him and His Sabbath gift (John 14:15). It is not meant to be a means of earning our salvation (Romans 3:20; Hebrews 4:9, 10). We respond to God's gift of rest by working for Him in His strength and for His glory (Exodus 20:8, 9; 2 Corinthians 9:8; Hebrews 13:20, 21).

Understanding the biblical basis of principle 10. I have often heard other Christians proclaim that those who attempt to keep the seventh-day Sabbath are hopeless legalists. And, yes, in my international study I found that some seventh-day Sabbath keepers admit that they keep Sabbath in order to be saved.

It's true that God's law contains a commandment about keeping the Sabbath, and any matter connected with law can sound legalistic. However, God didn't connect the Sabbath with a law when He created it. Genesis records no command that we keep the Sabbath. God made the Sabbath to give His children undivided love and attention. The first Sabbath was a very pleasant day of celebration and fellowship. God didn't have to say in a bossy way, "You *will* spend time with Me—or else!" I never had to tell my children, "You *will* have fun at your birthday party— or else!"

So, in the beginning, the Sabbath wasn't a command or a test of loyalty. But Genesis 2 does record a command that involved a test of loyalty—the tree test. And after sin, humanity became so reluctant to accept God's Sabbath love gift that He had to make it a command (Exodus 20:8–11; 31:13–17)—a "mandated gift," as Tilden Edwards put it.[5]

If we rely solely on the fact that Sabbath is presented in the law, then our approach to the Sabbath will be extrinsic—and possibly legalistic—

"because God said so" instead of "because I love Him and He loves me." However, even after sin entered the world, the Sabbath has continued to be about a love relationship between humanity and God, which is what God intended. The obedience part is derived from that relationship. Jesus said, "If you [really] love me, you will keep (obey) my commands" (John 14:15, AMP; brackets in the original). Our intrinsic motivation for keeping the Sabbath is based on that love relationship with God. In fact, we can keep the Sabbath meaningfully only when we have a personal relationship with God.

Jesus says we're to come to Him—relate to Him—and *then* He will give us rest (Matthew 11:28). Before sin, Jesus didn't need to say "Come to Me, and I will give you rest" because there was no weariness, and nothing separated His human children from Him. They were already together in Eden. Jesus took walks in the cool of the day to be with them (Genesis 3:8). But sin created a barrier (Isaiah 59:2), and that's when Jesus' invitation became necessary. So Jesus makes a point of inviting us to come to Him for relationship and rest—if we want to. We're not doing our own works during that sacred time. We've set our works aside, so we can't be earning salvation—or anything else!

In the Sabbath commandment, the law and the gospel are combined. Even though Sabbath keeping is part of the Ten Commandment law, the Sabbath commandment is also about the gospel—about resting because of God's finished work (Exodus 20:11). Out of that rest, we are empowered and enabled to live the rest of the law—the other nine commandments.

By keeping the Sabbath we reveal our willingness to accept God's will for our lives instead of depending on our own judgment. In so doing, we are not trying to make ourselves righteous. Rather, we observe the Sabbath as the result of Jesus' righteousness in justification and sanctification. True Sabbath keeping is a sign that Jesus has delivered us from sin and that we have received His righteousness (Exodus 31:13).

In fact, when God gave the law, He spoke about redemption before He gave any of the commandments (Exodus 20:2). He delivered His people from slavery—*therefore,* they would have no other gods before Him, they wouldn't worship idols or take His name in vain, they would keep His Sabbath, and so forth. Deuteronomy 5, the second iteration of the law, puts redemption right in the Sabbath commandment itself, as the reason for keeping the Sabbath (verse 15). We keep the Sabbath and the other commandments not in order to be saved but because we are saved.

Because of the fact that we are saved, we can rest in the joyous realization that we don't have to struggle on our own to measure up in order to *be* saved. Struggling wouldn't work anyway: "No one will be declared righteous in His sight by observing the law" (Romans 3:20, NIV). We must already be saved before we can keep the law.

What a relief! If salvation were all about how well I performed, I'd become exhausted just thinking about it! Hebrews 4:10, 11 unpacks the gift of true rest symbolized by the Sabbath: "Anyone who enters God's rest also rests from his own work, just as God did from his. Let us, therefore, make every effort to enter that rest, so that no one will fall by following their [the Israelites'] example of disobedience" (NIV). The Israelites tried to do it all themselves—and their efforts backfired! Do you see anything legalistic in God's alternative? I would say that the Sabbath rest alternative is the antidote for legalism!

A friend of mine once asked me a question that made me wonder about him at first. He asked, "Was the Sabbath Adam and Eve's first day or seventh day?" Of course, Adam and Eve's very first full day of life was their Sabbath rest with God—before they had a chance to do any work. However, even though that first Sabbath was Adam and Eve's first full day, it was God's seventh day.

Usually we work first, and then we rest because our work has made us tired. Our first parents didn't rest to recuperate on their first Sabbath because they hadn't yet worked and so weren't tired. Neither could they show any product of their labor. They had nothing to offer God on their first Sabbath with Him except a willingness to spend time with Him. All they could do was admire what God had done for them during Creation week. The Sabbath was a symbol that they were totally dependent on God's finished work. It pointed to a perfect and finished creation.

Noted theologian Karl Barth concluded, "God's rest day is man's first day. Hence man's life begins with the gospel, not the law, in freedom to celebrate with joy the festal day of God, not with an obligation laid upon him to perform some task, to labor and toil. Man rests before he works."[6]

After Adam and Eve first rested with God and celebrated His handiwork, they then worked to care for it (Genesis 2:15). When God reiterated the Creation Sabbath as part of the Decalogue, He cited the fourth commandment in a rest-then-work sequence. He said, first, remember to keep the Sabbath, and then work: " 'Remember the Sabbath day by keeping it holy. Six days you shall labor and do all your work' " (Exodus 20:8, 9, NIV).

When we rest with Christ on the Sabbath, the sign of rest and salvation, we then work out of the energy, power, renewal, and salvation we've obtained on the Sabbath. The cycle of first resting with Jesus and then working during the week has never changed since that first Sabbath at the dawn of earth's history. In that rest we absorb grace enough so we will "abound in every good work" (2 Corinthians 9:8, NIV).

The rhythm of the workweek demonstrates the divinely appointed rest-then-work sequence. There is a smaller rhythm that does the same—the biblical evening/morning sequence. Each day begins at evening—our rest time. Then, after we rest, we go about our daily work. "Notice the divine rhythm of rest and work, night and day, grace and law."[7]

By the way, the first Sabbath day was still within God's seven-day Creation week. God was just as much in charge of His creation process on the seventh day as He was during the other six days. The Sabbath rest was still part of His creative work. It was all about Him. Sabbath is still all about *Him*!

Ivan and Sara-May are my husband's and my children. I remember the days of their birth very clearly. Ivan was born in September. It was a sunny, pleasant day in Connecticut when I went into labor, and my husband and I decided that it was time to settle into Hartford's Mount Sinai Hospital for a few days. Ivan was born at 7:23 in the evening.

Sara-May was born on a cold, gray January day in Massachusetts. This time the beginning of my labor sent me and my husband to Worcester Memorial Hospital. Sara-May entered the "outside world" at 12:36 P.M. that day.

I worked—"labored"—before the births of both Sara-May and Ivan. Their first day of life was bonding time—they rested in my arms while I rested from my labor. (They rested in Gaspar's arms too.) After that, Ivan and Sara-May worked on the business of growing up.

These birthing experiences speak of that first Sabbath on earth, when Adam and Eve were newborn adults—the finishing step of God's "labor." They spent their first full day of life bonding and resting with their Parent. Can you see the first human beings experiencing marriage and Sabbath—with their heads on Jesus' shoulders and the arms of all of them entangled around each other! They basked in joy that day and then, the next day, they began to carry out their God-given work in the Garden, "to dress it and to keep it" (Genesis 2:15, KJV).

Acting on principle 10. Since keeping the Sabbath is a joyful response to God's love and grace, we need to relax more on Sabbath and let that

response happen. Note that Sabbath keeping is a *response*—a reaction. This is one case in which we do better to be reactive than proactive. Sabbath is a time when we don't have to put ourselves under the gun to be productive and busy. Nonproductive hours are OK as we visualize ourselves resting in Jesus' arms or sitting on His lap. If we work ourselves into a lather trying to qualify for God's approval in our attempt to keep the Sabbath, we are missing the mark and missing the blessing. That is why I try to clear my to-do list so my response mode can function. It does us no good to cram the Sabbath with as many activities as fill the other six days—even if the activities are religious and service oriented. Because the rhythm of life is rest before work and Sabbath is a resting, battery-charging, refueling time for our workweek both physically and spiritually, we need to let it happen.

We generally have a similar idea before we go on a car trip. I've noticed that most people fill the gas tank *before* they begin the trip—at least that's the sensible thing to do. If we don't fuel up first, we might run out of gas in the middle of our journey. Sabbath refuels us for our weekday work. If we go, go, go on Sabbath and end the day more physically and spiritually tired than when we began it, we probably have not allowed time for recharging and refueling. There is something wrong with that picture. How will we able to face the new week? We'll likely run out of gas.

God doesn't want us to become so involved even in spiritual activities that we wear ourselves out. We need to build some downtime into our Sabbath days. That doesn't necessarily mean that we should sleep away the whole Sabbath, but maybe a nap in His presence would be a good idea if we are physically exhausted.

The rest-before-work sequence also shows that God must come first in our thoughts and planning. Sakae Kubo pointed out that when we come to God before we do anything else in our workweek, we will have our priorities in the right order. Then we'll see the weekdays in the proper perspective.[8] This is the key to order in our private world.[9]

Here are some ideas for a balanced Sabbath afternoon:

- Time with family (If away from them, write a letter or make a phone call.)
- Time for rest or relaxation (All the family takes a short nap.)
- Time for personal spiritual growth (Do some reading and/or Bible study.)
- "Do-good" time
- Time for nature and/or physical activity

All these things yield delight, recharging, and balance. (But don't try to do them all on one Sabbath afternoon!)

Principle 11

Characteristic of the Personhood of God on which principle 11 is based. Jesus trusted His Father no matter how much Satan tempted Him to do otherwise (Luke 4:1–13). He demonstrated this trusting attitude as He suffered for our salvation (Matthew 26:39; Luke 23:46).

Principle 11—Trusting. Sabbath keeping means trusting God to take care of what we leave undone during the hours of the Sabbath (Exodus 16:14–30; 20:10; Psalm 5:11, 12; Matthew 6:33). It means learning to depend on God rather than on ourselves.

Understanding the biblical basis of principle 11. When the Israelites were wandering in the wilderness, the manna experience taught them to trust God to take care of what they left undone on the Sabbath. During the week, the laws of nature produced maggots in any manna kept overnight. But on the Sabbath, God pulled the plug on the maggot producers. (Maybe they were Sabbath keepers too!) Friday's leftovers remained worm-free and tasty on Sabbath (Exodus 16:14–30). God told the Israelites to leave undone the gathering and preparing of manna on Sabbath. This miracle happened every Sabbath for forty years (Exodus 16:26, 35; Joshua 5:12). That's 2,080 manna miracles! God proved Himself to be thoroughly trustworthy.

God promises to surround those who trust Him with a shield:

> Let all those rejoice who put their trust in You;
> Let them ever shout for joy, because You defend them; . . .
> For You, O LORD, will bless the righteous;
> With favor You will surround him as with a shield (Psalm 5:11, 12, NKJV).

When we keep the Sabbath, we give God the opportunity to show that He is trustworthy. Who would want to miss out on seeing that happen right before their eyes? It's very exciting!

Sabbath keeping and tithe paying both involve trust. Perhaps this familiar tithing passage can apply to Sabbath too: " 'Test me in this,' says the LORD Almighty, 'and see if I will not throw open the floodgates of heaven and pour out so much blessing that you will not have room enough for it' " (Malachi 3:10, NIV).

Isaiah passes on a promise and a feeling of regret in one verse:

"In repentance and rest is your salvation,
    in quietness and trust is your strength,
    but you would have none of it" (Isaiah 30:15, NIV).

I pray that we live everything in that verse but the last seven words.

Acting on principle 11. Sabbath provides us many an opportunity to
trust God. Some faithful Sabbath keepers have been threatened with losing
their jobs when they chose not to work at their secular livelihood on Sabbath. Others have chosen not to do other business on Sabbath even though
this put them at a disadvantage. For example, Kathy's aunt chose not to
allow her realtor to show her property on Sabbath even though she was having great difficulty in selling it. (See the introduction to this book.)

As I look back on my life, I have found that if I trust God to take care
of what I leave undone, I can rest from worry on Sabbath. Other people
have discovered that too. Recently, work was begun on an addition to
Florida Adventist Hospital. This project produced a testimony to the surrounding community and the larger world about what happens when one
trusts God no matter what. Taashi Rowe wrote the story.[10]

> It was supposed to take 26 hours. They had planned and
> prayed that everything would go right. After all, they closed down
> miles and miles of highway to make way for 1,400 trucks carrying
> enough cement to cover a football field five feet thick. They defied
> common sense and chose to start the cement pour on Saturday
> evening instead of Friday evening so they wouldn't disrupt the
> Sabbath.
>
> Even if everything went perfectly—if there were no weather
> problems, no mechanical hiccups, no traffic snarls—the pour
> would *probably* take 16 hours but everyone planned for 26 hours.
> Instead, one of the largest cement pours in Central Florida his-
> tory took only 10 hours. The cement pour laid the foundation for
> a new hospital tower for the Seventh-day Adventist-owned Florida
> Hospital Orlando.
>
> The cement trucks moved into action after a brief sunset
> prayer service Saturday, June 24. In ark-like fashion, they rolled
> two-by-two down Rollins Street between North Orange Avenue
> and U.S. Highway 17/92.

The cement pour was unique in several ways. It was not only one of the largest concrete pours in Central Florida's history and in Adventist hospital history, but according to hospital officials it was a testament to the "meaning and value of God's Sabbath." There was cause for worry when it rained the morning of the pour. With 5,000 people praying that all would go well, hope was renewed when the rain stopped. Oddly, once the foundation was laid out the rain started up again.

"If for some reason we [had] a breakdown we [would have] caused one of the worst traffic nightmares Orlando has ever seen on Monday morning because we chose to do it [after sundown] Sabbath," said Dick Duerksen, vice president for mission development at the hospital.

"The problem is that concrete can only stand for a certain amount of time before it begins to settle and becomes completely useless," said Tim Burrill, the hospital's vice president for construction. "So trucks must get to the site on a timely basis. Concrete pouring has to be done in one continuous process. Once it's started, you can't take a break."

"The construction company suggested that Florida Hospital begin the pour Friday evening after rush-hour," Burrill added. Because of the potential ramifications, an early start would seem to be a logical choice, but the hospital administration decided against it because it was the beginning of the biblical Sabbath observed by Adventists.

"We [went] on faith that we [would] be able to complete this pour by Monday morning," said Burrill.

"This [cement] pour is a test of our commitment to Sabbath rest," said Duerksen. "It is a test of our commitment to being a spiritual lighthouse in the community."

How does this cement-pour story connect with the "test of truth" that I presented in chapter 4 and that is applied throughout this book? The *precept*, or rule, was that even "the stranger that is within thy gates" was not to work—even to pour cement. If a person were following rules alone, he would demand that no one do the cement pour on Sabbath and leave it at that. However, a rationalizer might come up with some very convincing reasons to pour the cement on Sabbath "this time" because of the risks posed by waiting until Sabbath ended. So, on to the *principle* of the matter.

The hospital administrators believed the *principle* was trusting and obeying God no matter what disadvantages seemed to loom ahead. When they obeyed God's Sabbath commandment, His *precept*, they demonstrated their determination to love, trust, and worship Him. But there is something even closer to a helpful rationale for this particular decision—the *personhood* aspect of the paradigm.

What truth about God do this *precept* and this *principle* lead us to? During Jesus'—God the Son's—earthly ministry, He trusted His Father. He constantly modeled complete trust and submission to His Father's will. As our Lord, He asks us to follow His example by trusting and obeying Him. We may freely submit to His Lordship and fully trust in His care even if it appears that doing so will cause us problems.

The hospital administrators' trust in God explains their decision not to allow the cement pour to take place on hospital property during the Sabbath. If there was any doubt about whether or not it was OK to let the cement to be poured on Sabbath, they decided to err on the side of trust and obedience and to not let any stranger work within "their gates." They trusted God to take care of the results of their choice. Trust was at the center of this challenge.

This story was an eye-opener for me. It could seem that the administrators were nit-picking. But as I said in chapter 4, there are much bigger issues at stake in Sabbath keeping than quibbles over whether or not we are "doing work" in one situation or another.

The administrators had a deep, about-God reason for deciding whether or not to do something on Sabbath. They didn't decide simply to adhere to a list of rules with which they felt they could live. For them, Sabbath keeping was all about God and not just about them.

If we run this cement-pour situation through the "test of truth" that I described in chapter 4, the process might look like the following:

Precept	*Principle*	*Personhood*
Show trust/ obedience to God by not allowing the "stranger who is within your gates" to work (Exodus 20:10)— to pour cement	Trusting/ obeying God— responding.	Jesus is a model of trust/obedience.

What about you? Will you spend the coming Sabbath with God

- letting Him sanctify you?
- remembering Him and not just the day?
- worshiping Him in spirit and in truth with your family at home and in church?
- basking in His creation?
- responding to His love with obedience?
- trusting God to take care of what you leave undone on the Sabbath?

Questions for Reflection and Discussion

1. How have you shown that you trust God regarding the Sabbath?
2. Could a person use being out in nature as an excuse for breaking the Sabbath? How?
3. Revelation 3:18 counsels members of the Laodicean church to "buy" gold refined in the fire, white clothes to wear, and salve to put on our eyes so we can see. What does this kind of "buying" have to do with Sabbath keeping?
4. What ideas do you have for practicing principles 9 through 11?

Chapter 9
Vacation With God and With His Family—Part 1

My husband, Gaspar, struggled with his identity when he was growing up. Born in Puerto Rico and brought to New York City at the age of three months, he learned to blend into the Orthodox Jewish culture that was all around him. In the early 1960s, his neighborhood, Mount Eden Avenue near Claremont Park in the Bronx, was Little Jerusalem.

The little island of Puerto Rico that Gaspar's apartment represented was no match for the social opportunities that beckoned in the ocean of Judaism outside his doors. Gaspar bonded with his Jewish classmates at the local junior high school. In the absence of other activities, he would spend time with his schoolmates in the synagogue on Sabbath mornings. Most of his friends were caught up in planning for and celebrating their bar mitzvahs. The fellowship was more about the culture than about religion, and, while Gaspar found much ceremony, he didn't see much spirituality.

One day, when he was headed toward a synagogue with his *yarmulke* (skullcap) in his pocket, he noticed on a familiar corner a church sign that he had never stopped to read. It said Bronx Swedish Seventh-day Adventist Church. Gaspar's parents had once belonged to the Adventist Church, but over the years their relationship with the church had evaporated as the daily bustle crowded into the weekends and other things had become more important to them than worship or fellowship with other Christians. Gaspar's curiosity was aroused in part because of his family's Adventist background but even more by the fact that these Adventists were Swedish. He wondered what the Swedish language sounded like.

He soon found himself standing in the foyer of the church listening to the strange sounds coming from the sanctuary. A boy invited him in, promising that he would translate. The warmth of the whispered greetings, the kind acknowledgments from the pastor, and the pleasant expressions of worship made Gaspar feel welcomed and loved in spite of the language barrier.

After the church service, Pastor Sjøren spoke again to Gaspar. "We would really like to have you come to our home for lunch," he said. "Would you call your parents and see if that would be OK?"

Upon obtaining permission to go to the pastor's house across the river in New Jersey, Gaspar found himself in the pleasant company of the two Sjøren children, Kenny—the boy who had invited him into the church—and Marita. Mrs. Sjøren served a wonderful Swedish meal, which was followed by a leisurely walk. At sundown, the family sang a few songs and had a short devotional reading and prayer. Then they lingered in the living room to become better acquainted with their guest, and apples, popcorn, and table games seemed to appear from nowhere.

As Pastor Sjøren drove Gaspar home that night, Gaspar reflected on that life-changing Sabbath and thought, *This is the kind of home I want to have when I grow up. I feel so close to God when I am with them. I really want to stay in this circle and learn how to be more like them.*

The Sjøren family encouraged Gaspar to enroll in Greater New York Academy of Seventh-day Adventists in Queens. And it was through the mentoring of another Swedish pastor, Arnold Klingstrand, that Gaspar eventually entered the ministry.

A Puerto Rican kid, living in a Jewish culture, was nurtured spiritually by a Swedish family and taught what it means to belong. The stranger in a strange land had found his identity at last. He had found lasting peace in fellowship centered on Christ. For Gaspar, Sabbath fellowship was the catalyst for a relationship with Jesus and His family. It can be for you too. Let's talk about Sabbath fellowship.

Principle 12

Characteristic of the Personhood of God on which principle 12 is based. The Members of the Godhead are relational (John 15:15). God's relationship with us is the foundation of our relationship with each other (John 13:34, 35; 17:20–23). Jesus fellowshiped with others on the Sabbath (Mark 1:29–31; Luke 14:1).

Principle 12—Fellowshiping. Sabbath keeping means nurturing our relationships with family and friends (Mark 1:29–31; Luke 14:1). In the gift of the Sabbath, God provides time for focused fellowship with the whole family—even the family animals (Exodus 20:8–11). Sabbath and family go together (Genesis 1–2:25; Leviticus 19:3). This nurtures our "horizontal" relationships—those with our fellow human beings.

Understanding the biblical basis of principle 12. Bible-believing Christians believe that the Sabbath is set apart to be a day of communion with God and one another. God apparently had that purpose in mind during Creation week. He didn't create Eve after the first Sabbath was over. Right from the start He wanted her to enjoy Sabbath with Himself and Adam. On the sixth day,

> God said, "Let us make man in our image, in our likeness. . . ."
> So God created man in his own image,
>> in the image of God he created him;
>> male and female he created them (Genesis 1:26, 27, NIV).

On the next day, the first married couple enjoyed Sabbath together with God. This was their honeymoon, and it was God's gift to them (Mark 2:27). Charles Bradford called Sabbath "God's thoughtful wedding present."[1]

There are two Creation stories in the first two chapters of Genesis. Jacques Doukhan points out that we find the first one in Genesis 1–2:4. The seven sections that comprise it—the seven days—are climaxed by the creation of the Sabbath. We find the second story in Genesis 2:3–25. This story also comprises seven sections, which parallel the seven sections of the first story. The seventh section of the second story describes the creation of the family. Genesis, then, places the Sabbath and the family in parallel. In Hebrew thinking, this means that the Sabbath and the family are related.[2] Sabbath and marriage are the two institutions that God started in Eden. Therefore, neither Sabbath nor marriage were originated by the Jews, nor were they meant exclusively for them.

Leviticus 19:3 presents the Sabbath and the family together in one verse: " ' "Each of you must respect his mother and father, and you must observe my Sabbaths. I am the LORD your God" ' " (NIV). "The Sabbath and the family were alike instituted in Eden, and in God's purpose they are indissolubly linked together. . . . In His own day He preserves for the family opportunity for communion with Him, with nature, and with one another."[3]

Indeed, the Sabbath is the holy day of the Lord that is devoted to focused worship and study of the Holy Scriptures and nature. It is also a day that turns us toward others. However, our relationship with God should take precedence over our relationship with other people.

Commandments one through three of the ten deal mainly with our relationship with God, and commandments five through ten focus on our relationships with other people. The Sabbath commandment, which stands in the middle of the Decalogue, says a little about each. It lists specific behaviors toward both God and our fellow humans and has implications for both relationships. Roy Branson calls this commandment the hinge of the two tables of God's law.[4] In this chapter we will focus on our relationships with other human beings during the Sabbath.

God stated only two of the Ten Commandments in positive terms: the fourth and the fifth commandments (Exodus 20:8–12). In one of my many conversations with my mentor, Jacques Doukhan, I learned that the fact that these two commandments were written with the same orientation suggests that they are related. Herein lies another evidence that the Sabbath and nurturing human relationships belong together.

In New Testament times, Jesus placed principle 12 in the limelight when He fellowshiped with people on the Sabbath. Mark 1:29–31 says that He went to Simon and Andrew's house after Sabbath services, and Luke 14:1 pictures Him going to Sabbath dinner at a prominent Pharisee's house.

Not only does Sabbath fellowship nurture human relationships but it also emphasizes equality in all human relationships. On Sabbath, all come before their Maker on equal footing. On that day, they set aside their societal and cultural distinctions. The carpenter lays down his hammer; the dentist switches off her drill; the professor sets aside his lesson plans; the housewife closets her broom; the African mother puts aside her cassava mallet; the rickshaw driver parks his rickshaw; and together they worship their Creator. They are equal before Him and equally dependent upon Him.

The Sabbath experience is within reach of all, rich and poor. It is a demonstration of the social-justice mind-set that God wants all humanity to have during all seven days of the week.

> "Foreigners who bind themselves to the Lord
> > to serve him,
> to love the name of the Lord,
> > and to worship him,

all who keep the Sabbath without desecrating it
    and who hold fast to my covenant—
these I will bring to my holy mountain
    and give them joy in my house of prayer" (Isaiah 56:6, 7,
NIV).

Acting on principle 12. Sometimes I like to get away by myself, but generally, I enjoy vacations more when someone is with me. Most families do vacation together. The Sabbath vacation is family fellowship time at the highest level. *Family* can mean those related to us by blood, our church family, or other acquaintances that seem like family, such as neighbors and friends. Sabbath provides quality and quantity time to fellowship, connect with, and catch up on these significant people in our lives.

During the week, work and school may have separated the members of your household. Sabbath provides the opportunity for them to be together again. If your family members are generally separated on Sabbath too, something is wrong with your Sabbath observance practices. Family and Sabbath belong together.

Particularly on the Sabbath, we must cease our usual activities to make time for the people who are closest to us. In *A Touch of Heaven,* Greg Nelson calls this experience "incarnational Sabbath keeping."[5] It's about "presence" with our loved ones. If we have children, it's about focusing Sabbath activities on them. If we join other families for Sabbath fellowship, at least one parent should break away from the adult fellowship and spend time with the children, as I explained in chapter 7. Children can't always enjoy what adults enjoy, but adults can enjoy what children enjoy.

Whether or not you have had Sabbath traditions in the past, you can start some now. Sabbath family traditions help to anchor our children. They are a joyful routine. (Singles can also establish—and benefit from—Sabbath traditions that involve fellowship with others.)

Here are some practices that can become Sabbath family traditions.

- Play or sing the same music each week to start or close the Sabbath.
- Have a relational family worship to start and close the Sabbath. (In a relational worship, family members share personal feelings with each other—how their week went, things they are thankful for, etc.)

- Prepare a special Friday-night supper or Sabbath breakfast or dinner with your family.
- If it suits your situation, eat one meal each Sabbath with nearby relatives or special friends.
- Go on picnics and walks in nature with family and friends.[6]

It is "part of my religion" to call my children every Sabbath and wish them a happy Sabbath. Sara-May and Ivan may as well count on it, for it's generally going to happen. Since they're no longer home, I rely heavily on this time to catch up on what's happening in their busy lives. If you don't have children, you might wish to call a friend, write a letter, or get together after church with someone.

Pastors and their spouses may have to be very intentional about having family time on the Sabbath. When my husband was the pastor of the Niles Westside Church in Niles, Michigan, and Ivan and Sara-May were small, I remember that they sometimes felt that we gave low priority to fellowship with them on Sabbath. Gaspar and I had church responsibilities, meetings, social events with church members, outreach activities, etc. It wasn't easy to find special, quality time for our children. I realized that at the close of far too many Sabbaths they didn't feel like singing "Sabbath Is a Happy Day." It struck me that pastors, and their spouses, sometimes use Sabbath time to save the souls of strangers. They also need to observe the Sabbath in their families. In doing so, they will provide a setting in which God can save their family.

My husband and I finally became convicted that we needed to be more intentional about finding special Sabbath time with our children even if we had a busy church schedule. We tried to find a block of time every Sabbath to focus on our children and each other. Sometimes that was a half hour, and other times it was longer. Most of us take time to eat on the Sabbath no matter how busy we are. Sabbath family fellowship is at least as important as eating.

The Sabbath provides quality time for husbands and wives, as well as parents and children, to fellowship at a deeper level of intimacy than is common during the rest of the week. Occasionally, my husband and I go on a "couples retreat" for a weekend and spend the Sabbath hours getting in touch with each other in a new setting, away from our usual environment. At the time I'm writing this, our most recent retreats were a camping trip in a state park and a church-sponsored marriage retreat by the ocean.

Sabbath and sex

What about sex on the Sabbath? When my family served as missionaries in Russia, I learned that a common Russian translation of Isaiah 58:13 intimated that " 'finding your own pleasure' " (NKJV) has sexual connotations. Therefore, many readers of the Russian Bible have concluded that Scripture forbids pleasurable experiences, including sex, on Sabbath.

Family counselor Alberta Mazat has quipped that if sex is *only* for our *own* pleasure, it *would* be wrong on Sabbath—and wrong on Sunday, Monday, Tuesday, Wednesday, Thursday, and Friday too! The phrase "your own pleasure" in this passage actually means doing business as usual—not that it is wrong to have pleasurable experiences on Sabbath. If it is wrong to do things that bring pleasure on Sabbath, I'd have to stop going to church, for I enjoy church. I'd also have to stop keeping Sabbath the way God wants me to, for I consider most of that very pleasurable. However, we're not supposed to be miserable on Sabbath.

Only 9.3 percent of those who filled out my survey on Sabbath keeping in the Adventist Church reported that they usually or always had sex with their spouse on Sabbath. This is a private matter that couples should prayerfully and *mutually* decide on according to their consciences and under the guidance of the Holy Spirit. One partner should not force his or her views and preferences on the other. The New Testament abounds in counsel to be considerate, sensitive, and loving to "one another." This "one another" paradigm certainly fits the sex on Sabbath issue.[7]

I invite you to consider some of my thoughts regarding sex on Sabbath. I don't mean to push my preferences on this issue. I merely want to widen your horizons as you ponder this subject.

Let's go back to that Friday when God finished creating Adam and Eve. There was a garden wedding to beat all garden weddings. Can you picture Adam's first meeting with his new wife? Can you hear his exclamations? "Wow! Awesome!"

What excitement! With what indescribable joy he exclaimed,

> "This is now bone of my bones
>   and flesh of my flesh;
> she shall be called 'woman,'
>   for she was taken out of man" (Genesis 2:23, NIV)!

The Bible writer concludes, "For this reason a man will leave his father and mother and be united to his wife, and they will become one flesh" (verse 24, NIV).

In *Love Aflame,* Karen and Ron Flowers point out that Genesis 5:2 reveals a oneness so complete that God gave the two first people only one name, "Adam." Only after the story of the Fall do we read about the woman receiving a separate name, "Eve" (Genesis 3:20).[8]

God probably gave the new couple a sex-education lesson at some point. Maybe it was part of His wedding sermon. This education provided the how-to of "be fruitful and multiply."

Mr. and Mrs. Adam's honeymoon began on the first Sabbath. That day saw the strengthening of a love triangle: Mr. Adam, Mrs. Adam, and God. They had blessed fellowship and get-acquainted time on that Sabbath.

It's interesting that Jews, custodians of the Sabbath for thousands of years, prefer that their children be conceived on Sabbath. To them that is a special blessing. In *God Invented Sex,* Charles Wittschiebe wrote that Orthodox Jews, among the strictest of Sabbath keepers, consider Friday night a perfect time for sexual intercourse.[9]

Alberta Mazat has noted that some ancient Jewish writings instructed their readers to be ready for Sabbath an hour before sundown. Then, to appropriately prepare for the Sabbath, they were to read the Song of Solomon. Thus, as the holy hours of the Sabbath arrived, couples were to turn their thoughts to their love for each other and to God's love for His bride, His family of believers.[10] (Compare also Ephesians 5:25–32.)

When marital love takes on the Song of Solomon model, what could be more appropriate than sex on Sabbath? When a couple expresses the type of unselfish love, bonding, delight, commitment, and joy expressed there, it is consistent with the purpose and spirit of the Sabbath, which is a sign that we are also delightfully bonded and married to God! But if each human partner's purpose is to use sex for selfish ends, it is not appropriate on Sabbath or any other day.

As I ponder the issue of sex in relation to Sabbath keeping, it seems increasingly clear to me that sex—the intimate consummation of the marriage relationship—can be an illustration of and even a dramatic parable of the Sabbath experience. Marriage is the most intimate husband-wife link. Sabbath is the means through which we are most intimately linked to Jesus. Marriage and the Sabbath are the two institutions that have come to us from Eden. The subject of sex doesn't downgrade the Sabbath; instead, it can exemplify optimal oneness with God, our Beloved.

Below are a few comparisons between Sabbath and sex within marriage that have occurred to me. They also compare the intimate sexual aspects of a human marital relationship and the intimate Sabbath experience with our Husband—God. (See Exodus 31:13; Isaiah 54:5. Remember, "sanctify you" [KJV] can mean "am married to you"!)

Sabbath Compared to Sex Within Marriage

- For Sabbath and sex to be meaningful and fulfilling, unselfish love must be present.
- When one loves his or her beloved—one finds pleasure and fullness of joy in the beloved's presence (Psalm 16:11).
- Both Sabbath and sex are a celebration of love, embodying excitement, celebration, and ecstasy.
- Open communication is necessary during both.
- The partners' relationship in everyday life affects the joy of the experience.
- Sometimes disagreements and misunderstandings can arise regarding both.
- We can make both Sabbath and sex positive or negative experiences.
- There are counterfeits for both.
- Problems with both sex and Sabbath keeping are often linked to other relationship and communication problems. For example, if the partners have hard feelings or indifference toward each other, the experience is unfulfilling rather than special.
- Both quality and quantity time are necessary.
- Preparation is necessary.
- Reading Christian books on both subjects is useful.
- A "romantic" atmosphere enhances both (candles, music, etc.).
- In both cases, boredom can lead to unfaithfulness.
- Foreplay and afterglow are part of the experience.
- Both Sabbath and sex embody the most intimate level of the relationship.
- Mind-set is important. The partners' minds must be renewed (Romans 12:2).
- The couple must relax, screen out distractions and work, and focus on enjoying each other.
- Anxiety can dampen the experience.
- Distractions blunt the experience between partners.

- Sabbath and sex each provide special bonding time with one's spouse. Married couples need sex to deepen and maintain their relationship. Similarly, Christ's bride, the church, needs the Sabbath to do the same.
- Both Sabbath and sex include falling into our lover's warm embrace and letting go of all else.
- Both involve a "one flesh" experience with no barriers.
- Both provide a recharge and refreshment.
- Both contribute to health, if done according to God's will.[11]
- People should not participate in either if not married. (Sabbath keepers must be "married" to Christ.)
- The Sabbath and sex provide a special time for the married couple to renew and celebrate their commitment to God and to each other and time to enjoy intimate fellowship with God and each other.

Can you think of other comparisons?

Remember that Sabbath and sex are both centered on a relationship—an unselfish relationship that is lovingly focused on the other partner. The "one anotherings" in Scripture illuminate that unselfish love relationship. When we're truly unselfish, we experience pleasure and joy in giving as well as in receiving. So, seek out whatever it takes to deepen intimacy between you and both your earthly spouse and your heavenly Spouse!

Sabbath in a spiritually divided home

Now let's deal with another difficult family fellowship Sabbath issue. What if some family members don't want to go with you on your Sabbath vacation? Maybe your spouse doesn't hold God's seventh-day Sabbath in high regard. Maybe he or she dresses to go to work or to the mall when you are dressing for church. How should you relate to this?

Gum, my Burmese friend, told me that his father, a prominent member of Burmese society, refused to keep God's Sabbath because of social pressure. Gum's mother, in her zeal for guarding God's Sabbath, attempted to push her husband toward accepting the Sabbath. But her pressure and rigid Sabbath keeping turned her husband away from what seemed to him to be a very unappealing experience. Gum wished that his mother had instead focused on respecting his father and on making the Sabbath winsome. This attitude would have gone a long

way toward winning him to the deeper experience with Jesus that the Sabbath provides.

The apostle Peter recommended this mind-set: "Wives, . . . be submissive to your husbands so that, if any of them do not believe the word, they may be won over without words by the behavior of their wives, when they see the purity and reverence of your lives" (1 Peter 3:1, 2, NIV). He also admonished husbands to "be considerate as you live with your wives, and treat them with respect" (verse 7, NIV; see also 1 Corinthians 7:12–14). Gum's experience growing up in a spiritually divided home has led him to advise that those who have unbelieving family members should keep their Sabbath observance positive. For every No we say, we should try to say Yes to something else that's OK to do with them on Sabbath.

My friend Ella's husband isn't a Sabbath keeper. She shares Gum's attitude of being in the positive mode on Sabbath. Respect for her spouse is in the foreground as she lives each Sabbath. (See appendix C, her insightful essay "Sabbath Keeping in the Spiritually Divided Home.")

I can relate to Gum and Ella, for I too grew up in a spiritually divided home—my father never went to church with my mother, brother, and me. When it came to spiritual things, fellow believers became our family. We especially noticed this on Sabbath. Church members helped to make our Sabbaths happier than they would have been had we been on our own. I especially remember how Frances Foster helped me to run a story hour for neighborhood children at our apartment on Sabbath afternoon. My dad seemed to enjoy that. However, as I look back, I wish I had made even greater efforts to bond with him during Sabbath hours.

Facing Sabbath alone

What if you are single—either with or without children? Or what if you are married to a minister and feel as though you are single on Sabbath? When you come home from church, your empty house is waiting for you, but it doesn't help much. How can Sabbath possibly be a joy in such a situation?

When I was single, missionary activities sometimes took up my Sabbath afternoons. This really helped to replace Sabbath loneliness with Sabbath happiness. When I was focused on others, I felt better myself.

Sabbath meals can be a way to break your loneliness. Maybe you'd enjoy inviting someone to go on a potluck picnic with you. Sometimes you might want to have a special meal at home with pretty dishes, fa-

vorite food, candles, and flowers. This meal might be alone or with guests. One writer said that her aunt gave herself breakfast in bed on Sabbath.[12]

Judith, a musician friend of mine who was single, would often invite people to her home on Sabbath for a potluck. Even though I wasn't single, I felt right at home when I was invited to her home. She really ministered to me, the wife of a busy pastor. When she died last year in a car accident, memories flooded my mind of Sabbath afternoons at her house—the food, the joyful fun, the exciting biblical discussions, the singing around the piano. In my mind's eye, I can see her after the resurrection in her heavenly mansion with a houseful of happy people, including Jesus, enjoying fruit salad from the tree of life, and singing around a harp or some other amazing heavenly instrument.

Other suggestions: Go for a nature walk in a park you have been meaning to visit. Sit near a pretty waterfall and have a deep talk with God. Write a letter. Make a phone call to someone who is lonely. Try something new this Sabbath.

Sabbath fellowship with our church family

Corporate worship is important to God and to us. God the Son said, " 'Where two or three are gathered together in My name, I am there in the midst of them' " (Matthew 18:20, NKJV). The interactions between and the unity with brothers and sisters in Christ enhance the specialness and the dynamics of worshiping God. Groups of worshipers produce beautiful music that praises God. Spiritual gems seem even more precious when we hear them as we listen to a sermon or do a group Bible study with our spiritual family. And there is special power in corporate prayer.

Corporate worship is fellowship at its highest level. Every person who is fellowshiping in the worship mode stands at the same level before God's throne. This promotes a feeling of togetherness and respect for each other that we can experience in no other situation. However, the main focus of our corporate worship must still be the One who is our Savior.

Sabbath fellowship can also spawn spiritual growth and accountability groups. Evangelical writer and religious educator Dorothy Bass was the external examiner at my doctoral dissertation defense. When the examining committee was scrutinizing the results of my research, the issue of Sabbath-keeping laxness among some Adventists arose. I wondered what

Dr. Bass, a Christian who is not a member of the Seventh-day Adventist community of faith, thought about this in-house weakness. Dr. Bass commented that Adventists should use Sabbath afternoons as an opportunity to meet in small groups that are focused on helping other Sabbath keepers to grow spiritually and to be accountable to each other. When I heard this at my defense, I thought, *This would take our Sabbath afternoon fellowship to a new level. How can I make this a reality in my Sabbath afternoon fellowship?* What do you think?

As in all activities, balance is important in our church family too. Some churches hold meetings all day every Sabbath. But if we spend all the Sabbath hours in meetings, we can't focus as well on building relationships among family members, especially if a spouse or child is not a Sabbath keeper. If this is the norm for our Sabbaths, we lose opportunities for families and friends to enjoy restful, laid-back, enjoyable time with each other in the atmosphere that only Sabbath can provide. There is more to Sabbath than meetings at church. As I have stated previously in this book, Sabbath is multifaceted, and many different joys await us within the realm of holy time.

Some people also wonder about the appropriateness of having weddings and birthday celebrations on the Sabbath. I have attended two Adventist weddings on the Sabbath, one in Massachusetts and one in Russia. In both instances, I didn't attend the receptions held during the hours of the Sabbath. Events such as weddings pose a danger to Sabbath keeping. These events involve lots of stress, and people easily focus on the event and forget the Sabbath. Though the wedding ceremony can be very spiritual, the reception can become secular.

Sometimes Sabbath keepers get together to celebrate birthdays on Sabbath. This is consistent with the celebration aspect of Sabbath, if we focus on God's goodness in extending a person's life another year. There is nothing inherently wrong with eating birthday cake or blowing out candles on the Sabbath.

Fellowship with non-Sabbath keepers

Occasionally, we receive invitations from non-Sabbath-keeping relatives and friends to weddings, birthdays, and other celebrations and events. How should we respond to such acts of kindness? And is it appropriate to spend time on Sabbath visiting a next-door neighbor who couldn't care less that it's Sabbath?

Even though the biblical guiding principles that we have discussed provide helpful insights for keeping the Sabbath, they don't address every situation possible. Sometimes we find ourselves in a gray area, and we don't know what to do. Since I fellowship with many dear people outside my Sabbath keeping Adventist community of faith, I encounter many opportunities to "break" the Sabbath. If I participated in every activity that comes my way on Sabbath, I would rarely keep the Sabbath in a manner consistent with the biblical principles we have been discussing. Therefore, I have to prayerfully ask myself, "Will my decision to go or not go help or hurt my witness for God with this person or group?"

It seems to me that each situation is unique. When such opportunities arise, I talk to God about them each. I ask Him to help me to determine whether I should go, whether my Sabbath date with Him would be interrupted if I went, and whether He would want to go with me. Regarding such situations, Ellen G. White wrote, "The disciples, in doing the work of Christ, were engaged in God's service, and that which was necessary for the accomplishment of this work it was right to do on the Sabbath day."[13]

When I've felt impressed not to attend an activity to which I have been invited, I have sometimes said to the person who invited me, "Thank you for your kind invitation. I regret that I can't come. I have an appointment during that time." If my friendship with that person allows, I explain that my appointment is with my Lord and that I stop all secular activities to spend extraordinary, focused time with Him during His Sabbath.

Sometimes I have asked the Lord to be in charge of my thoughts and words and activities and then I have gone to weddings or otherwise fellowshiped with my non-Sabbath-keeping neighbors and friends. While there, I try to keep my mind focused on Him. It isn't easy to remember that it is Sabbath when everyone else is in another mode. When I visit my neighbors on Sabbath, I try to screen out what may be going on around me and focus on them to show that I care about them.

As we live the Christian life, we will continue to encounter gray areas—activities and events about which there is no clear permission or prohibition. And just as continually, God will be there for us. Isaiah 58, the backdrop chapter for true Sabbath keeping, reminds us " 'The LORD will guide you continually' " (verse 11, NKJV). Chapter 11 of this book will deal further with Sabbath "hot potatoes" and gray areas.

Principle 13

Characteristic of the Personhood of God on which principle 13 is based.
God is accepting, loving, and affirming (see Matthew 11:28; John 3:16;
Romans 8:38; Ephesians 1:3–10; Revelation 22:17).

Principle 13—Affirming. Sabbath keeping means rightly representing
the atmosphere of the Sabbath by a spirit of acceptance, love, and affirmation rather than a spirit of judgment and criticism (John 7:24).

Understanding the biblical basis of principle 13. This principle is connected with the concept of grace. Charles Scriven reminds us that we
need to see and live the Sabbath as a gift of grace and not merely a piece
of the law.[14] Of course, we balance that statement with Paul's description
of the law as holy, just, and good (Romans 7:12). When the law is misunderstood, it seems awful. Understood rightly, it is full of grace. This, of
course, is true of the Sabbath as well. Matthew 11:28 reflects the grace,
acceptance, love, and affirmation of the Lord of the Sabbath. He said,
" 'Come unto me . . . and I will give you rest' " (NIV).

When Jesus defended one of the miracles of healing that He performed
on the Sabbath, He said, " 'Stop judging by mere appearances, and make
a right judgment' " (John 7:24, NIV). A judgmental, critical spirit is in-
congruous with the spirit of the Sabbath. Jesus—God—is love (1 John
4:8), and so is His special day. In *Original Love,* Des Cummings sums
this up: "God is love in person, the Sabbath is love in time, and the
Church [and, I would add, home] is love in place."[15]

Acting on principle 13. We often hear the word *shalom* used in connection with the Sabbath. *Shalom* implies, first of all, a relationship.[16] It
implies a deep and caring interest in others. When we say "shalom" to
those around us, we express affirmation of them. May God help us to
really mean that affirmation when we say "Shabbat shalom" to someone.
The more we affirm people, the more we reflect the character of Jesus, for
He was all about building people up—remember what He said when
some self-righteous people dragged the woman caught in adultery before
Him to trap Him. (See John 8:3–11.)

As I mentioned in chapter 6, our Jewish friends have a beautiful practice of blessing family members as they welcome the Sabbath on Friday
night. The father brings each child close and recites a blessing for each.
For the sons he says, "May God make you like unto Ephraim and Man-
asseh!" For the daughters, "May God make you like Sarah, Rebekah,
Rachel, and Leah!" For everyone, the father says, "May the Lord bless you
and keep you. May the Lord cause His face to shine upon you and be

gracious unto you. May the Lord lift up His countenance toward you and give you peace." Then he blesses his wife by reciting Proverbs 31's commendations of the virtuous wife to her.

Jo Ann Davidson reminds us that blessing others is what Sabbath is all about.[17] God models that in His relationship to us during the Sabbath. Our heavenly Father wants to give us a blessing and to affirm us. Sabbath is not about us doing something for God, but about God doing something for us.

We can easily adapt for our own homes the Jewish Friday evening tradition of blessing family members. When Gaspar's and my children were home with us, we often used Friday-evening worship as a chance to affirm them for specific things we noticed in their lives during the week, and we affirmed each other as well. Since our children have left home, we call them each Sabbath to catch up with their lives. We affirm them for their accomplishments and pray with them for God's blessings and guidance in their lives for another week.

Gaspar and I have sometimes also used Friday sundown worship time to apologize to and make things right with family members whom we have wronged during the week. This has given us another opportunity to affirm these dear ones.

Gary Smalley and John Trent have written a whole book on the value of passing on the gift of giving blessings to our loved ones. They list the characteristics of a blessing.

- Meaningful touch: hugging, kissing, laying on of hands
- Spoken affirmation
- Verbal expression of high regard for the child (and the spouse)
- The picturing of a special future for the one being blessed
- Commitment to making this special future happen[18]

What better time than the Sabbath to nurture this type of experience in your family? If you haven't done it before, it's never too late to adapt it to your particular situation. Some families write little love notes to each other on Sabbath. Try this: on each love note, write the name of a member of your family and what that person means to you. Then sign the note and deliver it.

One family made a rule that no one can criticize another on the Sabbath day because Sabbath is a day of acceptance and ɪ ot judgment.[19] If we have something negative that we must say to someon ;, if at all possible, we

should wait until after the Sabbath to say it.

We may be tempted to make the Sabbath a time of criticism when we see someone doing what we consider to be "breaking" the Sabbath. An American Adventist told me disparagingly of the time he visited a European Adventist school and found a group of students playing soccer on Sabbath afternoon. These students weren't playing on organized teams or keeping score; they were just fellowshiping while batting a ball around. Who was the worst Sabbath breaker—the students or the person on the sidelines who was watching them with a critical spirit? That's something to think about.

What can we do to keep the Sabbath holy and yet not make it a day of criticism? The primary test is the question, What helps me in my relation with God? We should evaluate each Sabbath activity in terms of that question. Does this activity help or hinder my walk with God? If you are interacting with youth on Sabbath, you may be able to introduce an informal discussion with them about Sabbath keeping—in a noncritical way. Maybe you can ask what activities we can plan for Sabbath that will open our minds to God. After such an activity, debrief them. Did the activity open their minds to God? Would they do this activity again on Sabbath? Respect their ability to figure out the answers to these questions.

The close of the Sabbath provides opportunities for expressing affirmation and support to those around us. In this too, Jewish homes model Sabbath traditions that give us meaningful Sabbath-keeping insights. The *Havdalah*[20] ceremony marks the closing of the Sabbath. Jewish worshipers begin it when at least three stars are visible in the evening sky. They light the *Havdalah* candle and give it to someone—usually a young boy—to hold. This special candle has several wicks that have been twisted together to symbolize the joyful togetherness the family has experienced because of the Sabbath. It says that the companionship of the family is worth celebrating.

The worshipers put a goblet in a saucer and pour wine or grape juice into this goblet until it overflows into the saucer. Then they extinguish the *Havdalah* candle by dipping it into the wine in the saucer. This signifies that the Sabbath has overflowed with blessing and joy for the family. It also symbolizes the Sabbath influence spilling over into the workweek.

The family then passes around a special little Sabbath spice box called the *bassamen*. It represents the fragrance of life that they have just experienced in each other's company during the Sabbath. As they pass it around,

they say something like this, "May the fragrance of the Sabbath remain with you throughout the coming week." This act represents their wish that the memory of this fragrance will help carry loved ones through the pressures of the week until they are able, once again, to celebrate the Sabbath.

If you want to adopt these Sabbath-closing ideas in your family, you can purchase a *Havdalah* candle at a Jewish supply store, or you can make your own version by holding two long, thin taper candles over a steaming teakettle. When they become pliable, twist them around each other, starting at the base and working up toward the wicks. You can make a *bassamen* by filling a pretty little box with whole spices, such as cinnamon and cloves.

Can you truly say, as do many Jewish families, that the Sabbath hours have brought you closer to your family and friends? Can you say at the close of each Sabbath that the atmosphere in your family during its hours has been one of acceptance, love, and affirmation? If not, why not?

Questions for Reflection and Discussion

1. A faculty member doing Sabbath supervision in an Adventist boarding academy commented while watching students playing volleyball, "Which is better on Sabbath: letting the students be out in the fresh air and fellowshiping with each other while batting a ball around or sending them to their rooms where they will sleep, play secular video games, or gossip about just anything?" How would you answer that question?
2. Under principle 13 is found the statement, "When the law is misunderstood, it seems awful. Understood rightly, it is full of grace." How can the law be full of grace?[21]
3. How can we keep the Sabbath in a manner consistent with biblical principles and not be critical of others at the same time? How can we guide young people in a winsome way to keep the Sabbath in harmony with all the biblical principles?
4. What other ideas do you have for practicing principles 12 and 13?

Chapter 10
Vacation With God and With His Family—Part 2

When Seminary professor Jo Ann Davidson's children were young, she would take them to visit and sing to the patients in a children's hospital. She used to say to the sick children, "We are Seventh-day Adventists. We wish we could sing to you every day, but we don't have time because we are working. But today we don't have to work, so we came to share some of our Sabbath joy with you."[1]

When we serve other people during the Sabbath, we have golden opportunities to share our Sabbath joy with them. So, let's explore guiding principle 14—Serving.

Principle 14

Characteristic of the Personhood of God on which principle 14 is based. Jesus is a servant and proclaimer of the good news (Luke 4:18–21; Philippians 2:5–11). He went about doing good (Acts 10:38).

Principle 14—Serving. Sabbath keeping means serving other people in love and witnessing lovingly for God (Isaiah 58:7–10; Matthew 12:12, Mark 3:4, Luke 6:9; 13:12, 16).

Understanding the biblical basis of principle 14. Isaiah 58 gives a dramatic illustration of how true Sabbath keeping expresses itself in genuine concern for other people. Verses 7 through 10 admonish Sabbath keepers to share food with the hungry, provide the poor wanderer with shelter, clothe the naked, care for one's relatives, and more. Jesus said it is " 'lawful to do good on the Sabbath' " and " 'to save' " others (Matthew 12:12,

NKJV; Mark 3:4; Luke 6:9, NKJV). And Luke 13:12, 16 records His statement that the Sabbath is the day to free human beings from spiritual and physical bonds.[2] His attitude stands in contrast to that of the ruler of the synagogue, who felt that Sabbath consisted of obeying rules rather than loving people (Luke 13:14).

In the fourth commandment, God prohibits our doing our own work during His Sabbath. We are to do our work during the week: " 'six days you shall labor and do all your work.' " He asks us not to do "any work" on His Sabbath. Jim Wibberding points out that this is a reference back to the phrase "your work"[3]; thus we're free to do *God's* work on the Sabbath. Jesus believed that. After He healed a man on the Sabbath, He said, " 'My Father is always at his work to this very day and I, too, am working' " (John 5:17, NIV).

In 2004 I attended the first International Conference on Adventists in the Community at the world headquarters of the Seventh-day Adventist Church. I'm indebted to conference presenters Tony Campolo and Zdravko Plantak for expanding my understanding of how Sabbath is related to service and to reflecting God's love to others. They presented the idea that true Sabbath keeping extends beyond merely keeping the seventh day. We must have a "Sabbath attitude." This Sabbath attitude includes concern and care for humanity and our environment. If we truly observe the Sabbath, we cannot remain satisfied with only our own redemption, restoration, and liberation. We must show concern for our neighbors and the environment, physically as well as spiritually.

The doctrine of the Sabbath doesn't involve only the seventh day; it concerns the other six days as well. We should practice the Sabbath attitude throughout the week, even though a specific Sabbath day is also necessary. Leviticus 25 supports this idea. It shows that the Sabbath concern extends from the weekly Sabbaths to the sabbatical years. God specified that every seventh year was to be observed as a sabbatical year (Leviticus 25:1–7; cf. Exodus 21:2; Deuteronomy 15). And God set aside every fiftieth year, which followed seven sabbatical years, for the celebration of a year of jubilee (Leviticus 25:8–55).

There we have it: weekly Sabbaths, sabbaths of years, and the year of jubilee after seven sabbaths of years. All three of these kinds of sabbaths reflect an attitude of humanitarian concern. Thus, the Jews were taught about liberating and caring for the poor, widows, and orphans and about caring for the environment as well. Actually practicing the year of jubilee sabbath would have prevented unequal distribution of wealth.

The principles behind the three sabbaths portrayed in Leviticus 23 and 25 extend to Christians too.[4]

The Exodus 20 Sabbath tells us that God is the Creator of all who live on this earth. The common fatherhood of God means a common brotherhood and equality among human beings. Deuteronomy 5 presents the Sabbath as a reminder of redemption or liberation. Since God has freed us from sin, we are called to help humanity with issues such as poverty and injustice—see the job descriptions of the Messiah given in Isaiah 58 and 61. Isaiah 58 even uses jubilee sabbath terminology—" 'day acceptable to the Lord' " (verse 5, NIV). (Compare Isaiah 61:1, 2; Luke 4:19; Leviticus 25:10.) And the last verses of Isaiah 58 tie the weekly Sabbath to the serving-humanity theme.[5]

Richard Rice suggests that every practice that deprives human beings of their sense of dignity and worth contradicts the message of the Sabbath.[6] When Jesus was on earth, the religious leaders kept the Sabbath, but we know they didn't have the Sabbath attitude because we see that they didn't care about people. Isaiah passes on, direct from God Himself, this message about the need for social concern:

> "Stop bringing meaningless offerings!
>   Your incense is detestable to me.
> New Moons, Sabbaths and convocations—
>   I cannot bear your evil assemblies. . . .
>   Stop doing wrong,
>   learn to do right!
> Seek justice,
>   encourage the oppressed.
> Defend the cause of the fatherless,
>   plead the case of the widow" (Isaiah 1:13, 16, 17, NIV).

Those who cherish the true meaning of the Sabbath will seek to eliminate oppressive economic and social structures that hinder people from providing for themselves.

Because of who we are in Christ and because we follow His example, Sabbath-keeping Christians should be more active than anyone else in serving humanity and promoting justice, equality, and freedom. The end-time judgment scene of Matthew 25 drives home the importance of this conclusion. Whether or not we have cared for the poor and needy is a test that will reveal our eternal destiny.[7]

In chapter 4, I mentioned another great test of loyalty to God at the end of time. The keeping of the seventh-day Sabbath—the right day in the right way—serves as the basis of this test. It will be "an evidence of loyalty to the Creator."[8] What relationship do the two end-time tests—caring for the needy and the Sabbath truth—have to each other? Are they two unrelated tests or are they two parts of a single test?

I think that they are two aspects of a single test of our loyalty to God. The judgment scene at the end of Matthew 25 is a test of the Sabbath attitude as explained in the whole of Isaiah 58. Whether or not we keep the Sabbath *and* care for the needy will reveal the status of our relationship with Jesus—our loyalty to Him and our willingness to make Him and His earthly family a priority. They both are about how we treat Jesus, who will say, " 'Truly I tell you, just as you did it [or did not do it] to one of the least of these who are members of my family, you did it [or did not do it] to me' " (Matthew 25:40, NRSV; compare verse 45).

Acting on principle 14. Because we don't do our regular work on the Sabbath, we are free to focus on serving others. One of my most pleasant Sabbath memories as a teenager is of my regular visits to New Britain General Hospital. Other youth in my church and I ran a Sabbath afternoon worship service for some of the patients there. We would go to the patients' rooms and bring them to the meeting room. Joan Herman, a patient in the hospital, was confined to an iron lung. After studying with our pastor, she had become a Seventh-day Adventist Christian, and she invited many of her friends to attend these Sabbath afternoon programs. Because of the gift of Sabbath, my friends and I had time for this opportunity to serve—which served us too. This experience ingrained the culture of service in us at an early age. Through the years since, I have enjoyed other Sabbath activities, such as inviting people over for Sabbath dinner, visiting the sick and discouraged, passing out inspirational literature, and giving Bible studies.

Often, our weekdays are filled with secular activities. Our lifestyle doesn't easily accommodate acts of service. But we can construct our Sabbath rituals so as to give us opportunities to serve others and nurture relationships. For example, some families enjoy having a Friday-evening potluck meal together. Afterward they pull out instruments and sing gospel songs and choruses. It wouldn't take much effort to invite a few neighbors or friends from church or work to join in these informal times of worship and witness.

Some people enjoy entertaining visitors after the church's worship service by inviting them home for a meal. Some families pack picnic lunches and eat at a city park, taking enough food and drink to share with others in the park who may not have as much as they do. This gives an opportunity to reach out to people who are not part of one's normal social group. Consider planning a special social outreach activity at least once a month.

Lyndelle Chiomenti, one of my colleagues at work, spent many Sabbath afternoons doing pet therapy. She would take her dog, Elke, to institutions that house children with special needs—children who need some good company and encouragement. Friendly dogs provide that very well. And Lyndelle benefited from her outreach too; when Elke died, the memories of all the children Elke helped during her eight-year career as a pet-therapist dog tempered Lyndelle's sorrow.

Sabbath service challenges

We should keep in mind that we don't have to do all our ministry on Sabbath. I've noticed that on some of the Sabbaths when I've been very busy with service and ministry to others, my own soul ran dry. I wasn't stopping long enough to search for God myself on the day He has given me for that purpose. My Sabbaths were out of balance; I often ended them more tired than I was when they started. When that happens we need to ask ourselves why we think all our ministry has to be done on Sabbath. In making plans for the Sabbath, we need to keep in the forefront the most important reason God gave us that day—so we'd have time to spend with Him and to renew our experience of His indwelling.

Sometimes I have been invited to do service on Sabbath that involves regular work—the type of work I would do during the week. For example, I had a struggle deciding what to do when my Rotary Club first started doing "Christmas in April"—making repairs to a needy person's home as a gift of love. When I first heard about this project, I thought it was a wonderful, Christian thing to do. Then the club president announced that the project was scheduled for the last Saturday in April. That troubled me. I thought to myself, *Jesus said it is lawful to do good on the Sabbath [Matthew 12:12], and Isaiah 58 connects serving others with Sabbath keeping. This Rotary project surely fits these criteria. Anyway, I'm not the one who scheduled it on Saturday; I had no control over that decision.* But I also thought about the other side of the coin—the concept that I

shared in chapter 6, that we should avoid doing even good works such as "missionary" manual labor that would displace the chief biblical component of Sabbath observance—rest. Therefore, for myself, I have decided that it is better to schedule community outreach that involves manual labor on a day other than the Sabbath—taking the Sabbath attitude of concern for others into the weekdays.[9] I also concluded that because Jesus wants us to set the Sabbath aside from other days to seek Him and to rest with Him, I should kindly make it clear to my friends who are not Sabbath keepers that I distinguish the Sabbath from a regular work day.

The first year the Rotary Club planned to run their Christmas in April project, it rained on the Saturday on which they had scheduled it. They did the work on Sunday instead, so I wholeheartedly joined them, and many members of my church did too.

The second year it didn't rain. That year I brought breakfast and refreshments for the workers before I went off to church. They respected my decision to set apart the Sabbath as a special day, and the project wasn't jeopardized because I didn't spend the day working with them.

Through the years, I've had to ask myself whether the Sabbath is subordinate to service or service subordinate to the Sabbath. It is hard to come up with a good answer to this issue. Each of us needs to pray and ask the Lord of the Sabbath to send His Holy Spirit to guide us. We shouldn't judge someone who sees a gray-area Sabbath activity differently than we do—those matters are between the Lord and each individual. However, I spend lots of time with non-Sabbath-keeping friends, so I have many opportunities to join them in activities that don't serve the purposes for which God gave us the Sabbath. If I made exceptions every time I had such an opportunity, I would rarely keep the Sabbath according to the biblical principles that this book has shared.

Twenty-five years ago I had an unusual service opportunity. My husband, Gaspar, our baby son, and I were vacationing in Puerto Rico, my husband's homeland. While there, a fire destroyed the apartment of very close friends of his family. When the fire had been extinguished and the investigation was finished, the traumatized family desperately needed both emotional support and help with salvaging the personal belongings that had survived—and it was Sabbath.

Gaspar had to be away that day, but I was able to help them in their emergency. I had some special bonding time with this Catholic family as we spent the day going through the charred remains of their earthly possessions. A few of their things had escaped the flames, making the effort

worthwhile. They were moved that I would spend my Sabbath time helping them. By the end of that day I had Sabbath peace in my heart, even though on the outside I looked like a piece of charcoal!

When we are in the service of the Lord, we can never be totally sure of what situations we will face during the hours of the Sabbath. We can—and should—plan ahead, but sometimes things occur unexpectedly. When that happens, we should ask ourselves, "Will delay in responding to this situation cause harm?" If the answer is Yes, we might find ourselves doing things we normally wouldn't plan to do on Sabbath. This is consistent with the counsel of Ellen G. White that implies we should judge what will best serve God's purposes in the circumstances and that activities necessary for the accomplishment of His work are right to do on the Sabbath.[10]

Sometimes in the line of service on the Sabbath, we may have to travel farther than a tank of gas will take us, and we will have to buy gas. Or we may have to eat in a restaurant on the Sabbath. Of course, as far as possible, we should try to avoid making long trips on that day. However, if we must travel on the Sabbath, by God's grace we can keep our minds on Jesus. We can commune with Him even then.[11]

Principle 15

Characteristic of the Personhood of God on which principle 15 is based. God supplies all our needs all the time (Exodus 16:26, 35; Joshua 5:12; Matthew 6:25–33; John 5:16, 17; Philippians 4:19), and He advocates that we care for the needs of all His creatures (Matthew 12:1–14; Mark 2:23–28; Luke 6:1–5).

Principle 15—Caring. Sabbath keeping means caring for physical needs on Sabbath; no creature—animal or human—should be allowed to suffer on Sabbath (Exodus 23:12; Matthew 12:1–14; Mark 2:27).

Understanding the biblical basis of principle 15. This principle is related to the principle of service on the Sabbath. I designated it as a separate principle to draw attention to the importance of caring for the physical needs of the healthy as well as of the ill on the Sabbath. The grainfield-snack story recorded in Matthew 12:1–8, Mark 2:23–26, and Luke 6:1–5 illustrates this principle. "One Sabbath Jesus was going through the grainfields, and as his disciples walked along, they began to pick some heads of grain. The Pharisees said to him, 'Look, why are they doing what is unlawful on the Sabbath?' He answered, 'Have you never read what David

did when he and his companions were hungry and in need? In the days of Abiathar the high priest, he entered the house of God and ate the consecrated bread, which is lawful only for the priests to eat. And he also gave some to his companions' " (Mark 2:23–26, NIV).

It's obvious in this passage that Jesus condones taking care of personal needs such as hunger on the Sabbath. In the next verses, Jesus made a summary statement regarding the Sabbath grainfield-snack dilemma: "Then he said to them, 'The Sabbath was made for man, not man for the Sabbath. So the Son of Man is Lord even of the Sabbath' " (verses 27, 28, NIV).

Jesus' point in telling the story of David and Abiathar seems to be that if it was right for David and his companions to eat the holy bread that belonged to the priests, it is even more appropriate for the hungry disciples of the Son of David to violate the scribal rules about the sacred Sabbath.[12] It is likely that David did not eat the bread that was currently in God's presence on the table in the Holy Place but rather that he ate the week-old bread after it had been replaced with fresh loaves (1 Samuel 21:6). The bread was replaced on the Sabbath, and some rabbis believe it was on that day that David took the bread. Scripture doesn't state the day of the week on which this happened, but if it was indeed the Sabbath, David's example would be even more apropos.[13]

Ángel Rodríguez has observed that the Pharisees treated the Sabbath as though humankind were created to serve the Sabbath rather than the Sabbath created to serve humankind. But Jesus, the Creator, intended the Sabbath to benefit all of us. In His humanity, He knows human needs. In His divinity, He has the authority to declare how His Sabbath should be used.[14]

Exodus 23:12 portrays a God so caring that He extends the "care for physical needs" principle to animals, slaves, and aliens as well: " 'Six days do your work, but on the seventh day do not work, so that your ox and your donkey may rest and the slave born in your household, and the alien as well, may be refreshed' " (Exodus 23:12, NIV).

Jesus said both His Father and He work on the Sabbath (John 5:17). While God rested from creating new things on the Sabbath of Creation week, He doesn't rest from sustaining His creation on that day. He keeps the oxygen flowing, the world spinning, the sun shining, people's wounds healing, plants growing, and our hearts beating.

Acting on principle 15. Sick people need both emergency and basic care twenty-four hours a day, seven days a week. That is why many Sabbath-

keeping medical personnel take shifts during Sabbath hours. Providing such care may also mean that in an emergency we will have to go to a pharmacy and purchase medicine. We should do whatever is necessary to preserve life and health on every day, including the Sabbath.

Jesus agreed with this principle: "There was a certain man before him which had the dropsy. And Jesus answering spake unto the lawyers and Pharisees, saying, Is it lawful to heal on the sabbath day? And they held their peace. And he took him, and healed him, and let him go; And answered them, saying, Which of you shall have an ass or an ox fallen into a pit, and will not straightway pull him out on the sabbath day?" (Luke 14:2–5, KJV).

Have you had any "ox fallen into a pit" Sabbath experiences lately? For me that has meant helping someone to push their car out of a snowbank and running to a pharmacy to get medicine for my sick child.

Jesus wants His children to have an abundant life (John 10:10). It is especially appropriate to experience this abundant life on the Sabbath. That means our Sabbath keeping shouldn't leave anyone feeling deprived or hungry or suffering in any other way if we can help it. Ellen White wrote, "Every false religion teaches its adherents to be careless of human needs, sufferings, and rights. The gospel places a high value upon humanity as the purchase of the blood of Christ, and it teaches a tender regard for the wants and woes of man."[15] "God's holy rest day was made for man, and acts of mercy are in perfect harmony with its intent. God does not desire His creatures to suffer an hour's pain that may be relieved upon the Sabbath or any other day."[16]

I pray we will act accordingly.

And so . . .

We have finished looking at fifteen guiding principles that are based on three general principles: (1) Sabbath is a special vacation; (2) during that vacation we strengthen our ties with God; and (3) during that vacation we also strengthen our ties with God's family and with ours.

I have dedicated many pages in this book to sharing with you a process that has helped me to choose Sabbath rules and practices for my own life. This process consists of realizing that Sabbath is about deepening my relationship with Jesus and reflecting His character. That character manifests itself in principles found in the Bible. When I make personal decisions regarding Sabbath keeping, I first factor in the applicable

aspect of God's character. Next, I find the principle derived from His character. And then I figure out the rule—the practice—that fits the particular situation.

Don't accept the "rules" mentioned in this book merely because of what I say or do. If I endeavored to spell out what you should and should not do in each situation you might encounter, I would be taking on the role of the Holy Spirit and interfering with your personal relationship with Jesus—and that I should never do! I've presented the examples in this book to give you concrete ideas about how to keep the Sabbath in a principled way. I've shared my struggles and imperfect cogitations in the hope that some of them may be helpful to you. We all need to ask Jesus for the "eye salve" that He offers (Revelation 3:18) so that it will be clear what is the best thing to do in each situation. God will guide you to find Sabbath-keeping practices that fit your situation and culture. As He is doing so, He wants you to think and pray things through for yourself. That is an important part of your spiritual growth. Our Sabbath keeping practices will grow and improve along with the rest of our spiritual growth. So, "Grow in grace, and in the knowledge of our Lord and Saviour Jesus Christ. To him be glory both now and for ever. Amen" (2 Peter 3:18, KJV).

Remember, Sabbath keeping is all about *Him*!

Questions for Reflection and Discussion

1. Is the Sabbath subordinate to service opportunities or are service opportunities subordinate to the Sabbath? Why?
2. What's the result of not making the Sabbath an issue when a service opportunity arises? What's the result of making the Sabbath an issue and trying to arrange service opportunities for another time? How would you go about doing the latter?
3. With which of the options below do you agree? Why? What biblical principles apply?
   a. On Sabbath, one should provide help only in emergency situations.
   b. On Sabbath, one should provide any kind of help that has a compassionate purpose even in nonemergency situations.
4. What "ox fallen into a pit" situations have you experienced?

Chapter 11
Real Bumps in Real Life

"Do you have the sunblock and your swimsuit?" I asked my husband, Gaspar, as he, our daughter, Sara-May, and I prepared to leave for the airport. Gaspar, Sara-May, and I had packed many summer clothes in our luggage, even though it was December-cold outside our house. We shivered in our light jackets as we loaded our luggage and ourselves into the car that took us to the airport.

A warm tropical evening greeted us when we deplaned in Santo Domingo, Dominican Republic. Zoila, a close friend of Gaspar's father and stepmother, met us at the De Las Americas International Airport and helped us rent a minivan. Our son, Ivan, and his girlfriend, Crystal, had flown in from California and Tennessee, respectively, to enjoy our vacation with us. We picked them up in the bus terminal, for they had landed in La Romana and had ridden a bus to Santo Domingo. What a joy it was to see them again after a long separation!

Zoila led us to her lovely home on the outskirts of town. After we prayed to thank God for the safe trip and the happiness of being together, we enjoyed the sumptuous meal that Zoila lovingly prepared and served. We were grateful for the hospitality and fellowship that we enjoyed in her home.

After a good night's sleep, we piled our luggage and ourselves into our rented Sienna minivan and drove to the home of Gaspar's father in Santiago. We had come to the Dominican Republic to visit him and his wife, Fior. For the first time we saw their new condo in person. We didn't need to use our imagination any longer—we were there!

For the next ten days we ate delicious Dominican food, explored the island, visited points of interest, enjoyed scenery, learned about the history of the country, met new friends, attended church, took care of my father-in-law—who was recovering from a stroke, witnessed to a Haitian young man (when we returned home, we sent him a French Bible and Bible lessons), soaked in the sun on various beaches, picked up souvenirs, and so forth. The list could go on and on. All in all, we enjoyed this vacation immensely. But to a large degree, we enjoyed it so much because we were with members of our family whom we dearly loved.

But we also had some confusing and apprehensive times. Many people in the Dominican Republic don't pay much attention to traffic signals. Red lights are just a suggestion that drivers stop if they deem it necessary; many drive right through the lights as if they weren't there. Some drivers crossed double yellow "no passing" lines, and some passed on curves. There seemed to be no absolutes when it came to traffic laws.

Not only were some of the drivers a problem, but the roads on which we drove were also a challenge. I especially remember our trip to Sosua beach on the northern coast of the island. We had to travel many kilometers on mountain roads. On our way to the beach we bounced along on some very bumpy roads with all sorts of obstacles, such as slow pickup trucks loaded with people. Some of the roads were in bad repair and full of potholes—a very "holey" experience indeed. When we arrived at the beach, we discovered that our rented minivan had lost a hubcap because of the holes and bumps on the way.

As bad as our trip to the beach had been, our return that night was even worse. It was dark, foggy, and rainy, and we had a hard time staying on the potholed mountain road back to Santiago. Because there were no street lights and the fog and rain were thick, at times we didn't know where to go. We watched, prayed, and checked our road map often. What a relief it was when we finally saw the lights of Santiago piercing through the fog! We descended the mountain into the city thankful that we were safe and glad for the rest we were soon to enjoy.

Bumps, fog, hazards, and dilemmas

In many ways, my Dominican Republic vacation reminds me of my Sabbath experience. I've had many happy times and much sweet fellowship with my earthly and heavenly family, but sometimes I've also experienced frustration when people in the church and the world ignore God's

absolutes. (Of course, I haven't always been as careful as I should have been about God's directions either.) Then there are the bumps and foggy times that have confused me about which way to go. How should we deal with the difficult parts of our Sabbath experience on this side of heaven?

Even after we've considered all of the fifteen principles, we may still have questions about living the Sabbath that we don't find easy to answer. We have the sense that God is with us, but we're still in the fog. And we encounter people both outside and inside our churches who share the road we're on but who don't take the laws of the road very seriously.

The Sabbath cuts across the general flow of life on planet Earth today. It seems that many people aren't willing to get out of their stressful rat races to stop and recharge in God's presence on His day of divine appointment. Apparently, they consider doing this too incompatible with their lifestyle. Also, the postmodern prejudice against law, against absolutes, disparages our taking seriously any specific command from God. Against this backdrop, we can expect some difficulty and confusion regarding Sabbath keeping.

To help me be more realistic as I addressed this issue of Sabbath-keeping difficulties, I circulated a two-item questionnaire to a number of my friends around the world. Thirty friends from North America responded, and four from other parts of the world. Here are the questions:

1. List some specific, concrete Sabbath-keeping situations in which contemporary Adventists find themselves, and which demand a decision. (E.g., eating in restaurants on Sabbath, travel on Sabbath, swimming on Sabbath, soccer on Sabbath, etc.) List any others that you think I should address in my book.

2. What biblical principle-based suggestions and insights can you give me so that I can provide relevant, solid guidance on how to keep the Sabbath in the situations that you listed? (E.g., regarding eating at restaurants on Sabbath.) I may have a blind spot on some of these issues and need a variety of angles from which to approach these situations. That's why I need your help.

In the preceding chapters, I've often written about some of the challenges I've faced in keeping the Sabbath. However, many people are more interested in their own challenges. That is why I'm addressing a sample of

the confusion with which other people are grappling. My goal is not to condemn the Sabbath-keeping practices of others but to practice applying biblically based principles on confusing situations. We need to take our thinking to a new level to sort out some of these things. To avoid overdosing you, I will share a very small sample of the responses from my friends to my urgent plea. Their responses have been condensed and paraphrased.

Nitpicky Sabbaths

One of my friends sent me a lengthy response about her childhood Sabbath experiences, of which the following is a small part:

I couldn't play outside with the neighbors as I could on other days, but I could play outside with church friends who had come for dinner.

I couldn't play Go Fish with my regular game cards, but I could play Go Fish when using the cards from the Butterflies or Trees or Rocks nature games.

I couldn't play house, but I could play branch Sabbath School.

I couldn't ride my bike, but I could take a walk.

I couldn't wear shorts or pants, but I could wear an everyday dress when taking a Sabbath afternoon walk.

I couldn't swim, but I could wade up to my knees on a Sabbath afternoon walk.

I couldn't snorkel to see the fish and coral, but I could take a Sabbath afternoon walk and look at birds through binoculars.

We could go to the zoo—until they started charging a parking fee.

Mother could reheat the Sabbath dinner casserole but not bake it. Later, when we got an oven with a timer, she started baking the casserole while we were at church. Of course, this is rational and a principle of good stewardship because it saves electricity by not heating the oven twice.

Rather than eating in a restaurant on Sabbath when we traveled in Asia and Europe, we carried with us a mix of granola and powdered milk to which we added water for our meals.

My take on these remarks is that my friend's parents seemed to be trying to do their best to set the Sabbath apart from other days of the week. A number of our Jewish friends have a similar mind-set: some Orthodox Jews pretear their toilet tissue, paper towels, and sheets of aluminum foil for Sabbath. Their Sabbath-keeping rules forbid tearing things or changing something from an unusable form to a usable form on the Sabbath.[1] How's that for conscientiousness?

As important as it is to be intentional about living the Sabbath, in doing so we must not lose sight of the *who* of the Sabbath—Jesus Christ. Otherwise, we could get stuck in a *Mishnah* mentality. The *Mishnah* is a compilation of rabbinic laws made at the close of the second century A.D. In it you will find detailed advice for life, such as "A man may fold up his garments [that he wears on the Sabbath] as many as four or five times."[2] If such advice is practiced without principle-based thinking and outside of a vibrant relationship with God, the Sabbath can become hollow and cumbersome.

Upon reading my friend's lengthy response, I am reminded that Sabbath is not meant to be about nitpicking. It's meant to be big and grand. I wonder whether the parents of this friend of mine put as much thought and effort into how their family could enjoy unstressful, undistracted, exquisitely delightful time with Jesus on the Sabbath, as they apparently did into establishing the rules. In their home, was the Sabbath all about *Him* or was it about them and their performance? Were they more concerned about breaking the Sabbath than about breaking their relationship with God? Did my friend's parents lead their family in activities that focused on praising Jesus for His beautiful creation and that celebrated His bountiful blessings in their lives during the past week and on the Sabbath? Did they also try to make real the truth that Jesus was "with them" in a deeper sense than during the other six days of the week?

God didn't intend the Sabbath to be the "don't day." The Sabbath commandment is one of only two commandments phrased in a positive manner in the Decalogue. I think the biblical principles of basking, celebrating, and sanctifying could have benefited my friend and her family.

When the focus is off Jesus, we tend to fixate on all manner of less important things. Did my friend's family seek to develop a delightful relationship with Jesus on His day? If they had, rules about what they wore and what they did on Sabbath would have made more sense and brought more joy.

Don't get me wrong, I do believe that God has sanctified the Sabbath—that He has set it apart from the other six days of the week. Bound-

aries are important to the Sabbath—or any other holiday. If we didn't have boundaries for these special days, they would blur into all the ordinary days, and we wouldn't be able to sense their specialness.

Clear boundaries on basketball courts and football fields enable the players to enjoy the game better. Without them, the players would have to expend lots of energy trying to sort out where they and the ball should and shouldn't be. Though the Bible doesn't pretend to give instruction on every possible Sabbath-keeping situation, biblical Sabbath-keeping principles that are based on God's character establish boundaries to help us enjoy His day and understand its meaning. Ask God to help you to turn these biblical principles into rules and practices for your situation and culture. Ask Him to make you sensitive to His leading. He will give you "sanctified common sense"[3] and Holy Spirit guidance. Then enjoy the "game"! *He* is the whole point of it all. You win when you find *Him* in what you're doing.

Let's consider other responses to my two-item questionnaire. I will present only one sample response from each of the following categories: spending money on Sabbath, recreation on Sabbath, traveling on Sabbath, secular distractions on Sabbath, Sabbath work issues, Sabbath in the military, celebrations and family events on Sabbath, and concerns from cultures outside North America.

Spending money on Sabbath

Many responses to my two-item questionnaire involved the issue of spending money on Sabbath. Here's one.

> What about eating in a restaurant on Sabbath or in a cafeteria in a Seventh-day Adventist institution and having to pay cash or use a credit card? Or what about buying items at a store after church to throw together a lunch for some unexpected company?

A friend commented that if she decides to get together with her friends for an unplanned Sabbath lunch, she doesn't hesitate to stop at the store on the way home from church to buy whatever ingredients they don't already have so that they can throw the lunch together.

As we consider this situation, let's use our spiritual imagination: Jesus is personally with you and will be taking part in the activities of the day with you. Even though He is always with you, your relationship on the

Sabbath is not in the everyday mode but in a romantic, dating mode. You don't want to spend most or all of your time with Jesus being bogged down in nitpicking and analyzing and focusing on minutia, which is cumbersome and not restful, romantic, or delightful. The paralysis of analysis might set in, and you might get stuck staring at a pixel of the Sabbath scene and not move back to enjoy the whole picture.

With that in mind, which of the fifteen biblical principles that reflect His character shed light on the issue of buying food on Sabbath, especially when it enhances fellowship? Principle 1, preparing, admonishes us to prepare for the Sabbath ahead of time. Principle 2, resting, presents the Sabbath as a gift of time when we can rest from secular concerns and distractions, such as commercialism. Principle 12, fellowshiping, encourages fellowship on the Sabbath. Principle 14, serving, covers the idea of loving service and witness for God. And principle 15, caring, supports caring for physical needs on the Sabbath. If you put all these biblical principles—and any other relevant ones you can find—together, you have tools to help you evaluate the matter of spending money on Sabbath in a way that is in-line with the meaning of God's day.

Recreation on Sabbath

Some of the responses asked about recreation on the Sabbath: "What about ball playing or swimming, snorkeling, or other water sports on the Sabbath?"

What biblical principles shed light on where we should go with this one? There seem to be several. For example, principle 3, renewing, admonishes us to choose activities that renew us. Principle 5, celebrating, promotes a happy, delightful atmosphere. Principle 7, remembering, reminds us to include Jesus and His creation in our thoughts. Since these recreational activities are often done outside in nature, we would do well to see if principle 9, basking, which promotes basking in nature and enjoying it, is relevant. Then, of course, these activities often involve fellowship, so it wouldn't hurt to check out principle 12, fellowshiping, which advocates spending time with family and friends.

Then there is principle 6, sanctifying—the principle of setting the Sabbath and its activities apart for a special focus on God. How can we combine the principles I listed above—or any others that come to mind—with this principle of setting the Sabbath apart for a special focus on God, His Word, and His agenda? Ask the Lord of the Sabbath to help you sort this out.

Since many of my Adventist friends refer to a passage that Ellen White wrote when they address the issue of sports on Sabbath, I will address it before moving on to another issue. Here is the passage: "Every working of Christ in miracles was essential, and was to reveal to the world that there was a great work to be done on the Sabbath day for the relief of suffering humanity, but the common work was not to be done. Pleasure seeking, ball playing, swimming, was not a necessity, but a sinful neglect of the sacred day sanctified by Jehovah."[4]

As I pondered these two sentences and their context, I noted that the author is listing a series of things that are commonly done on the weekdays. Her point is that Christ's miracles were done to provide for a necessity, with a purpose, and the Sabbath also has a purpose. It's not a common day. Ellen White is listing examples of activities appropriate to common days; actions that don't support the purpose of the Sabbath—its specialness and sanctity. (See principle 6, sanctifying.) In whatever we do on the Sabbath, we need to keep in mind the sanctity of the day and not treat it as a common day. It is not business—or pleasure—as usual.

This doesn't necessarily mean that we can't go near or into a body of water or do things that bring us pleasure on that day. However, it does mean that pleasure must be focused on Him. Remember, He's set this day aside to spend with us, as if we were on a date. Regarding all that we do on the Sabbath, we should be able to give a positive answer to the question, "Does this activity bring us closer to Him?" In keeping with the theme of this book, I will say again: our Sabbath keeping is not about us. It should have a purpose beyond ourselves—the purpose of focusing on Jesus.

Traveling on Sabbath

One response to my brief questionnaire asked about traveling on Sabbath for pleasure or for business. When I looked at my list of biblically based Sabbath-keeping principles while considering this question, I realized that most of them have some relevance to the issue of traveling on Sabbath—depending on the reason for the travel. I challenge you to look at the list of principles and choose and apply those that fit. Take into consideration that the answer to this question may vary depending on whether the travel being considered is being done on a routine basis or as an exception. It seems to me that if we restrict such travel to exceptional situations, we will expend greater effort to keep the Sabbath holy during the trip.

Secular distractions

Let's look at a couple of related responses that were sent to me about media and secular Sabbath conversation:

> Reading a newspaper and listening to or watching the news on Sabbath seems wrong, yet when we get to church we talk about— and sometimes the sermon mentions—the news that is carried by those very media!

When I fellowship on Sabbath, must I talk only about God?

Once again, let's remind ourselves that Jesus is the Center in this situation too. When I have a friend with me, I should try to talk about things he or she finds interesting. On the Sabbath, we set aside everyday things so we can have more time to focus on our Friend Jesus. Would He enjoy talking about what's in the newspaper or in the news on TV? Since you have a strong relationship with Jesus during the week, you know Him well enough to know the answer to that question. If He would want to talk about the news, then go ahead. Sometimes the news provides good illustrations for spiritual truths.

The point is that we should remember that Jesus is with us on a special date, and we wouldn't want to exclude or ignore Him. Principle 7, remembering, implies that we can converse with and about Jesus by remembering and reflecting on the reality that He created our world, He redeemed us, and He will be coming to take us to heaven, where we can talk to Him face to face. Principle 6, sanctifying, factors in here too. How does that affect your Sabbath conversation?

Sabbath work issues

I received several questions on this subject. Here's one: "What about owning in full or in part a business that operates on Sabbath—e.g., trucking companies, printers, restaurant chains, etc."

Again, Jesus is the Center. He's the Lord of the Sabbath and of this situation. What principles that reflect His character can guide us in this particular case? It seems to be related to the principle of resting from work, from life's burdens and secular concerns—principle 2. Exodus 20:10 seems to apply: " 'The seventh day is the Sabbath of the Lord your God. In it you shall do no work: you, nor your son, nor your daughter,

nor your manservant, nor your maidservant' " (NKJV, emphasis added). Then, of course, there is Isaiah 58:13, which admonishes us not to do as we please—or not to do business as usual—on the Sabbath. What we own is our responsibility. Since Sabbath is about *our* relationship with Jesus, His Holy Spirit will guide in each situation—if we ask.

Celebrations on the Sabbath

Here's a question that deals with the issue of family celebrations and other family events in relation to the Sabbath: "What about holding or attending family centered events such as birthday celebrations, graduations, family reunions, or weddings on the Sabbath? (In Russia, weddings are sometimes part of a Sabbath morning worship service.)"

A friend recounted the following experience:

> My husband's uncle died about five months ago. He and his second wife were not Adventists. Since his death, we have tried to be supportive of the aunt by including her in family functions. Just a few weeks ago, we received an invitation to a surprise sixtieth birthday party that her sisters were throwing for her. They were having special entertainment—a bluegrass band. The party was scheduled for a Saturday afternoon.
>
> My husband's and my immediate response was that since it was on Sabbath, we wouldn't go. Then we talked it over with other Adventist family members and decided that we would go and be supportive of the aunt but wouldn't stay all day. So that's what we did—bluegrass band and all!
>
> The aunt is aware of our customary observance of the Sabbath. Our presence at her party that day sent a stronger message of our love and support for her than our witness for the Sabbath would have provided had we not gone. We're thankful that God impressed us with the right thing to do in that situation.

What biblical principles can you find that would help guide you, if you were the one making the decision regarding my friend's situation or other family events? As I look at the list, principle 2, resting, seems to be relevant because often these events involve out-of-the-ordinary work and distractions for those who are holding the events and those who are

guests. Principle 5, celebrating, seems also to apply.

We would need to ask ourselves if our holding or attending the family event would enhance or compromise our focus on and intimacy with God or that of others—see principle 6, sanctifying. Would we remember Jesus and His spiritual presence during the event, or would our minds be diverted in other directions? (See principle 7, remembering.) Principle 10, responding, also seems to be relevant to this decision.

Principle 12, fellowshiping, is very directly related to the issue of family social events—as is principle 13, affirming. One purpose of birthday parties, graduations, family reunions, and weddings is to affirm the people involved. You might also be able to link any of these events with service and witnessing for God, principle 14.

If you mix together all of the above principles with a good dose of prayer and Holy Spirit guidance, what do *you* conclude? (You will need to consider that not all birthday celebrations, family reunions, graduations, and weddings are created equal.)

Sabbath in the military

Jim was drafted into the army during the Korean War. One of the first "bumpy" issues he ran into was keeping the Sabbath. He reminisces about his army Sabbath experience.

> There were three of us Adventists in the outfit. We determined that, come what may, we would find a way around working on Sabbath.
>
> Fortunately, we had an excellent Adventist chaplain on the base who had prepared the way for us. Unfortunately, there were other Adventists (so-called) on the base who had signed "waivers" that allowed them to carry weapons and work on Sabbath and still retain their 1AO (conscientious cooperator) draft classification. They did that to get out of pulling a lot of unpleasant duties like KP (kitchen police) that we Adventists inherited. Their behavior raised a lot of questions from our buddies in the outfit.
>
> As it turned out, however, the main problem was not getting Sabbath free. We worked that out, thanks to the chaplain. The main problem—we thought—was our relationship with the other guys in the outfit who would naturally think that we were getting special treatment, even though we worked on Sundays to make

up for being free on Sabbaths. (Since they usually had Sundays free, they didn't realize we were in the barracks working.)

Every Friday night was a "GI party"—the term for having to scrub the floors in the barracks, clean rifles, scrub the latrines, etc. The most amazing thing was that even though we left at sundown Friday and didn't return until lights out after the GI party, and we left again early Sabbath morning before roll call, the Lord seems to have worked a weekly miracle, because the rest of the guys never missed us and didn't even realize we were gone. We spent endless hours at the chapel until we were eligible for weekend passes. Then we spent the time after church in the local library.

When basic training was over, I actually got the Outstanding Soldier award by vote of the other guys in the outfit, and I never even carried a weapon! Amazing what the Lord can do when you are faithful even in small things.

As your research points out, I probably did a better job of keeping Sabbath in the army than I have as a pastor, since pastors work just about every Sabbath of the year.[5]

Not every soldier is as fortunate as was Jim regarding Sabbath keeping in the military. One prominent American Adventist military chaplain wrote the following:

Military personnel serve God and country in a 24/7/365 capacity. Sometimes there is training on Sabbath that has to do with lifesaving or that can help you save your own life. Then there are times when one is called to duty on Sabbath: such as a radar person on a ship at sea or an air-traffic controller at a military airport or a person who is trained to remove unused explosives from a warplane when it lands. (You don't leave those hanging on the plane for days!) Often, there was no one with whom you can trade duty—especially if the unit is deployed. Refusal to "do duty" on any day can lead to a court martial and a felony conviction. So, what is an Adventist Sabbath keeper to do in these situations, especially if the unit is depending on your participation to safeguard the unit members—or potentially to do so? You just never know. "Don't join" is a lame answer if you are already there. It's too late to back that cat out of the bag.

When I consider an issue such as the one just described, a question comes to my mind, Is the Sabbath subordinate to service, or is service subordinate to the Sabbath? Does Mark 2:27 shed light on that question? What if human life is threatened? What biblical guiding principles that reflect Jesus' character can help us here? And, of course, we must remember that Jesus is in the center of this situation. What would Jesus do if He were a GI?

For me, the principle of preparing comes to mind. When possible, a military person should at least try to prepare the way to observe the Sabbath by informing commanding officers that he or she is a seventh-day Sabbath keeper. Even when in life-or-death situations, soldiers need to follow the principles of resting and renewing. The ideal would be on Sabbath—the appointed day of rest. But if one is in a situation such as the chaplain describes above, the principles of serving and caring also kick in.

When Jesus cared for the physical needs of the man at the pool of Bethesda one Sabbath (John 5), enabling him to take up his bed and walk, He indicated His concern for the well-being of the people He had created. When church leaders censured Him for His behavior, He calmly replied, "My Father worketh hitherto, and I work" (verse 17, KJV). It's true that God ceased creating on the Sabbath, but He didn't and doesn't cease maintaining whom and what He created.

The military chaplain commented on having a Christian mind-set when the situation demands doing duty on Sabbath:

> Why would I do duty on Sabbath—to avoid being in trouble or to honor God by serving His people? If all I'm doing is avoiding trouble, I have a very self-centered focus. What *can* I do on Sabbath to honor God? Maybe I can tell the commander that even though it is Sabbath, I will honor the command, my fellow soldiers, and God by being at my place of duty on whatever day that duty demands. What is the motive? Selfish or selfless?

What other principles would you apply to a military situation?

Concerns from outside North America

Here are some additional "bumpy" issues that people shared as I gathered data for my dissertation. If you met these people in person, what

biblical guiding principles for Sabbath keeping would *you* share with them to help them enjoy an optimal Sabbath?

Sometimes the very activities or atmosphere of my church prevent me from coming closer to God on Sabbath. (Colombia)

My family stays at the church all day for various meetings, and we have very little time together as a family. How should I relate to this? (France)

I know that Sabbath is a family day, but I stay away from my family because they are not Sabbath keepers. I fellowship with a sister in my church all day Sabbath. (Russia)

I have children, which makes Sabbath morning such a hustle. I arrive at church; get to Sabbath School; potty, feed, and play with the kids outside of church during the worship service so they don't disturb anyone; and then go home ready to sleep. It sounds like I ignore Jesus—at least it feels that way. How can I relate to Him on Sabbath in my situation? (Côte d'Ivoire)

School in my country is held on the Sabbath. If I did not go to school on Sabbath, I would fail my education. Is this an ox-in-the-pit situation and therefore is it OK for me to attend school on Sabbath? (Côte d'Ivoire)

God blesses our efforts

A colleague of mine, Dr. Kathleen Kuntaraf, ran into the school-on-Sabbath issue as she went through medical school in Indonesia. Here's her story as adapted from *College and University Dialogue:*

Somehow with the grace of God, I managed to solve the Sabbath problems for the first five years that I was in the school of medicine in one of the state universities in Indonesia. Any theoretical or practical exams that fell on Sabbath could be replaced with an oral exam arranged on one of the weekdays so that I never attended any lectures or did any lab work or sat for any kind of examination on the Sabbath day.

However, when it was time to take my exams from the fifth year to the sixth year, there was a change in the examination regulation, with no more oral exams. Everything would have to be written. The exams covering six subjects would be held one per day from Monday through Saturday.

As soon as I knew of the changes, I went to see the president of the student association to inform him of my problem with the pediatrics exam, which was to be given on Sabbath. He suggested that I go ahead and sit for the rest of my exams, and he would try to arrange for the dispensation I had previously received.

So, on Monday I sat for my internal medicine exam. I had not received any word whether the pediatrics exam that fell on the Sabbath day could be given on another day. On Tuesday, I sat for the second subject, obstetrics-gynecology, and waited again. Nothing happened.

I thought to myself, *This is going too slowly.* So I went to see the president of the university. *Who knows?* I thought. *I might get support from him!*

I was happy when I met him to discover that as a Moslem, he was supportive of the Adventist conviction regarding Sabbath keeping. He advised me to report to the chairman of the exam committee, and if a green light was given, to discuss this problem with the director of the department of pediatrics. Walking out of the president's house, I felt delighted, realizing that the man who held the highest position in the university was very supportive of me.

However, when I met the chairman of the exam committee, I found him furious at me because of the Sabbath problem I faced. He said, "Do you think the angels will chop off your head the moment you do your exam on the Sabbath day? How can the regulation of the state university be changed because of one Seventh-day Adventist student? Impossible!"

Oh, I was sad when I left the house of the chairman of the examination committee. I just knew that I would surely flunk the whole exam. At that time, the regulations were that if you failed one subject, no matter how well you scored in the other five, you still had to retake the exams for all six subjects.

My friends were not very supportive. They didn't understand why I was so particular about my religion. They said, "Entering the state university was already so difficult for you, and now you

are adding more problems. Don't be a fanatic. Go ahead and take your exam and then ask God for forgiveness."

Despite the little support I received, I took my exams on Wednesday, Thursday, and Friday. On Sabbath I went to church fully aware that when the results came out, I would be announced as having failed them. And it was true—when the results came out, I had failed because I had received no grade for pediatrics. I would have to take the exams for all of the subjects over again after three months. I was extremely sad, but I remembered 1 Corinthians 10:13, which says that God does not allow you to be tested beyond your power to remain firm.

The week after the depressing results came out, I went to see the president of the student association again to arrange for the next exam schedule to be held just on weekdays. He said, "This is too early. Come and report two weeks prior to the exam."

Two and a half months went by swiftly, and it was time for me to see the president of the student association again. To my surprise, he told me, "We have tried to reschedule the exams but have not been successful. Six subjects have to be taken within six working days, from Monday to Saturday, so you have no alternative but to change your attitude."

I went to the academic dean, thinking I might have his support. A pharmacology professor had heard about me—the fanatic student who was willing to accept failure because of her religious convictions. While I was waiting to see the academic dean, he came directly to where I was sitting and said, "I've asked the oldest Christians in the world, the Roman Catholics, and they said that you have to keep Sunday holy."

I didn't know how to answer him because there were so many doctors surrounding me, some Moslem, some Catholic, and some Protestant! Then I remembered Matthew 10:18, 19, " 'You will be brought before governors and kings . . . but . . . do not worry about what to say or how to say it. At the time you will be given what to say' " (NIV). So I quickly prayed, "God, please give me the right answer," and then I heard a small Voice whispering into my ear, "Answer with this, 'Oh, I am just following what the Bible says!' "

When I said that, the pharmacology professor put the folder he was holding under his arm and with his finger pointing to all

the doctors who had surrounded me, he said, "You all have sinned against God. The Bible asks you to keep Sabbath holy and not Sunday. Be converted!"

I felt so grateful because he had done the preaching for me. Then I went to see the academic dean. We talked for about a half hour. He said, "Be logical with your religion."

I answered, "I realize that religion is illogical at times. For instance, some people, when they pray to God, have to face a certain direction. Is that logical? No! God is omnipresent, so you can call to Him anywhere and at anytime. Then why do people keep on doing such a practice? It is because that is their conviction.

"When you finish reading a textbook, you can just simply dump it into a wastepaper basket and nobody will condemn you. But you can't do that to a Bible or a Koran. Instead, you would treat them respectfully even though they might be made of materials inferior to those of the textbook. Isn't that illogical? But it is our conviction, so even though it is illogical, we continue to do it."

He was silent, realizing that it was true that religion is illogical at times. Finally, he said, "I'm sorry. I want to help you, but I just don't know how. My suggestion is that you go straight to the pediatric professor."

I told myself this would be my last effort. If I didn't succeed, I would just fly abroad to attend an Adventist medical school. I might have problems but at least there was hope I would be a medical doctor someday.

I brought this matter to our prayer meeting. The church elders disagreed with my plans to go abroad if my meeting with the pediatrics professor failed. They said, "You are a pioneer. You have to be patient and fight for the Sabbath. What's going to happen to the rest of the Adventist medical students in the lower levels? They don't have the money to go abroad, so what's next? Let's bring this matter to God in prayer!"

The whole church prayed for me that night. Then I went to see the pediatrics professor. My, he was really upset at my firm religious principles and said, "There is no way to change the regulation of the university because of only one Seventh-day Adventist student."

It so happened that his wife, who is a lawyer, was sitting with us in the living room. She defended me right away, saying, "No,

Daddy. This is a *pancasilais* country. Everyone has the right to have religious liberty."

A debate ensued between husband and wife while I sat there with bowed head, silently praying that the Lord would bless this debate to the glory of His name. And God answered my prayer. Eventually, the pediatrics professor said, "OK, we will reschedule the pediatric exam for you."

I was asked to sit for the pediatric exam on Friday after the surgery exam. I was isolated in the house of one of the pediatric staff until the students sat for the exam on the following day, the Sabbath day, at eight o'clock. Then I was released to go to church. When results came out, praise the Lord, I passed the exam!

Later, in each department in which I worked—internal medicine, obstetrics-gynecology, surgery, etc.—I was allowed to leave the hospital on Friday before sunset and return to work on Saturday after sunset. I had to work longer in each department to make up for the many Sabbaths I had missed. After I finished one department, I had to wait for the next batch of students before moving on to another department, which made my schooling take much longer than that of the other students. Yet I was happy to be able to observe the Sabbath all through my years of schooling in a non-Adventist school of medicine.

When graduation time came, I had one more problem. All the graduation services are conducted on Saturdays. Again I went to see the president of the student association. He said, "Please give in just this once. We will no longer bother you anymore after you have graduated. You know, it is impossible to have all the professors march for you, the only graduate, on a weekday." I was asked to come again the following week after the president of the student association negotiated this matter with the academic dean.

When I returned, I received word that I had to wait for another two weeks because the academic dean and the dean of the school of medicine found it difficult to solve my graduation problem. I had to go back and forth for several weeks for repeated discussions. Finally, after two months, they agreed to make a special graduation for me on a weekday with all the doctors marching and me as the only graduate. I really praise God for the strength He gave me to endure these problems and finally win the victory.

As a result, when the Adventist medical students who were in the lower levels were ready to graduate, they, too, were given a special graduation. I do praise God for His mercy and His goodness and His greatness.

May we always have such a close relationship with God that nothing can prevent us from keeping the Sabbath holy, for the Bible says, " 'If you love me, you will obey what I command' " (John 14:15, NIV).[6]

Questions for Reflection and Discussion

1. John 10:10 says that Jesus came so we can have life more abundantly. Does keeping the Sabbath mean that we will have life more restrictedly instead of more abundantly? Why or why not?

2. How does the following quote apply to Sabbath keeping? "Obedience must be rendered from a sense of principle, and the right must be pursued under all circumstances."[7]

3. An *Adult Sabbath School Bible Study Guide* lesson about relationships asked the following: "How does one determine what Sabbath-keeping practices belong to an unchangeable core of our beliefs in contrast to what are mere cultural expressions and can, therefore, be changed to fit the context of various groups? Why, for the sake of unity, must we be able to distinguish between the two concepts?" How would you answer?

4. How do the words of the following hymn apply to keeping the Sabbath?

> God be in my head, and in my understanding.
> God be in mine eyes, and in my looking.
> God be in my mouth, and in my speaking.
> Oh, God be in my heart, and in my thinking (*Sarum Primer*, 1558).

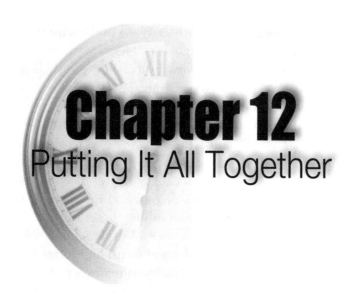

Chapter 12
Putting It All Together

Let's revisit Principle International Airport (PIA)—portrayed in chapter 5 as the imaginary departure point for our weekly Sabbath vacation. Several Sabbath-keeping families have just arrived at PIA late Friday afternoon with their Sabbath plans luggage. They come from many cultures. The divine Airport Official checks their ID at the check-in counter to determine whether their identity is "in Christ." If they pass the identity check, the Official directs them to gate 7.

Some travelers don't have a deep relationship with Jesus, so they can't proceed past the check-in counter. (They wouldn't enjoy spending a vacation with Someone they didn't really love anyway.) Some of those who were turned away at check-in had luggage packed with plans that would be incompatible with Sabbath Land. The luggage screener would have rejected their luggage.

Those who have the proper ID head for the gate area. They look at the flight departure monitor on the way. It says that the flight to Sabbath Land is on time—it will leave one hour before sundown Friday night from gate 7.

Arriving at the gate area, the vacationers line up for the screeners. Even though these people have a relationship with Jesus, going through the weekly screening still serves a good purpose, for keeping Sabbath is something people grow into, and there is always something new to learn. The luggage screener checks their Sabbath plans luggage against the fifteen Bible-based principles that are a guide to an optinal Sabbath vacation experience. The people screener checks their persons to be sure they aren't

wearing or carrying unsafe items, such as wrong motives for their Sabbath behaviors and practices.

After the screenings, these frequent flyers board the Shalom International Airlines flight. As they go airborne and ascend above their daily routine, they breathe a sigh of relief. They're not only riding on "the high places of the earth" (Isaiah 58:14), but even higher than that—to a new level of spiritual growth! The passengers muse, *God is so kind to provide this weekly vacation on which we can rise above our daily routine and relax in a new environment. That's what it takes to recover from the stresses of the daily grind.* (When I sing "As We Come to You in Prayer," I think this same joyous thought. You might want to sing that song right now.[1])

At sundown the vacationers arrive in Sabbath Land, the land of *Shabbat Shalom*—Sabbath peace. Sabbath Land is currently located on our sinful planet, but it is like a "palace in time" that removes us from the weekday environment.[2] When the Sabbath travelers deplane, they feel the difference in the climate. They were cold when they boarded the plane, but they step into a warm, pleasant tropical evening as they get off the plane.

The passengers celebrate entry into Sabbath Land by gathering for Friday sundown worship. Jesus, the Lord of the Sabbath, is waiting for them there. His arms are spread wide, and He welcomes and hugs each traveler (Matthew 11:28). They are overjoyed that they can be with Him in a relaxed yet focused way. Yes, He has been with them through their hard, busy week, but they had felt so rushed that they found it difficult to bask in His presence. Sometimes they were even too busy to notice Him. But not now. Jesus seems closer than ever.

Children and parents, husbands and wives, singles and friends sing together, and then they share Bible verses that especially fit their experiences during the past week. They talk to their Creator, thanking Him for a safe trip into this land of love, joy, and peace. They trust God to take care of the weekday responsibilities they have set aside during their vacation time. This palace in time is truly a foretaste of heaven.

After a good night's sleep, the vacationers have a special breakfast and then go to a worship service at the Shabbat Shalom Church to celebrate and honor the Lord of the Sabbath. The Father, Son, and Holy Spirit are in church with them—along with myriads of angels.

The church is appropriately named, for Sabbath is about *shalom*—peace. On this day, church members can focus undistractedly on God. He will keep in perfect peace those whose minds are stayed—focused—on Him (Isaiah 26:3).

The worshipers celebrate the goodness of their Lord during the past week. Songs of joy and praise fill the air. They gather in groups to study Jesus' love letter, the Bible. More music follows that praises the Divine Trinity. Then a Holy Spirit–filled preacher makes a portion of God's Word come powerfully alive. The worshipers are spiritually recharged to live another week for God.

After this spiritual feast, the people move on to another feast—a scrumptious Sabbath dinner prepared the day before. The delicious food and fellowship are some of the many delights of Sabbath Land—just a taste of all God's gifts to them. They invite several strangers and lonely ones to join them, and they all bask in the friendship and joy that surrounds them. At one of the tables, a group of friends excitedly gather to visit—for this is alumni weekend. It has been fifty years since they graduated from high school!

When the meal is finished, the vacationers involve themselves with various activities. A mother and father and their two children go to the edge of Sabbath Land and excitedly tell those there about Jesus and the vacation they are enjoying with Him. Two young people bring Sabbath School to a group of strangers by holding a branch Sabbath School. A single person sits under an inviting shade tree for some personal Bible study. Not far away, some friends are involved in an informal discussion group about a biblical or spiritual issue. A youth group finds sick or discouraged souls and brings them flowers, fellowship, and joy. (After all— the vacationers are in the earthly Sabbath Land—and earth's imperfections and problems are not far away.)

Families rejoice that they can do something fun together after a busy week that took them in different directions. Fathers, mothers, boys, and girls from different cultures have no trouble finding something to do that is consistent with the biblical principles that govern Sabbath Land. Two families go out to explore the beautiful nature scenery and wildlife in the woods and hills. They thank and praise Him for His handiwork. Three friends walk along the beach with the Lord. Their footprints are a reminder of their daily walk with Him. Out in the middle of a lake, a young couple leisurely paddles a canoe as mallard pairs swim around them. As the canoeists approach a shore, they spot a beaver dam and a blue heron. Other Sabbath vacationers enjoy many other activities. Some lie down for a while in one of the lush green meadows and enjoy a short nap while basking in the sun— and in the presence of the Son. Each adds their culture's special touch to their Sabbath experience. Jesus is with all of them at the same time.

The earthly Sabbath Land is a foretaste of heaven. However, because it is located in an imperfect world, the Sabbath vacationers run into bumpy roads and fog on the edges of Sabbath Land. They experience frustrations and confusion from time to time. The Sabbath vacationers have learned that when this happens, they do well to consult their maps and guidebooks immediately. These travel aids contain biblical Sabbath-keeping principles that are based on Jesus' character traits. They've found that when problems arise, it really helps to refocus on the Lord of the Sabbath. After all, Sabbath is all about *Him*! When the vacationers remember to do this, He helps them find their way through the rough spots and back to the peaceful center of Sabbath Land. The rough spots will disappear forever when the vacationers keep Sabbath in the earth made new. There all the roads will be smooth—and paved with gold!

Return trip

When the afternoon has passed and the sun is about to set, the Sabbath vacationers meet together again for sundown worship. They reflect on their Sabbath experience with Jesus, celebrate the day, and launch their new week. As they sing and pray together, they feel that their souls have been restored through the undistracted vacation time they've enjoyed with God and His family. They have gained courage for the coming week through the affirming and healing words and activities they have experienced.

They join hands for a closing worship prayer: "During this Sabbath, You have taught us Your ways, O Lord, that we may live according to Your truth. May the fragrance of this Sabbath spill into our new week and give us purity of heart—undivided hearts—that we may honor You. In the name of the Lord of the Sabbath, Amen."[3]

By now, a few stars glimmer in the darkening sky. Regretfully, the vacationers board their Shalom International Airlines flight to New Week. Never once during the Sabbath did they query when it would end so they could do what they want (Amos 8:5).

The vacationers happily look over the souvenirs they have collected to take into their new week: restored sanity, recharged physical and spiritual batteries, a renewed appreciation for God's creation, the joy of the Lord that is their strength (Nehemiah 8:10), greater trust in God, courage to face the new week's challenges, closer ties with their family and friends, a deepened understanding of God's Word, and more.

As the plane lands at sundown Saturday evening, the passengers think about what they will take from their Sabbath experience into their new week. They know that as the new week progresses, they will live out what they have renewed during the Sabbath. What they do on the Sabbath embodies the whole life of sanctification.

As the Jewish *Havdalah* wine that overflows the cup into the saucer (see chapter 9), the Sabbath sanctification, the Sabbath experience, spills into the new week. "He who from the heart obeys the fourth commandment will obey the whole law. He is sanctified through obedience."[4] Similarly, the Sabbath experience will spill over from this old world into the new earth.

Last flight out

Blind songwriter Fanny J. Crosby could see the final glorious flight in her mind's eye.

All the way my Savior leads me;
O the fullness of His love!
Perfect rest to me is promised
In my Father's house above.
When I wake to life immortal,
Wing my flight to realms of day,
This my song through endless ages,
Jesus led me all the way.

Other writers have seen a similar vision of the hereafter. It appears at the end of the Tamid tractate in the Jewish *Mishnah:* "A Psalm: a Song for the Sabbath Day; a Psalm, a song for the time that is come, for the day that shall be all Sabbath and rest in the life everlasting."[5] Greg Nelson says, "The Sabbath is a present experience of the future heaven."[6] Don Postema calls Sabbath "a vacation with God planned from the beginning to be enjoyed into eternity."[7] Mark Buchanan says that though the Sabbath isn't eternity, it's close. He sees it as a dress rehearsal for things above; things that we anticipate forever in the Sabbath.[8] The great expositor of the meaning of the Sabbath, Abraham Joshua Heschel, observed, "Unless one learns how to relish the taste of Sabbath while still in this world, unless one is initiated in the appreciation of eternal life, one will be unable to enjoy the taste of eternity in the world to come."[9] And Norman Wirzba views the

Sabbath practice as a sort of training ground for life in eternity, "a preparation for the full reception and welcome of the presence of God."[10]

When we prepare for Sabbath on this earth, we are also preparing for Jesus' second coming, the portal to heaven. Our Sabbath experience now is a rehearsal for heaven. It points to the perfect creation, redemption, and restoration to be realized in the glorious earth made new. "And when Eden shall bloom on earth again, God's holy rest day will be honored by all beneath the sun."[11] Isaiah tells us that " 'from one Sabbath to another, / All flesh shall come to worship before Me,' says the LORD" (Isaiah 66:23, NKJV). We may be in the minority now when we keep the seventh-day Sabbath, but in the heaven that Isaiah describes, *everyone* will keep it!

Signs all around us cry out that it's high time for Jesus to come. It's time now to take the Lord and His Sabbath more seriously, for it is a sign to the world of our relationship with Him (Exodus 31:13). Before Jesus comes, His people will proclaim the Sabbath more fully through the power of the Holy Spirit.[12] I hope this book and our lives will support that sacred endeavor.

Until He comes, however, we will find ourselves in situations where we need to take a stand for the Lord and His Sabbath. Are you willing to take that stand over and over again by His grace? If so, pray this prayer with me: "Lord of the Sabbath, I take a stand for You and Your Sabbath right now. I choose to commit [or recommit] myself to You and to taking Your Sabbath more seriously in these end times as I prepare for Your second coming. I long for the day when I will be in heaven with You. Until then, keep me faithful. In the name of Him who is able to keep me from falling and to present me before His glorious presence without fault and with great joy.[13] Amen."

Final advice

"For yet a little while, and he that shall come will come, and will not tarry" (Hebrews 10:37, KJV). We are still waiting—anxiously and expectantly—to take our flight to the land of fadeless day. How shall we live in the time of waiting? I wrote this book to help you answer that question. I pray that it has educated your conscience, deepened your understanding of living the Sabbath, and provided helpful guiding principles to diminish the guesswork of doing so.

Just as I experienced fog on my journey in the mountains of the Dominican Republic, so we will experience fog in living the Christian life on

this planet before Jesus returns. Paul wrote, "Now we see through a glass, darkly"; now we "know in part" (1 Corinthians 13:12, KJV). Sometimes we might think to ourselves, *I can't see what's wrong with doing that on the Sabbath.* I hope that this book has put you on the path toward seeing more clearly God's will for how we should live His Sabbath gift while we wait for the time when we "shall know fully."

In closing, I will share with you some final thoughts on using the principles for living the Sabbath that I have presented in this book.

1. Don't follow one principle to the neglect of others. The principles interact with each other; they have a synergy. For example, you shouldn't regard rest on the Sabbath as negating the need for regular worship with your church family. Both are important; they work together.

2. You should avoid incorporating into your Sabbath keeping any elements that aren't based on biblical principles. Instead of *synergism*, in which several biblically sound Sabbath-keeping principles interact positively with each other, this would be *syncretism*, an attempt to unite that which shouldn't be united. Mark Buchanan put it this way, "Just as we ought not pull asunder what God has joined, so we ought not to join what God has pulled asunder."[14]

3. Obviously, you can't live all the fifteen principles in one Sabbath but must spread them out over several Sabbaths. For example, you might do service one Sabbath, bask in nature another, focus on family fellowship another, rest at home on another, have people over for Sabbath dinner on yet another, etc.

4. However, you should also keep in mind that you must follow certain principles every Sabbath or the day wouldn't be a Sabbath. For example, every Sabbath should involve rest from work, worship, etc.

5. Balance is an overriding principle that helps us live the guiding principles. It will help you decide which principle-based activities to choose. If you've done active service for others all week, maybe on Sabbath you should get away by yourself for a while and meditate and read or go out in nature. If you don't have time during the week to be involved in service activities, a Sabbath that includes some service activities would provide beneficial balance for you.

6. All of the three p's—precepts, principles, Personhood (character) of God—are important in living the Sabbath and in our Christian life in general. However, when deciding your Sabbath practices in a given situation, start with the relevant character trait of God, find the related principle, and then make the rule for actual life. When testing rules that already exist, be

sure they point to a biblical principle that reflects God's character. Don't focus on the rules alone.

7. *The Bible lists some Sabbath-keeping commands at the rule level that are based on specific situations in Bible times*—see Exodus 20:10; 16:22–30; Numbers 15:32–36; Nehemiah 10:31; 13:15–22; Jeremiah 17:21–24; etc. However, God generally provides guidance at the principle level, which we have explored in this book. We may often find ourselves in situations that the Bible doesn't specifically address at the rule level, which means we must seek principles and use them to establish rules for our unique situations.

8. *In the May 5, 2005* Adventist Review, *I wrote an article about the essence of Sabbath keeping that covered in a very brief way the subject of this book.*[15] Some blog writers on a Web site for former Adventists reacted to that article, arguing emphatically that to worry about specific practices and even principles of keeping the Sabbath was to be legalistic. Our lives, they said, should focus "only on Jesus."

I own a book titled *365 Ways to Say I Love You.* When we love someone, we want to communicate that love in intentional, practical ways. If we don't express our love in definite ways, the person we love might wonder about our feelings for him or her. So we try to think of creative ways in which to celebrate birthdays and do other special things for the person we love. Doesn't Jesus deserve expressions of love that are just as tangible? Some of us less creative creatures appreciate ideas that get us started in deepening our relationship with our human loved one, and some people may appreciate the same kind of help regarding our Divine Loved One— the Lord of the Sabbath. That is why I wrote this book.

Principles should not supersede precepts—each of the three *p*'s is important. But they will help us to choose the precepts that best say "I love You" to Jesus on the day created for love and undistracted time with Him.

9. *We should live the Sabbath principles from the inside out.* We must be filled with Jesus and His Spirit or we will focus only on behavior rather than on the inner person. Focusing only on behavior is like putting a new label on an old can filled with spoiled food.

10. *We need to view any differences in Sabbath practices that we see in differing cultures with sensitivity and understanding, because the challenges that people of various cultures face may be very different.* Labeling people is inconsistent with Christlike, unconditional love. It is better to focus on the biblical Sabbath-keeping principles that unite all cultures than to fo-

cus on differences in the application of these principles. There is plenty of room for the Holy Spirit to guide the application of a biblical principle within a particular culture. (Of course, it should be the Holy Spirit who guides the application of the principle to the culture rather than the culture that guides the application of the principle.) Believers truly need biblical principles as a compass to guide them to the Sabbath experience that is right for their individual situations. Operating at the principle level will not lower the standards. Rather, it will bring high, Christ-empowered standards within the reach of all.[16]

11. If no biblical principles directly address a specific situation in which you find yourself, consult less specific biblical principles that touch upon the issue. Make sure that they truly are principles—timeless, universal foundations for practices. Don't confuse rules with principles. Here are some sample general principles in question form.

- Would the activity that I am considering detract from or enhance the meaning of the Sabbath? (See chapter 3 for a description of the meaning of the Sabbath.)
- Will this activity draw me even closer to Jesus?
- "Does this activity naturally lead me to think of God and His character, or does it tend to divert my attention from Him to the activity or to myself?"[17]
- What are the likely consequences of my choice? Might it cause someone else to stumble? Would my choice make Jesus and His Sabbath look ridiculous?
- Is this action consistent with who I am as a child of God? (Sabbath keeping is not just *doing*, it's *being*—reflecting God's being.)

12. Mark Buchanan writes about a funny tendency that emerges among Sabbath keepers: First we overdo it, piling rule on rule (legalism). Then we become weary of that and push toward minimalism, making excuses as we look for loopholes, exemptions, and shortcuts. For example,

So we say we won't shop. Not at all. And then one Sunday [Sabbath] afternoon we see that if the kids are to have breakfast Monday morning, we need milk. We explain to ourselves that this falls under the category of a bull falling into a well on the Sabbath. *Of course you pull it out.* Well, likewise, if the kids don't eat breakfast

or eat their cereal dry and without the recommended daily requirements of calcium and vitamin D, then they will have insuf-
ficient strength that day—not to mention bad attitudes—and
will struggle to concentrate, and then they'll fall behind in their
schoolwork, and then they'll fail third grade, and then their self-
esteem will plummet, and then they'll turn to a life of crime and
waste and dissipation to fill the void—and all this because I was
too hidebound to go out and buy a jug of milk.[18]

I get tired just thinking about this logic. Sabbath is bigger than nitpicking. If we look at each Sabbath rule only by itself, we have only a
tightfisted, wobbly obedience. Most Christians who observe the American Thanksgiving or Christmas holiday don't minimize these special days.
In fact, their practices are often rather extravagant. They usually plan well
ahead of time. Why? Because there is a big picture. It is about Jesus and
their loved ones and friends. Do we have the same mind-set for the Sabbath? Do we see each rule and practice in terms of the big picture—that
Sabbath is a celebration day on which we take a vacation with Jesus and
with His family?

The more careless we become about the Sabbath and about keeping
the focus on Jesus, the more we focus our Sabbath keeping on us—our
needs and our wishes. I suspect we could easily answer many if not most
of our questions about Sabbath observance if our relationship with Jesus
were what it should be. (Remember chapter 3?) Both an anything-goes
attitude and a rigid approach to the Sabbath can be problematic if our
mind-set is all about us.

*13. Now that you've read this book about the process of choosing Sabbath
practices—the* what *(the precept or rule), the* why *(the principle), and the* who
(God's person or character)—give the process a try by God's grace. I've found
that when I "make every effort to enter that rest" (Hebrews 4:11, NIV)
and intentionally create a Sabbath experience, I enjoy the Sabbath so much
more. I realize that my intentionality is worth the effort.

*14. "Trust in the Lord with all your heart [the heart religion described in
chapter 3], / And lean not on your own understanding; / In all your ways
acknowledge Him [using principles based on His character, because it's all
about* Him!*], / And He shall direct your paths [so you will know what practices to follow—what rules to make]" (Proverbs 3:5, 6, NKJV).* " 'The Lord
will guide you continually' " (Isaiah 58:11, NKJV)—that includes on the
Sabbath. "Those who study the Bible, counsel with God, and rely upon

Christ will be enabled to act wisely at all times and under all circumstances. Good principles will be illustrated in actual life."[19] How's that for a bold assurance!

The big picture

In this book we have been moving toward trying to understand better the big picture of living the Sabbath. We have used various metaphors—three lenses or three *p*'s; glasses in a cereal box; Ping Pong balls, marbles, and rice in a jar; luggage screeners; etc.—as different ways to illustrate the point that in order to see clearly what Sabbath rules we should establish in our individual cultures and lives, we must base those rules on biblical principles that, in turn, are based on Jesus' character—for Sabbath is all about *Him*!

Biblically based Sabbath-keeping principles are like sections of a picture of the character of Jesus, and rules are like pixels within those sections. *Each pixel must be in the picture for the picture to be clear.* The principles and the resulting rules are an expression of the character of the Jesus whom we serve.

The rules and principles find their real importance only when they reveal Jesus. We need to ask ourselves, "Will my pixels—my personal rules for Sabbath practice—help make the picture look like Jesus, or will they make a blurry picture—or worse, one that looks like someone or something else?"[20]

You will be traveling life's road with people who are legalists, piling rule upon rule. Keep your eyes on Jesus! You will be among people who are minimalists—who go to the other extreme and try to find shortcuts in Sabbath keeping. Keep your eyes on Jesus! No matter whom you are with or where you are on your earthly journey—keep your eyes on Jesus!

If you were in an elevator and someone you met there were to ask you about the Sabbath, what would you say about it in the short time you would have till one of you reached your floor? I might say something like this, "I keep Sabbath because I love Jesus and He loves me. We both clear our schedules on His seventh-day Sabbath—the day *He* has set apart for us to spend special time together. It's our divine appointment. As I spend this special time with Him to strengthen our ties, I pray that I'll better reflect His character to those around me every day of my life.

"I don't keep the Sabbath to be saved by works but because Jesus wants me to take the Sabbath day off from work every week to rest with

Him. That makes fifty-two days off per year—seven and a half weeks of vacation with God and with His family. Wow!"

What's the big deal?

As we have traveled together through this book, you probably have noticed that we didn't focus on Sabbath theology and doctrine. Those topics have already been covered very well. Instead, we focused on the spirituality of the Sabbath. A key definition of Christian spirituality is "the *lived* experience of Christian belief."[21]

Why have I attempted to explore at such length the many dimensions of living our Lord's Sabbath? I've done so because I believe we must consider more fully and understand better the deeper meaning behind the doctrine of the Sabbath. The Christian life is made up of spiritual disciplines as well as of doctrinal truth. The Sabbath is the queen among the spiritual disciplines.

George Barna warns that when we are given broad instruction in a doctrine without being informed how to carry it out in our lives, we often find it hard to find the focus and energy to accomplish the task God has set before us.[22] Tilden Edwards calls for balance by reminding us that *orthopraxy*—right practice—must complement *orthodoxy*—right believing.[23]

The Christian world is waking up to the significance of living the Sabbath experience. A chorus of Christian writers are turning up the volume of the call to rediscover the Sabbath. We have sampled some of their insights throughout this book. Dorothy Bass, director of the Valparaiso University Project on the Education and Formation of People in Faith, reminds us that the Sabbath is God's gift to us and that it is the most challenging—and necessary—spiritual discipline for contemporary Christians.

Notice Professor Norman Wirzba's conclusion regarding the whole matter:

> It makes sense . . . to think of Sabbath observance as one of our most honest and practical indicators of authentic religious faith. The extent and depth of our Sabbath commitment is the measure of how far we have progressed in our discipleship and friendship with God. Our Sabbath commitment bears witness to whether or not we have brought our habits and priorities in line with the ways and intentions of God. When we fail to observe the Sab-

bath, we miss out on the chance to experience creation and each other as God desires it. We forfeit the opportunity to live our days in the modes of care, celebration, and delight—all marks of the first Sabbath day.[24]

Who wouldn't want to relive that first Sabbath day over and over to eternity? The joy and delight it brings comes from Jesus. It's all about *Him*! And it's *for us*! *Enjoy!*

Questions for Reflection and Discussion

1. Which principles must be followed every Sabbath? Which principles can be practiced occasionally rather than every Sabbath?
2. To what extent is the choice of a Sabbath practice a personal decision between the soul and the Savior?
3. How do you relate to the story in Numbers 15, which tells about an occasion when God punished with death a man who gathered wood on the Sabbath? Could this story be saying that constantly working on the Sabbath will kill us?
4. Share your sixty-seconds-or-less "elevator" version of why you keep Sabbath.

Sabbath keeping changes our character. We will be irrevocably transformed by the commitment to a special day set aside for our relationship with God, and that transformation will result in thinking and attitudes and emotions and behavior consistent with the character of the God who is the focus of our Sabbath keeping.
—Marva Dawn, *Keeping the Sabbath Wholly*

When the character of Christ shall be perfectly reproduced in His people, then He will come to claim them as His own.
—Ellen G. White, *Christ's Object Lessons*

Appendix A
Ideas for Celebrating Sabbath in Your Family

When you experience the love of God, the joy of the gospel, and Sabbath rest in Jesus and have conceptualized some principles of Sabbath keeping, the next step is to visualize your ideal of a perfect Sabbath. What would it look like, feel like, taste like, and sound like? You can then choose activities that will fit with the principles and values of the inspired counsel in God's Word, which are based on God's character. The goal of this resource is to pull together into one document ideas from many different sources to get you started toward an optimum Sabbath experience. Some of the Sabbath practice ideas listed below were discussed in this book.

Preparation for the Sabbath
- Have each family member describe their ideas of a perfect Sabbath, and make a list of the food, activities, and places they mention. Invite each family member to take a turn choosing a favorite activity and food for a Sabbath. Then have all the family work together to create that family member's special Sabbath. Give another family member the opportunity to choose an activity and food for the next Sabbath.
- The Our Sabbath Plan form can be helpful in your planning. The family scribe can fill it out during the discussion of Sabbath plans. (See chapter 5 for a more complete explanation.)
- Have the children share in the work of preparing for the special

Our Sabbath Plan

Friday Night

• Meal

• Activity

Sabbath Morning

• Meal

• Activity

Sabbath Afternoon

• Meal

• Activity

Sabbath Evening

• Meal

• Activity

guest—Queen Sabbath, who brings the King with her. They can take baths and help clean, prepare food and clothing, etc. (See Ellen G. White, *Child Guidance,* 528.)

• Place something special from God's creation, such as freshly cut flowers or a single flower or beautiful autumn leaves on your dinner table for Sabbath.

• Have clothes and Bibles laid out and ready for Sabbath morning.

• Plan special family worship activities to open and close the Sabbath hours.

• Remove distractions from the atmosphere you wish to create in your home for the Sabbath by putting away secular magazines, newspapers, etc. The television should be turned off. Consider hanging a card that says "Preempted for Spiritual Prime Time" on the television.

• Use a reversible bedspread, reserving one side just for Sabbath.

• Aim to be ready one hour before sundown.

• Prepare a Sabbath basket with toys that are to be played with only on the Sabbath. Change the toys in the basket every two months, putting some away to bring back later.

- Start playing sacred music during Friday afternoon cleaning to put your family in the mood for Sabbath.
- Before you go to church, be sure you are ready to seek and share God.
- Avoid doing things, such as church-related business, heavy sermon preparation, choir rehearsals, etc., on Friday night and Sabbath. Keep the Sabbath as restful as possible.
- If you plan to have guests for Sabbath dinner, try to be aware of their personal interests and have in mind some ideas for Sabbath conversation with them during their visit. You might keep a little notebook handy during the week to jot down ideas from your devotional reading, from the pastor's sermon, etc.
- Settle differences between family members and with anyone else with whom you need to make things right. "Let all bitterness and wrath and malice be expelled from the soul. In a humble spirit, 'confess your faults one to another, and pray one for another, that ye may be healed.' James 5:16." (Ellen G. White, *Testimonies,* 6:355, 356) Wouldn't it be wonderful if every Seventh-day Adventist did this every week? If all differences in the family or between church members were never more than a week old, would there be any divided families or divided churches?

Friday night

- Play or sing the same music each week to start Sabbath. This can serve as a "trigger" to remind the family of Sabbath. Other triggers could be scented candles, a fire in the fireplace, air freshener, etc.
- Wear an outfit that is casual and comfortable but special, which you reserve for Friday nights only.
- Make Friday-night supper simple, special, and fun with candles, special dishes, etc. (e.g., soup and muffins or tostadas).
- Don't try to reform table or conversational manners on Friday night. Instead, do affirming activities, such as telling what you like about the person on your left. Or, ahead of time, prepare slips of paper by writing questions on them or fill-in-the-blank statements such as: The thing I like best about you is _____. If Jesus were here tonight, I know He would do _____ for you. When I think of you, I think of the Bible verse that says _____. At supper or sometime else during the evening, choose someone to be the

person of the night. Then have the other family members draw the slips of paper from the basket, read them, and fill in the blanks regarding the person of the night. Keep the conversation spiritual and affirming.

- Try saying a blessing *after* your Friday-evening meal. Jews do this in keeping with Deuteronomy 8:10, 18.
- After Friday-night supper, clean up the table and set it for breakfast.
- Have a campfire or lit fireplace for Sabbath opening worship.
- Activities you might include in Friday-night worship: singing favorite Sabbath songs, teaching the Sabbath School lesson with felts, playing charades (acting out Bible stories), or memorizing Scripture.
- Kneel in a circle, and let each person pray.
- Have "hug time" or "tickle time" after worship.
- Play a special "I spy" game during Friday-night worship—an activity in which each family member tells how God has worked in his or her life during the past week. Then pray together. (One study showed that the best family worships are life integrated. It does us no good to know a Bible story unless we know what relevance it has for our life.).
- Play the above "I spy" game at Friday-night bedtime (if you don't do it at worship time). Everyone piles in a bed with one candle in a dark room to play the game.
- Get the kids to bed early.
- Write love notes to family members during Friday-evening worship.
- Lie in bed with your children with candlelight and soft music in the background. Talk about the following: "I am so glad that . . ." "I wish that . . ."
- Go to bed early on Friday night to have a clear, alert mind for the Sabbath day.
- Have a "Friday night" box in which you've placed a treat or surprise for each child, such as a special food treat, small trinket, or special activity. You could use a heart-shaped box.
- Play Memory Verse Catch with a knit ball. When the ball is tossed to you, you must say a memory verse.
- After the kids are in bed, put on your favorite Sabbath music.
- Have a special nightie or pajamas you wear only on Friday night.

Sabbath morning

- To avoid Sabbath morning madness, get up a few minutes early rather than a few minutes late.
- Put on Sabbath music.
- Upon waking up, pray for a Sabbath blessing.
- Plan a special treat for breakfast—e.g., muffins, sweet rolls, special juice, etc.—and serve it in special dishes or bowls used only on Sabbath.
- For Sabbath morning breakfast, use napkins on which you or your children have written special messages.
- Listen to *Your Story Hour* or other Sabbath story CDs during Sabbath breakfast.
- Dress small children after breakfast.
- Reward children with a special Sabbath story if they are ready on time and for good behavior.
- Arrive at church fifteen minutes early. Pray for and feel the presence of God.
- Sit together as a family close to the front of the church.
- To a young child, the sermon might as well be preached in a foreign language. So, bring a Sabbath bag with quiet Sabbath activities, books, etc. I believe that children should participate in prayer and singing and use the Sabbath bag only during the sermon and that parents shouldn't give their children food in church.
- Cover your child's mouth on the way out of the sanctuary if the child is crying.
- Don't allow children to run around in the church.
- Avoid using the mother's room during the church service except for emergencies.

Sabbath afternoon

- Keep visits brief after church.
- Have simple meals in special dishes.
- During Sabbath dinner, discuss what the children learned in Sabbath School and from the sermon. Have Bible guessing games or memorize Bible verses.
- Don't complain about the pastor or the church service.
- Occasionally, invite single people to join your family during Sabbath afternoon.

• Have a picnic in a park or somewhere else out in nature. After eating, sit on a blanket and read stories.
• Take time to catch up on what's happening in the life of each member of the family.
• Read books that are spiritual and inspiring to the children.
• Think of object lessons inspired by your surroundings.
• Create Bible scenes from objects found in nature.
• Have a scavenger hunt. Pass out a list and look for the items on a walk. Make spiritual applications of what you find.

During Sabbath hours, service to others is more enjoyable than is merely trying to entertain your children. Isaiah 58 implies that service and Sabbath go together. Those who serve will " 'ride high' " (verse 14, *The Message*). So, take a blessing to your community. Visit people in nursing homes and hospitals and other lonely people.

Other suggestions of Sabbath blessings that you can bring your community:

• Bring a loaf of homemade bread and *Steps to Christ* to people who have come to the local Community Services Center. Ask them if they need any further assistance.
• Do clown ministry in a park. The youth can give balloons away to little kids and write the kids' names with a "God loves you" note on the balloons.
• Set up a table in a nearby city and feed the hungry.
• Work with a local food bank on a can collection. Advertise well ahead of time.
• Help serve a meal to the guests at a local mission or soup kitchen.
• Do babysitting at a facility for homeless women and children.
• Run a health-age-appraisal booth at a public location, and advertise an upcoming smoking cessation clinic or nutrition school.
• Write appropriate cards ("I'm sorry," "Thank you," or "Congratulations") to people mentioned in the local newspaper.
• Deliver "a present from Jesus to someone He loves." (You decide what the present should be.)

To keep your Sabbath afternoon activities balanced and delightful, you might want to vary them. Here's a suggested monthly plan for Sabbath afternoons:

- One Sabbath per month for Christian hospitality. (Have planned activities for the children.)
- One Sabbath per month for service—visiting sick people, old people, etc.
- One Sabbath per month for nature-oriented activities. Picnic. Look at leaves, pick berries, look for birds. Give each child a bag or jar for collecting things, etc. (See Eileen Lantry's book *Sabbath Nature Activities*.)
- One Sabbath per month for just the family. Take a nap, and then do something special with the children.

Closing Sabbath

- Sabbath evening worship should be special as you bid farewell to the day. Sing songs and have prayer.
- Play or sing the same song every week to close the Sabbath.
- Try using a homemade twisted candle at the close of the Sabbath. You can make your own by holding two thin taper candles over a steaming teakettle. Starting at the bottom of the two candles, twist them together up to the top. At sundown Saturday evening, light the twisted two-in-one candle, which represents the togetherness that the Sabbath has brought the family.
- Before your worship you might relight the candles that you lit to open Sabbath. Then light some incense just before blowing out the candles at the end of worship. Let the incense represent the fragrance that the Sabbath experience gives to the new week.
- Pass around a pretty box full of spices, such as cinnamon or cloves, and say, "May the fragrance of the Sabbath remain with you throughout the coming week."
- Have a family Sabbath review to evaluate how the Sabbath went. Start to plan the next Sabbath.

The ideas compiled here were drawn from or contributed by Gaspar Colón, Don and Diane Crane, Debbie Cox, Laurel Damsteegt, Richard and Jo Ann Davidson, Jacques Doukhan, Ron and Karen Flowers, Linda Friday, Fritz Guy, Donna Habenicht, Abraham Joshua Heschel, Noelene Johnsson, Karen Mains, C. Mervyn Maxwell, Gordon Pifher, Ruth Satelmajer, Nancy Van Pelt, Nancy Wilson, John and Millie Youngberg, and Martha Zimmerman. I originally prepared this list for the General Conference Department of Family Ministries, and it is used by permission.

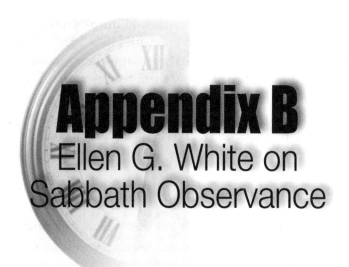

Appendix B
Ellen G. White on Sabbath Observance

Below you will find a sampling of principles and values that I have gleaned from the writings of Ellen G. White on the subject of Sabbath observance. The books referred to are *Education* (Ed), *Child Guidance* (CG), and *Testimonies for the Church* (T).

- The Sabbath and the family belong together; therefore, Sabbath should be a family day (Ed 250).
- The Sabbath is a religious education tool and aid that is beyond estimate. Use it for that purpose (Ed 250).
- The Sabbath is a memorial of God's creative power. Thus, nature should be a significant part of our Sabbath activities so that we will be better acquainted with God and His works (Ed 251).
- The Sabbath should give opportunity for intellectual training in the Scriptures (Ed 252).
- The Sabbath is a day to be devoted to the service of God (CG 527).
- The needs of the soul are to receive special attention (CG 527).
- The Sabbath is not ours but God's (CG 529).
- Sabbath time is too precious to sleep away (CG 530).
- Attend public worship with your children (CG 530).
- "Special" and Sabbath go together: i.e., wear special clothes for public worship on Sabbath (CG 531), and provide special treats at mealtime (CG 532).
- Parents should spend much of the Sabbath with their children (CG 532).

- Plan suitable reading and conversation on the Sabbath (CG 532).
- Don't be indifferent to children's activities (CG 533).
- If they can, parents should spend time out-of-doors in nature with their children instead of allowing them to play as usual either indoors or outdoors (CG 533).
- Sabbath should not be tedious or burdensome: i.e., don't weary children with tedious exhortations and long prayers (CG 534).
- Make Sabbath the most interesting and joyful day of the week (CG 536, 537).
- The Sabbath should bring change from the regular routine (CG 536).
- Families should worship God at home as well as in church during the Sabbath hours. Have a special Sabbath worship time together (CG 529, 536, 537).
- Sabbath keepers are not to follow the lax practices prevailing among Sunday keepers (6T 353).
- "Remember the Sabbath" all through the week (6T 354). However, Friday is the "preparation day" on which to do the final preparing of food, clothing, and person, and on which to put away differences (CG 528).
- When traveling, keep your mind stayed upon God and commune with Him (6T 360).
- On Sabbath, relieve those who suffer and help those in need (6T 360).
- When meeting with others on Sabbath, rather than complaining about the dark chapters in our experience, we should praise God for His mercy and love (6T 367).

Appendix C
Sabbath Keeping in the Spiritually Divided Home

by Ella M. Rydzewski

Sam targeted his gaze at the television screen, where he was watching an international golf tournament and his favorite player, Tiger Woods. Emily, Sam's wife, sat reading on the living-room couch, her legs stretched out in front of her and her back to the screen. She was aware that Tiger was winning because of Sam's occasional comments. But she had learned to immerse her thoughts in whatever reading material she had, in spite of the almost continuous sound of the television.

The day was Saturday, Sabbath—a normal Sabbath for Emily. In her lap was the church paper, containing, ironically, an article on Sabbath keeping. Such articles amused yet troubled Emily because most of the suggestions didn't fit her life with Sam and hadn't for the thirty years of their marriage. For all this time, Emily had attended church alone–one of the many "church widows" in North America. Emily has sisters all over the globe.

Many church members—I don't know the percentage, but it is very high—are married to people not of their faith or of no faith. Most Adventists in such situations are women. Sometimes they have become Adventists or have become active as Adventists after marriage, but a significant number of active members marry outside the church. Many make that choice due to circumstances. For one thing, almost two-thirds of Adventist members are women, and in some countries, such as Sweden, the percentage is even higher. Thus, the number of Adventist men available for marriage is limited.

Those of you who know the joy of conversing about spiritual matters with your spouse can only imagine what it is like for those in marriages

where such insights are out of bounds—where if one expresses spiritual insights, they will be ignored, scorned, debated, or even laughed at. Such responses can cut like a knife. Living in such circumstances is like living in a different dimension from one's mate. Unfortunately, the thing one holds dearest in life cannot be apprehended by the person who shares one's life. If believers aren't careful, this sad situation can cause them to drift away from their faith. It can imperil their soul. (See Ellen G. White, *Testimonies*, 5:364.)

Sabbath keeping may not be a problem when the relationship begins. But in time, the Christian believer may become convicted that Christ wants him or her to keep His Sabbath. If the spouse rejects this change in their lifestyle and relationship, stress and arguments often follow. Then Sabbath keeping becomes a challenge.

Imagine experiencing a particularly joyful time in a refreshing spiritual atmosphere among friends who love the Lord and then, upon walking in the door of your home, being met by the blaring of a television and pressure to make lunch—even orders to do it quickly, before you've had time to change your clothes. The Sabbath may seem to have died at the door!

Sabbath keeping in a spiritually divided home meets a particularly strong challenge in cultures where women are not considered equal partners in the marriage relationship. They can be subject to the whims of the husband and to his needs to the point that Sabbath becomes like any other day. If the wife is lucky, she may have a kind husband who allows her to attend church, which in some cultures can continue all day and provide spiritual fellowship for her. In other cases, should she refuse to serve her husband, the day can be filled with tension, threats, and even physical abuse. Most converts to Adventism in those cultures don't face such overt familial persecution, but almost all will have challenges to their Sabbath keeping that require some sort of accommodation.

However, the reasons for spiritually divided marriages lie in the individuals' pasts. How should one live once the deed is done?

From their perspective

If you want a pleasant home life, you must be able to put yourself into the skin of your spouse and see things from their perspective. Imagine if your world was turned upside down by your spouse finding a new lifestyle or some new "truth" and expecting you to abide by it, or at least live with

the effects. Perhaps the two of you enjoyed some traditions for your weekends, but now your spouse sees you leaving the house for several hours each Saturday and then coming home and doing "Sabbath things" that do not include him or her. How would you feel if your beloved partner believed you were eternally lost? How would you feel about living with someone who regarded you that way? Would you be comfortable with them?

Though you may suffer in a spiritually divided home, you should provide as little reason as possible for disharmony. Some say, correctly, that it never pays to argue over religion or politics because arguments about those topics don't change minds—they merely reinforce individual opinions. You need to avoid subjects that cause argument. Human nature defends itself. Religion can quickly become the scapegoat and cause your spouse to associate it with tension. Then it becomes easy for them to blame problems in the relationship on "that Adventist Church"—whatever the actual roots of the problems.

When you are married to a dedicated believer of another faith, you should respect that faith as you would like your faith to be respected. If you want your partner to accompany you to your church, you need to attend your partner's church as much as is practical. When both partners embrace Christ as Savior, many barriers come down at the altar of family worship and Bible study. If the barriers don't come down in such circumstances, one or both of you aren't praying and studying as you must to open your hearts to the Holy Spirit and His compassion. No Adventist should push his or her interpretation of the Bible on their spouse unless the spouse wants to hear it.

Many households break up because the believer insists on making the rest of the family follow her or his practices. A friend of mine who married an agnostic pressured him to give 10 percent of his salary to her church. Being a kind man, he did so for a while, but this expectation soon wore out his patience. Why should he support with his money the promulgation of ideas he didn't believe?

A vital element

In the matter of Sabbath keeping in a spiritually divided home, planning ahead is vital. Nothing can crush Sabbath feelings quicker than an unprepared response to the day. So, you must plan and prepare even more carefully than do those who are united in their faith. This includes

guiding your children to enjoy the Sabbath, which becomes a challenge when the unbelieving spouse differs regarding what children should do on that day. Here the believing wife often has to accept the husband's decision.

When the believer presents the Sabbath as a pleasant day of special family time, children associate it with happiness, and so do spouses. Nature trips offer the most enjoyable way to spend Sabbath together. But don't expect your spouse to talk of religion or to avoid secular conversation, and don't scold him or her for Sabbath lapses. If your spouse wants to buy you an ice-cream cone, enjoy it. I can remember walking through large, air-conditioned shopping malls on Sabbath afternoons when the Southern California heat was overwhelming. I didn't buy anything, but we enjoyed good walks together.

Sabbath trips yield delightful family memories for the future. I would suggest taking a whole day on occasion for such a trip. However, avoid missing more than one Sabbath at a time of church attendance, except during vacations. Nonattendance can become habitual, and church fellowship is necessary for the sanctified life.

Sabbath can be a time to invite other believers home from your church so your spouse can become acquainted with them. Just be careful not to invite someone who might be judgmental or who carries an air of self-righteousness.

Creeping, or otherwise, compromise is not always a bad word in spiritually divided homes. In fact, it is necessary for keeping the peace and treating each other with respect.

Of course, some things are not up for compromise. The believer is "placed under stronger obligation to be faithful to his companion, however widely they may differ in regard to religious faith; yet the claims of God should be placed above every earthly relationship, even though trials and persecution may be the result. With the spirit of love and meekness, this fidelity may have an influence to win the unbelieving one" (Ellen G. White, *Patriarchs and Prophets*, 175).

So, the Adventist member needs to decide what things can and what things cannot be compromised. To make Sabbath a Sabbath—a rest—you will need to shun those things identified with the workday world. That generally means not working for a paycheck. You cannot, however, bind your spouse to this limitation.

In some countries, Adventists accept the playing of sports with the children; in other countries, it is out of bounds. Watching television on

those dreary days when children can't go outside may be a viable option because some channels have programs appropriate for Sabbath viewing. Unfortunately, in North America, advertising distracts from these programs. However, you can also obtain appropriate nature and other videos. Otherwise, you can plan appropriate games for or with your children.

One area of conflict for many members is that of eating in restaurants on Sabbath. Believers must each make their own decision, of course, but rejecting spousal custom on this matter can cause unnecessary tension. If you decide to spend time with your spouse in a restaurant on Sabbath, do your homework first. Try to find a restaurant with a quiet, low-key atmosphere. Sabbath is not a fast-food day.

Many church widows find Sabbath companionship with other members who attend church alone. I've heard of a group of ladies in Russia who go to the apartment of a single lady each Sabbath. There they worship and spend the day, experiencing a weekly spiritual retreat together and avoiding the problems of Sabbath keeping at home. Fortunately, they're married to understanding husbands. Such an idea may not work everywhere with everyone, but it does suggest an option.

There are instances in which the relationship of husband and wife in a spiritually divided home works well, but I suspect they are few and far between. Despite all one's efforts, it's unlikely that the unbelieving spouse will ever feel comfortable with the believing spouse's choices regarding Sabbath observance. Acceptance of this fact is one of the hurts such a relationship entails.

Scriptural hope

There is a Bible text that does bring hope to many spouses. It works for spiritually divided children and parents as well—and even for extended family and friends. The apostle Paul wrote, "The unbelieving husband is sanctified by the wife, and the unbelieving wife is sanctified by the husband. . . . For what knowest thou, O wife, whether thou shalt save thy husband? or how knowest thou, O man, whether thou shalt save thy wife?" (1 Corinthians 7:14, 16, KJV).

"Sanctify" and "sanctification" are biblical words that mean, basically, to set apart as holy. We sanctify the Sabbath by keeping it unto the Lord (Deuteronomy 5:12). We might define becoming holy as growth toward spiritual maturity with resultant good actions. Believers are to become loyal, helpful, kind, gentle, joyful, patient, and self-controlled. These are

the fruits of the Holy Spirit, and they witness to God's character. In close family relationships, we might use the word *influence*—believers have a good influence on the other members of the family and teach them about the character of God by the way they behave and love the family. The power of influence also spreads to the second family in a relationship—the in-laws. Wary at first, they will ultimately embrace the Adventist member who exhibits the fruits of the Spirit.

These spiritual fruits may sound a bit intimidating. We aren't perfect human beings, and trying to become perfect is a real burden, especially in an environment of conflicting values. The most important role you can take in relationship to your family is that of someone who prays and who studies the Word. This opens the mind to the influence of the Holy Spirit, who in turn gradually changes our thoughts and lives in accordance with God's will. But even under the power of the Spirit, we often—especially at the beginning—will slip and indulge our own selfish will and desires. When we do so, asking forgiveness before the day ends is vital to our Christian experience.

Being married to a spouse who does not share the same Christian faith can place one on a lonely road on which one frequently feels isolated. The responsibilities are great. Adventists in such a relationship tend to hold the dream that one day their spouse will embrace the faith. Some eventually do. Hope is health-building and positive. But only by accepting and adjusting to the reality of the present will you be able to live by the Spirit and leave your life in the hands of our Savior. Only He knows your spouse's true spiritual condition, and only He can convert your spouse.

Some days will be discouraging, and our self-worth will be threatened because we seem to have made little difference in the life of our loved one. Yet this is a ministry we have chosen—usually before we ever comprehended its perplexities. Just remember, our Lord takes our hand, for we are yoked forever with Him.

"Whosoever shall compel thee to go a mile, go with him twain" (Matthew 5:41, KJV).

Endnotes

Preface

1. May-Ellen N. Colón, "Sabbath-keeping Practices and Factors Related to These Practices Among Seventh-day Adventists in 51 Countries," (PhD diss., Andrews University, 2003).

Introduction

1. See Robert Gorle, "Soccer on Sabbath?" *College People* 5 (January–February 1985):12.

Chapter 1: The Adventist Church's Sabbath-day Journey

1. See C. Mervyn Maxwell, *Tell It to the World* (Mountain View, Calif.: Pacific Press® Publishing Association, 1977), 73. Before the Great Disappointment of 1844 (the fact that Jesus did not return when William Miller and his followers had expected Him), J. A. Begg, a Scottish student of prophecy, had called the attention of Millerites to the issue of the seventh-day Sabbath.

2. Those who followed William Miller were called Millerites.

3. Theodore Lucas, ed., *Pioneer Stories Retold* (Washington, D.C.: Review and Herald® Publishing Association, 1956), 53, 54.

4. Ibid., 17.

5. Ellen G. White, *Life Sketches* (Mountain View, Calif.: Pacific Press®, 1915), 95.

6. Ellen G. White, *Testimonies for the Church* (Boise, Idaho: Pacific Press®, 1948), 1:75.

7. See Roger Coon, *A Gift of Light* (Hagerstown, Md.: Review and Herald*, 1983), 21. Seventh-day Adventists believe that Ellen G. White had the spiritual gift of prophecy (spoken of in Romans 12:6; 1 Corinthians 12:28; Ephesians 4:11; Revelation 12:17; 19:10), which was sometimes manifested in visions that she received from God. White handwrote more than one hundred thousand pages (twenty-five million words), giving counsel to the Adventist Church on many different subjects.

8. Arthur White, *Ellen G. White: Messenger to the Remnant* (Washington, D.C.: Review and Herald®, 1969), 34.

9. James White to Stockbridge Howland, 2 July 1848, Record Book I, 116, 117; quoted in Arthur White, *Ellen G. White: Messenger to the Remnant,* 35.

10. James White, "Time of the Sabbath," *Advent Review and Sabbath Herald,* December 4, 1855.

11. John N. Andrews, "Time for Commencing the Sabbath," *Advent Review and Sabbath Herald,* December 4, 1855. In addition to presenting clear scriptural evidence that Sabbath begins at sunset rather than 6:00 P.M., Andrews pointed out that if 6:00 P.M. was the appointed time, for five thousand years Sabbath keepers wouldn't have known for sure when Sabbath started because clocks weren't invented until about 1658. Andrews admitted that his previous views about when the Sabbath starts were wrong after they were tested by his personal and thorough investigation of Scripture. He declared: "I frankly acknowledge my own fault. It is always duty to correct our errors when we see them; and however sincerely we may have acted in the past we can no longer act so, if when we see a fault as such, or a mistake, we refuse to acknowledge it" (78).

12. James White, "Time to Commence the Sabbath," *Advent Review and Sabbath Herald,* February 25, 1868.

13. Arthur White, 36.

14. The *Review and Herald* (the name has varied slightly through the years) has been the flagship journal of the Adventist Church throughout its history. Official statements and counsel have been regularly disseminated through this publication.

15. If you would like to read a more comprehensive survey of Adventist writings that reflect Adventist Sabbath practices from the beginning of the church to the present, see chapter 2 of my dissertation.

16. G. D. Ballou, " 'Bless' and 'Blessed,' " *Advent Review and Sabbath Herald,* October 1, 1895.

17. Ella White Robinson, *Over My Shoulder* (Washington, D.C.: Review and Herald®, 1982), 86.

Chapter 2: Good News, Bad News

1. See my PhD dissertation, referenced in the preface. Friends at the General Conference of Seventh-day Adventists and in foreign countries helped me to scatter my Sabbath Observance Exploratory Survey (SOES) all around the world. I wish that I could have also studied Sabbath keeping among other communities of faith, but obtaining this data would have been too difficult with my time constraints.

2. The name has been changed.

3. See Matthew 2:5; John 7:21–23. See also Ellen G. White, *The Desire of Ages* (Mountain View, Calif.: Pacific Press®, 1940), 285.

4. Barna Research Online, "Religious Beliefs Vary Widely by Denomination," www.barna.org (accessed June 25, 2001), quoted in Russell Burrill, "Can Dying Churches Be Resuscitated?" *Ministry* 75 (December 2002): 14.

5. Des Cummings Jr., *Original Love* (Fallbrook, Calif.: Hart Books, 2001), 71.

6. For example, compare Robert Gorle, "Soccer on Sabbath?" *College People,* January–February 1985, 12, and John Hayward, "Editorial Heresy," *College People,* July–August 1985, 5.

Chapter 3: What's a Sabbath Keeper to Be?

1. Pathfinders is an organization that provides a Christian character-building program of activities for boys and girls from ten to fifteen years of age. Pathfinders wear uniforms, and their activities are similar to those of the Boy Scouts and Girl Scouts.

2. My family's last name is Colón. My husband and our children are descendents of Cristobal Colón—Christopher Columbus. I've piggy-backed onto that honor by marriage!

3. F. D. Nichol, ed., *Seventh-day Adventist Bible Commentary* (Washington, D.C.: Review and Herald®, 1980), 7:202, commenting on Colossians 2:9, which says, "Within Christ dwells the sum total of the nature and attributes of God."

4. Cummings, 13.

5. See Rick Warren, *The Purpose-Driven Life* (Grand Rapids, Mich.: Zondervan, 2002), 117–121.

6. Cummings, 39.

7. "All true obedience comes from the heart. It was heart work with Christ. And if we consent, He will so identify Himself with our thoughts and aims, so blend our hearts and minds into conformity to His will, that when obeying Him we shall be but carrying out our own impulses." (Ellen G. White, *The Desire of Ages* [(Nampa, Idaho: Pacific Press®, 1940]), 668.)

8. Ellen G. White, *Christ's Object Lessons* (Washington, D.C.: Review and Herald®, 1941), 312.

9. Ellen G. White, *Patriarchs and Prophets* (Mountain View, Calif.: Pacific Press®, 1958), 213, 214.

10. In expressing this point, Paul used phrases such as "Christ in me," "in Christ," "Christ in you," and "you in Christ." Sangster said thirteen epistles because he didn't consider Paul to have written the epistle to the Hebrews.

All the Sangster material in this chapter comes from "the Secret of the Indwelt Life," General Conference Ministerial Association *Ministry* Tape of the Month, December 1984

11. Paul prayed "that Christ may dwell in your hearts through faith" (Ephesians 3:17, NKJV). In *Ephesians: Chosen for Christ* (Hagerstown, Md.: Review and Herald®, 2005), 66, John Fowler points out that the Greek word translated "dwell" is *katoikeo*, which indicates permanent residence. We need Christ to be a permanent part of our lives, not just a guest.

12. Colón, "Sabbath-keeping Practices," 25, 26.

13. George White, "Wordswithoutspacemakenosense," *Alive Now!* July/August 1989, n.p.; quoted in Martha Whitmore Hickman, *A Day of Rest: Creating Spiritual Space in Your Week* (Nashville: Dimensions for Living, 2002), 13. Quoted with George White's permission.

14. B. B. Taylor, "Remember the Sabbath," *The Christian Century,* May 5, 1999.

15. Tilden Edwards, *Sabbath Time* (Nashville: Upper Room Books, 1992), 136.

Chapter 4: How's a Sabbath Keeper to Decide What to Do?

1. George Vandeman, *A Day to Remember* (Mountain View, Calif.:

Pacific Press® Publishing Association, 1965), 54.

2. James Robertson, "The Regatta," *Cornerstone Connections,* August 13, 1997.

3. Philip Yancey, *What's So Amazing About Grace?* (Grand Rapids, Mich.: Zondervan, 1997), 235.

4. Cummings, 15.

5. See Josh McDowell and Bob Hostetler, *Right from Wrong: What You Need to Know to Help Youth Make Right Choices* (Nashville: W Publishing Group, 1994), 97. Diagram used by permission.

6. Nancy Vyhmeister, "Principles," unpublished paper, Andrews University, n.d., 24.

7. Ellen G. White, *Christ's Object Lessons,* 315.

8. See John Brunt, *A Day for Healing* (Washington, D.C.: Review and Herald®, 1981).

9. See McDowell and Hostetler, *Right from Wrong.* McDowell and Hostetler's book focuses especially on right vs. wrong choices (moral temptations). The precept-principle-person pattern is also helpful with right vs. right choices (ethical dilemmas), where two important moral principles are in conflict with each other. For an interesting and helpful discussion of dealing with right vs. right choices, see Rushworth M. Kidder, *How Good People Make Tough Choices* (New York: Simon & Schuster, 1996).

10. Ellen G. White, *Testimonies,* 4:88.

11. Lightly edited.

Chapter 5: *Vacation* With God and With His Family—Part 1

1. Ellen G. White, *Mind, Character, and Personality* (Nashville: Southern Publishing Association, 1977), 1:89.

2. These questions are adapted from my dissertation.

3. Kidder, 99.

4. Marva Dawn, *Keeping the Sabbath Wholly: Ceasing, Resting, Embracing, Feasting* (Grand Rapids, Mich.: Wm. B. Eerdmans, 1989), 203.

5. W. Gary Phillips and William E. Brown, *Making Sense of Your World: A Biblical Worldview* (Chicago, Ill.: Moody Press, 1991), 195.

6. Dorothy Bass, "Receiving the Day the Lord Has Made," *Christianity Today* (March 6, 2000), 64.

7. Ellen G. White, *Christ's Object Lessons,* 333.

8. Martin Weber, *Adventist Hot Potatoes* (Boise, daho: Pacific Press®, 1991), 80.

9. Don Pate, *52 Sabbath Activities for Teen Groups* (Hagerstown, Md.: Review and Herald®, 1995), 18.

10. Ellen G. White, *Testimonies*, 6:355; emphasis added.

11. Martha Zimmerman, *Celebrate the Feasts* (Minneapolis, Minn.: Bethany House, 1981), 24.

12. Karen Burton Mains, *Making Sunday Special* (Nashville: Star Song, 1994), 93. This book has many practical insights that are very useful for observing the seventh-day Sabbath as well.

13. Ibid., 99.

14. You can easily make a "sundown clock" by drawing a clock face on a sheet of paper and pasting it to a piece of cardboard for durability. Stick a couple of hands on it and a magnet on the back so you can hang it on your refrigerator. If you have children at home, you might make the task of creating this clock a Sabbath afternoon project.

15. Richard Davidson, *A Love Song for the Sabbath* (Hagerstown, Md.: Review and Herald®, 1988), 97.

16. Ellen G. White, *Testimonies,* 6:356.

Chapter 6: *Vacation* With God and With His Family—Part 2

1. Don Postema, *Catch Your Breath: God's Invitation to Sabbath Rest* (Grand Rapids, Mich.: CRC Publications, 1997), 45.

2. Mark Buchanan, *The Rest of God: Restoring Your Soul by Restoring the Sabbath* (Nashville: W Publishing Group, 2006), 87.

3. See Dorothy Bass, *Recieving the day: Christian Practices for Opening the Gift of Time* (San Francisco: Jossey–Bass, 2000), 65.

4. Ellen G. White, *Testimonies,* 6:356.

5. See Wayne Mueller, *Sabbath: Finding Rest, Renewal, and Delight in Our Busy Lives* (New York: Bantam Books, 1999), 83.

6. See Bass, 48.

7. Edwards, 136.

8. *I'm Soooooooo Tired,* Hardinge Lifestyle Series (Loma Linda, Calif.: Loma Linda University School of Health, 1988), 11–13. In a March 25, 2008, e-mail to me, Dr. Kathleen Kuntaraf explained that this article says that during World War II, manufacturers of war material tried to increase production by asking their employees to work seven days per week. However, they found that when they shortened that to a forty-eight hour work week, production increased by 15 percent. On July 29, 1941, English prime minister Winston Churchill told the House of Commons that if

the Allies were to win the war, it would be by staying power, and for that reason they must have one holiday per week and one one-week holiday per year, which was then voted into law. Isn't this what God, our Creator, said in Exodus 20:8 long before Churchill's time?

9. Samuele Bacchiocchi, *Devine Rest for Human Restlessness: A Theological Study for the Good New of the Sabbath for Today* (Rome: Tipographia, 1980), 224.

10. See Eugene H. Peterson, "The Good-for-Nothing Sabbath," *Christianity Today,* April 4, 1994, 34–36.

11. Bass, 66.

12. Mains, 103.

13. Oswald Chambers, *My Utmost for His Highest* (Uhrichsville, Ohio: Barbour & Company, 1963), 40, 42.

14. Brunt, 45.

15. Jo Ann Davidson, telephone conversation, March 25, 2008. See John 5:1–16; Luke 6:6–11; Mark 3:1–6.

16. Ellen G. White, *The Desire of Ages,* 207.

17. Brunt, 60.

18. Céleste Perrino-Walker, *Making Sabbath Special* (Nampa, Idaho: Pacific Press®, 1999), 18.

19. Vandeman, 15.

20. Richard Davidson, 160.

21. Dwight L. Moody, *Weighed and Wanting* (Chicago, Ill.: Fleming H. Revell, 1898), 54.

22. Abraham Joshua Heschel, *The Sabbath: Its Meaning for Modern Man* (New York: Noonday Press, 1951), 30, 31.

23. John and Millie Youngberg, *Family Sabbath Traditions to Bless Your Heart and Home* (Nampa, Idaho: Pacific Press®, 2001), 53.

24. Jan Kuzma, quoted in Kay Kuzma, *Fit Forever: One-a-Day Devotionals for Body, Mind, and Spirit* (Hagerstown, Md.: Review and Herald®, 2005), 45.

25. Ellen G. White, *Child Guidance* (Washington, D.C.: Review and Herald®, 1982), 536.

26. For more ideas, see appendix A; see also Karen Holford, *100 Creative Activities for Sabbath* (Nampa, Idaho: Pacific Press®, 2006).

Chapter 7: Vacation *With God* and With His Family—Part 1

1. Dawn, 100.

2. Richard Davidson, 97.

3. Ellen G. White, *The Desire of Ages,* 556.

4. James Richard Wibberding, *Sabbath Reflections* (Telford, Penn.: Big Fish Publishing, 2006), 77.

5. Jacques Doukhan, "Loving the Sabbath as a Christian: A Seventh-day Adventist Perspective," in *The Sabbath in Jewish and Christian Traditions,* eds., T. C. Eskenazi, D. J. Harrington, and W. H. Shea (New York: Crossroad Publishing, 1991), 154.

6. See Kuzma, 318.

7. Ellen G. White, *Testimonies,* 6:351.

8. See Richard Davidson, 89, 90.

9. Charles Scriven, *Jubilee of the World* (Nashville: Southern Publishing Association, 1978), 15.

10. Heschel, 89.

11. Adapted from Buchanan, 33.

12. Richard Davidson, 97.

13. Ellen G. White, *Child Guidance,* 532.

14. Ellen G. White, *The Great Controversy* (Mountain View, Calif.: Pacific Press®, 1950), 599.

15. Ellen G. White, *Testimonies,* 2:585.

16. Ellen G. White, *Child Guidance,* 533.

17. Heschel, 22.

18. Ellen G. White, *Child Guidance,* 532.

19. Ellen G. White, *Testimonies,* 6:356.

20. Doukhan, "Loving the Sabbath," 151.

21. See Ellen G. White, *Education* (Oakland, Calif.: Pacific Press®, 1903), 251, and "The Sabbath Endures," *The Signs of the Times,* September 23, 1908, 210.

22. Dorothy Bass, *Receiving the Day: Christian Practices for Opening the Gift of Time* (San Francisco: Jossey-Bass, 2000), 48.

23. Bacchiocchi, 146, 147.

24. Jacques Doukhan, "Loving the Sabbath as a Christian: A Seventh-day Adventist Perspective," in T. C. Eskenazi, D. J. Harrington, and W. H. Shea, eds., *The Sabbath in Jewish and Christian Tradition* (New York: The Crossroad Pub. Co., 1991), 153.

25. Ibid., 153, 154.

26. Ibid., 154.

27. Nancy Van Pelt, "The Art of Making Sabbath Special," cassette recording (Fresno, Calif.: Heart & Home Seminars, 1991).

28. Ellen G. White, *Education*, 250.

29. Jim Nix, "Growing Up Adventist: No Apologies Needed," *Adventist Review*, March 23, 2006, 8–13. See also Ellen G. White, *Testimonies*, 6:353.

30. See Ellen G. White, *Child Guidance*, 529, 530.

31. For more ideas, see Linda Kirk, "Food and Friends: How to Have Wonderful Sabbath Fellowship," *Adventist Review*, May 26, 2005, 27. Also, the Chicken Soup for the Soul series has an excellent line of conversation-starter cards, many of which are appropriate for the Sabbath. See http://www.educationallearninggames.com/chicken-soup-for-the-soul-cards-games.asp.

32. See Ellen G. White, *The Desire of Ages*, 283.

33. Ellen G. White, *Child Guidance*, 531.

34. Ellen G. White, *The Great Controversy*, 438.

Chapter 8: Vacation *With God* and With His Family—Part 2

1. See F. D. Nichol, *Seventh-day Adventist Bible Commentary*, 3:881.

2. See Ellen G. White, *Child Guidance*, 533, 534.

3. Weber, 76, 77.

4. Ellen G. White, *Child Guidance*, 534.

5. Edwards, 136.

6. Karl Barth, *The Doctrine of Creation*, III.4, *The Command of God the Creator*, 56, 57, quoted in Gregory P. Nelson, *A Touch of Heaven: Finding New Meaning in Sabbath Rest* (Nampa, Idaho: Pacific Press®, 1999), 31. In finishing redemption—our re-creation—Christ followed the same sequence as He did during Creation week. He worked first, and then He rested on the Sabbath—this time, in the tomb. Since the Cross, the rest-first-and-then-work cycle remains (see Hebrews 4:9).

7. Nelson, 28.

8. See ibid., 31.

9. Gordon MacDonald, *Ordering Your Private World* (Nashville: Thomas Nelson Publishers, 1984), 164.

10. Taashi Rowe, "United States: Prayer Cited As Reason For Problem-Free Large-Scale Cement Pour," *Adventist News Network Bulletin*, June 26, 2006. Used by permission.

Chapter 9: Vacation With God and *With His Family*—Part 1

1. Charles Bradford, *Sabbath Roots: The African Connection* (Silver Spring, Md.: Ministerial Association of the General Conference of Seventh-day Adventists, 1991, 51.

2. Jacques Doukhan, *The Genesis Creation Story: Its Literary Structure* (Berrien Springs, Mich.: Andrews University Press, 1978), 78, 79. See also Doukhan, "Loving the Sabbath," 158.

3. Ellen G. White, *Education,* 250, 251.

4. Roy Branson, "Festival of Fellowship," in *Festival of the Sabbath*, Roy Branson, ed. (Takoma Park, Md.: Association of Adventist Forums, 1985), 72.

5. Greg Nelson, *A Touch of Heaven* (Nampa, Idaho: Pacific Press®, 1999), 113.

6. See John and Millie Youngberg, *Family Sabbath Traditions to Bless Your Heart and Home* (Nampa, Idaho: Pacific Press®, 2001), for more ideas about Sabbath fellowship traditions.

7. Karen and Ron Flowers have an extensive list of what they call "New Testament 'One Anotherings' "; see Karen and Ron Flowers, *Family Faith* (Nampa, Idaho: Pacific Press®, 2005), 11, 12.

8. Karen and Ron Flowers, *Love Aflame,* (Hagerstown, Md.: Review and Herald®, 1992), 78, 79.

9. Charles Wittschiebe, *God Invented Sex* (Nashville: Southern Publishing, 1974), 91.

10. Alberta Mazat, *Questions You've Asked About Sexuality* (Boise, Idaho: Pacific Press®, 1991), 85.

11. Among the health benefits sex provides are stress relief, boosting of immunity, weight loss, improvement of cardiovascular health, boosting of self-esteem, reduction of pain, reduction of prostate cancer risk, and better sleep. See Kathleen Doheny, "10 Surprising Health Benefits of Sex," http://www.cbsnews.com/stories/2008/03/24/health/webmd/main3961979.shtml.

12. See Lorna Arthur, "Solo Sabbaths," *Adventist Review*, May 17, 1990, 14, 15.

13. Ellen G. White, *The Desire of Ages,* 285.

14. Will Eva, Roy Branson, Andy McRae, and Charles Scriven, "The Meaning and Role of the Sabbath," *Ministry*, May 1997, 23.

15. Cummings, 27.

16. For more on the meaning of *shalom*, see Jacques Doukhan, "Shalom: The Hebrew View of Peace," *Shabbat Shalom* 48 (Spring 2001): 12–14.

17. Jo Ann Davidson, in an oral presentation at the Adventist Family Conference, July 22, 2002, at Andrews University, Berrien Springs, Michigan.

18. Gary Smalley and John Trent, *The Blessing* (New York: Pocket Books, 1986), 27.

19. Edwards, 132.

20. Lisa Katz, "Havdalah," About.com: Judaism, About, Inc., A part of *The New York Times Company*, http://judaism.about.com/library/3_Blessingsprayers/bl_havdalah.htm. "The name *havdalah* comes from the Hebrew word *l'havdeel*, which means to distinguish or separate. Havdalah is a ceremony that distinguishes between the holy Sabbath day and the secular work week." Lisa Katz, "Havdalah," About.com, http://judaism.about.com/library/3_blessingsprayers/bl_havdalah.htm.

21. Just a thought: the law gives us concrete guidance in deepening our relationship with a loving God. He empowers us to live this law, which enhances our quality of life.

Chapter 10: Vacation With God and *With His Family*—Part 2

1. Jo Ann Davidson, in an oral presentation at the Adventist Family Conference, July 22, 2002, at Andrews University, Berrien Springs, Michigan.

2. See Bacchiocchi, 196, 197.

3. Wibberding, 196.

4. These festivals illustrate the Sabbath attitude, but this doesn't mean that we are to observe these festivals now. See Colossians 2:16, 17.

5. Pastor Larry Lichtenwalter portrays this theme as an Oreo cookie—those cookies comprised of two chocolate wafers and a cream filling in the middle. The first wafer is compassionate service as explained in Isaiah 58:1–12. The second wafer is integrity and the restoring of justice for the oppressed as presented in Isaiah 59. Sabbath (Isaiah 58:13, 14) is the filling.

In order to make compassionate service a way of life and in order to obtain integrity and the desire to bring justice to the oppressed, we need the Sabbath (the filling). The Sabbath provides us with the time and motivation to "absorb" God's holiness, His character. Then we can live out the Sabbath attitude as shown in the rest of Isaiah 58 and 59 (the wafers).

The Sabbath attitude and mode is not something we can switch on Friday night and switch off Saturday night. It is lived out all week. And just as the Oreo must have the cream to enhance the flavor of the wafers, so we must have the Sabbath to make compassionate service a part of our

lives. Thus, the Sabbath will bring us to the higher level of spiritual growth to which Isaiah 58:14 points us.

6. Richard Rice, *The Reign of God: An Introduction to Christian Theology from a Seventh-Day Adventist Perspective* (Berrien Springs, Mich.: Andrews University Press, 1997), 320.

7. See also Ellen G. White, *The Desire of Ages,* 637–641.

8. Ellen G. White, *The Great Controversy,* 605.

9. Of course, emergencies are an exception. However, the Rotary activity was not an emergency.

10. See Ellen G. White, *The Desire of Ages,* 285.

11. See Ellen G. White, *Testimonies,* 6:360.

12. See Walter F. Specht, "The Sabbath in the New Testament," in Kenneth Strand, ed., *The Sabbath in Scripture and History* (Washington, D.C.: Review and Herald®, 1982), 94, 95.

13. Ibid., 95.

14. Ángel Rodríguez, "The Biblical Sabbath: The Adventist Perspective." Retrieved June 28, 2003, from http://biblicalresearch.gc.adventist.org/documents/sabbath-catholic2002.htm.

15. Ellen G. White, *The Desire of Ages,* 287.

16. Ibid., 207.

Chapter 11: Real Bumps in Real Life

1. Blu Greenberg, *How to Run a Traditional Jewish Household* (New York: Simon & Schuster, 1983), 40.

2. See Herbert Danby, trans., *The Mishnah* (London: Oxford University Press, 1933), 113.

3. Jonathan and Kathleen Kuntaraf, "Principles of Life," in *Thy Word Is a Lamp Unto My Feet: The Bible for Today, Adult Sabbath School Bible Study Guide* (Washington, D.C.: General Conference of Seventh-day Adventists, 2007), 59.

4. Ellen G. White, *Selected Messages* (Washington, D.C.: Review and Herald®, 1980), 3:258.

5. Courtesy of Jim Zackrison.

6. Adapted from Kathleen Kuntaraf, "Sabbath or Medical School?" *College and University Dialogue,* 2:33. Reprinted with permission.

7. Ellen G. White, *To Be Like Jesus* (Hagerstown, Md.: Review and Herald®, 2004), 45.

Chapter 12: Putting It All Together

1. This hymn is no. 671 in the *Seventh-day Adventist Hymnal.*
2. Heschel, 21.
3. My version of Psalm 86:11.
4. Ellen G. White, *Testimonies,* 6:350.
5. Danby, 589. The portion quoted was written about Psalm 92.
6. Nelson, 95.
7. Postema, 15.
8. Buchanan, 213.
9. Heschel, 74.
10. Norman Wirzba, *Living the Sabbath* (Grand Rapids, Mich.: Brazos Press, 2006), 24.
11. Ellen G. White, *The Desire of Ages,* 283.
12. Ellen G. White, *Early Writings* (Hagerstown, Md.: Review and Herald®, 1963), 33.
13. See Jude 24.
14. Buchanan, 89.
15. May-Ellen Colón, "Of All the Week the Best," *Adventist Review,* May 5, 2005, 16–20.
16. In 2006, Cheryl Doss, a missiologist who teaches at the Seventh-day Adventist Theological Seminary in Berrien Springs, Michigan, shared with me in conversation some additional insights regarding choosing practices for Christian living within a given culture. She spoke of a process called "critical contextualization" that can be applied to Sabbath keeping. Every generation should apply this process to the spiritual practices. The process includes the following:

1. Look at current practices.
2. Go to the biblical record and look at all texts that deal with that subject (e.g., Sabbath, what to wear, etc.).
3. Apply those texts to current practices.
   a. E.g., if a practice is to wear a red dress at weddings, does the Bible forbid the wearing of a red dress at weddings?
   b. What do we need to get rid of? (E.g., in India, women wear eyeliner to keep the evil eye off them.)
   c. Find a functional substitute for whatever you throw out.
   d. If you can make a cultural practice biblically acceptable by modifying it, do so. (E.g., in a culture where people undergo some kind of initiation before marriage, keep the practice of

initiation but change the content of the ceremony if that's necessary to make it biblically acceptable.)
4. Evaluate—try it and see if it works. E.g., "in our community we will allow our kids to ride bikes on Sabbath if they do so in nature." Try this practice and see if it works.

For more information, see chapter 4, "Critical Contextualization," in Paul Hiebert's *Anthropological Reflections on Missiological Issues* (Grand Rapids, Mich.: Baker Books, 1994), 75–92.

17. Richard Davidson suggests this question in *A Love Song for the Sabbath*, 102.

18. Buchanan, 122, 123.

19. Ellen G. White, *Testimonies,* 5:43.

20. This idea can be used for living other Bible doctrines too.

21. E. H. Cousins, "What Is Christian Spirituality?" in *Modern Christian Spirituality: Methodological and Historical Essays,* ed., B. C. Hanson (Atlanta, Ga.: Scholars Press, 1990), 41; emphasis added.

22. George Barna, *Transforming Children Into Spiritual Champions: Why Children Should Be Your Church's #1 Priority* (Ventura, Calif.: Regal Books, 2003), 62.

23. Edwards, 46.

24. Wirzba, 13.

Have you found this book helpful? You'll want to read these as well:

If you are a Christian, you are a leader!
Ellen White on Leadership
Cindy Tutsch

Part of our responsibility as followers of Jesus is to use our influence to lead others to follow Jesus. We do this in different ways, according to our spiritual gifts.

Ellen White did not invent the term *servant leadership,* but as the messenger of the Lord, she lived it. While Seventh-day Adventists officially hold that Ellen White's writings are authoritative, her writings are also considered subordinate to the Scriptures. You will find insights on service and leadership, as well as surprising personal anecdotes of Mrs. White's responses to situations you may encounter.

ISBN 13: 978-0-8163-2251-0   ISBN 10: 0-8163-2251-1
Paperback, 160 pages.

Let the Bible in your hands be God's power in your life!
Exalting His Word
Shelley Quinn

Shelley Quinn knows firsthand the power and victory not only of reading the Word, but of speaking the Word—affirming promises of God aloud. This book will take you beyond claiming the promises to confessing the promises. You'll discover how God causes His way of thinking to become your way of thinking. If your heart's desire is to break free from the "three-steps-forward, two-steps-back" routine, and to finally experience God's transforming power in your life, it's time to start *Exalting His Word*!

ISBN 13: 978-0-8163-2147-6   ISBN 10: 0-8163-2147-7
Paperback, 176 pages.